GOLGOTHA'S GROANING

Other Best-selling Books
by Carl Gallups
from Defender Publishing

Eyes to See (August 2024)
Yeshua Protocol (November 2022)
Glimpses of Glory (March 2022)
The Summoning (January 2021)
Masquerade (March 2020)
The Rabbi, the Secret Message, and the Identity of Messiah (February 2019)
Gods of the Final Kingdom (July 2019)
Gods of Ground Zero (October 2018)
Gods and Thrones (October 2017)

DEFENDER

CRANE, MO

Golgotha's Groaning: Stunningly Unique Biblical Disclosures, from Genesis to Revelation, That Will Shake the End-Times World

By Carl Gallups

Defender Publishing
Crane, MO 65633

© 2025 Defender Publishing

All Rights Reserved. Published July 2025.

Printed in the United States of America.

ISBN: 978-1-94014-93-9

A CIP catalog record of this book is available from the Library of Congress.

Cover design by Jeffrey Mardis
Interior design by Katherine Lloyd

Unless otherwise indicated, all Scripture quotations are from The ESV® Bible (The Holy Bible, English Standard Version®), copyright © 2001 by Crossway, a publishing ministry of Good News Publishers. Used by permission. All rights reserved.

Hebrew translations of the English New Testament taken from the Greek New Testament are derived from the Delitzsch Hebrew New Testament.[1]

For Marlene.
You've been an almost lifelong surrogate mother,
sister in the Lord, unshakable cheerleader, prayer warrior,
and invaluable confidant to me.

I thank the Lord for putting you in my life!
I love you.

My God, my God, why have you forsaken me?
Why are you so far from saving me,
from the words of my groaning?
(Psalm 22:1)

For we know that the whole creation has been
groaning together in the pains of childbirth until now.
(Romans 8:22)

CONTENTS

A Note from the Author xiii

Part One
HIDDEN IN PLAIN SIGHT

1 Behind the Veil 3
2 Gruesome Agendas 6
3 They Don't Know 9
4 A Kingdom of Priests 12
5 A Traitor in the House 16
6 Show Us The Father 20
7 Only God 24
8 A Garden 28
9 A Rectified Crime 32
10 The Denial 36
11 Peter and John 39
12 The Journey 43

Part Two
THE INVISIBLE BECOMES VISIBLE

13 From the Beginning 47
14 The Scarlet Thread 49
15 Indisputably Unique 51

Part Three
FOUNDATIONS

16 Letters That Become Ideas 57
17 The First 60
18 The Last 62

19	The Eth	65
20	Words That Are Pictures	68
21	Magnified	72
22	Twelve Supernatural Words	74
23	The Mirror Image and the Gift	77

Part Four
PILLARS OF THE TEMPLE

| 24 | Prophesying Pillars | 83 |
| 25 | What's in a Name? | 85 |

Part Five
THE PATH OF GROANING

26	The Trail of Tears	91
27	The Garden Link	95
28	The New Testament Icon	98
29	Abraham's Groaning	101
30	Abraham's Longest Walk	105
31	Abraham Longed to See My Day	109
32	Origins	112
33	Pentecost and Abraham	114
34	The Compounding of Psalm 22	117
35	David's Agony	119
36	The Rabbi's Discovery	122
37	In the Dust of Death	124
38	Take Him Away!	126
39	Casting Lots	129
40	Isaiah and the Arm of the Lord	132
41	The Interlude	136
42	Isaiah's Groaning	138
43	Death and Resurrection	141
44	Isaiah's Criminals	144

Part Six
A LAMB AND A HIGH PRIEST

45 The Lamb 151
46 When I See the Blood 154
47 The Lamb of Sacrifice 158
48 The Messenger of the Covenant 161
49 Passover Fulfilled 164
50 Golgotha's Groaning 168
51 The High Priest of Old 172
52 Our Great High Priest 175

Part Seven
FROM FIRST TO LAST

53 Show Us the Father 181
54 The Word Became Flesh 184
55 God So Loved the World 187
56 The Alpha and Omega 189

Part Eight
WHERE, OH WHERE?

57 The Cavernous Mystery 195
58 Golgotha's Trail 197
59 Goliath's Head? 201
60 New Testament Confirmation 204

Part Nine
THE RELEVANCY

61 What We Don't Know 211
62 Stick a Fork in It 214

About the Author 219
Acknowledgments 221
Notes 223

A NOTE FROM THE AUTHOR

Throughout this book, the English word "Jesus" is often written as *Yeshua*, the Hebrew rendering of His Name. You will also see the Hebrew words *HaMashiach* ("the Messiah"), *Adonai* ("Lord and Master"), Yahweh ("Lord of All," "the Great I Am"), and *Tanakh* ("Old Testament").

These terms are used to maintain the Hebraic tone in which the book was researched and written, and to highlight the ancient Hebrew letter representations that create one of the world's most iconic images.

Also, you may wish to know the precise protocols I employed in order to bring you these staggering revelations. You can read them at this endnote.[2]

Thank you for turning the next pages. And thank you for taking this journey with me. I am honored you are doing so.

I pray you'll be blessed for having read it, to the glory of Yeshua. Enjoy!

Part One

HIDDEN IN PLAIN SIGHT

Jesus said to him, "Have I been with you so long, and you still do not know me, Philip? Whoever has seen me has seen the Father. How can you say, 'Show us the Father'"? (John 14:9)

1

BEHIND THE VEIL

> *The mystery that has been kept hidden for ages and generations, but is now disclosed to the saints. To them God has chosen to make known among the Gentiles the glorious riches of this mystery, which is Christ in you, the hope of glory.*
> (Colossians 1:26–27, NIV)

What you'll encounter in the following pages will be, at times, mindboggling.

In large part, I'm speaking of the legendary image of Golgotha: three crosses, with *Yeshua HaMashiach* spiked to the middle one. The awe-inspiring visual representation of it is hidden in plain sight throughout the Word of God.

But those seemingly encoded Golgotha portrayals are only visible to those who know what they're looking for. The ancients never could have understood the true meaning of their presence. In fact, they wouldn't have even noticed them. However, not only are we now able to *see* them, but we're also able to *understand* them in their truest contextual sense. They appear to have been meant for our generation!

From Genesis to Revelation

What makes this matter even more startling is that the Golgotha representations are found from the very first page of Genesis all the way to the very last page of Revelation, and their presence is undeniable. That's right! When the New Testament is translated into Hebrew, they are *there,* also—right where they might be expected.[3]

However, there's much more to this exploration than just recognizing the images. Their systematically placed locations also tell a remarkable story that unifies and magnifies the entire Word of God in a beautifully divine manner. Assisting you in this journey are more than eighty vivid illustrations to validate and punctuate what you're about to experience.

A Messianic Rabbi Weighs In

Messianic Rabbi Zev Porat is my dear friend and longtime ministry partner. Born and raised in Israel, He speaks, reads, and writes Hebrew as his first language. He was certified to be a Sanhedrin rabbi not long before he surrendered his life to *Yeshua HaMashiach*. With a huge ministry following, Zev teaches, preaches, and ministers the gospel message all over the world, even in the darkest corners of several nations known to be anti-Christian, and in the underground churches within those nations. Zev and his wife, Lian, reside in Tel Aviv, Israel.[4]

I sent the entire manuscript of this book to Zev before publication so he could review the content, including the use of the Hebrew language and the imagery that results from it. Following is his response, published with his approval:

> These revelations are spectacular! They *had* to have been implanted in the Word of God from the beginning! There are simply too many human complexities and impossibilities involved for them to have *not* been supernaturally encoded. There's no other rational explanation. These are not mere coincidences. The readers are going to be shocked when they see this for themselves!

Bringing It Alive

I'm convinced that the larger substance of this book will be more appropriately unwrapped if you're able to *feel* something of what this exploration is really tied to. So, the chapters of part one will be as though you're reading a short novel. But, in reality, you'll be personally engaged, through *the theater of your mind,* as you *experience* the account of how the unseen realm of darkness was finally shaken to its core.[5]

BEHIND THE VEIL

We'll begin our journey by going back in time almost two thousand years to an upper-room hideaway in downtown Jerusalem where Yeshua and His original twelve disciples are celebrating the annual Feast of Passover. This is Yeshua's last meal with his closest companions before He submits Himself to one of the most hideous forms of execution known to humanity: Roman crucifixion.[6]

Spring, AD 33—Downtown Jerusalem[7]

Yeshua is at the table. Seated around Him are the men who have been with Him from the beginning. He is acutely aware that one is a heartless traitor, harboring vile intentions that will eventually unfurl and engulf them all. Just a few short hours from now, their lives, and the world itself, will be changed forever.

And Yeshua knows what's coming next—every groaning detail.

≡ 2 ≡

GRUESOME AGENDAS

Yeshua knew all of these truths. He knew them before the first tidbit of those details had even come to pass, and He knew much more than that.

Yeshua is keenly aware that He now has less than one full day to live. As He glances around the room, He looks at His disciples, pausing a moment as He thinks of each of their lives—and their futures. The crushing reality of what lies ahead is a huge weight upon His spirit. But He forces a smile and winks at Peter, who is now looking right at Him with a huge grin spread across his face, as if to say, "Are you having fun, Master?" Yeshua's heart melts, as He nods his head "yes."

He is also aware that by tomorrow night, His dead body will be wrapped in grave clothes and tucked away in a musty, dungeon-dark tomb. The entrance will be sealed with a gigantic stone bearing the signet of the Roman emperor, Tiberius Julius Caesar Augustus, who is currently the most powerful man on the planet.

Yeshua knows, too, that while in the crypt, His horrifically disfigured body will be guarded by a Roman military attachment. The specialized unit will be comprised of sixteen hardened soldiers who will ultimately answer to the emperor himself. Each will also be under the threat of execution if something should go awry under their watch—if the body they will be guarding should go missing, for example. However, unbeknownst to them, the very thing the guards will be dreading will, in fact, *go wrong*. Terribly wrong.[8]

Three days later, the nature of that affair will detonate into Satan's dark domain, a devastating eruption that no one other than the One who sits on the throne of Heaven itself could have possibly seen coming.[9] Against all human odds, Yeshua's body will vanish from the tomb.

That flash of unbridled cosmic panic will unfold early in the morning, on the first day of next week, when several of Yeshua's female disciples will be the first to discover the empty tomb.

Tomorrow

By about this time tomorrow evening, the guardsmen will be placed at Yeshua's tomb under the frantic urging of the Jewish Sanhedrin council and the order of the Roman governor, Pontius Pilate. But first, there will be a gathering of the top tier of the political and religious elite of Jerusalem.

Heaps of drama will be served up as the centerpiece of the ensuing raucous discussions. Agendas from each faction will be presented through a variety of demands laden with seething disdain for the opposing party. Of course, Rome will have no desire to be involved in the internal religious interactions of the largely Jewish population of the area. At the same time, the Jewish religious elite will greatly prefer Rome to simply stay out of the affair altogether. They will claim the issue to be solely a Jewish one, therefore subject only to Jewish law.

That reasoning will not abide well with the Roman authorities. Practically everything the Jews do matters to Rome, on one level or another. They know fully well that these Jewish rulers would love to have a monopoly in matters of regional authority. With that coveted power, they would simply execute Yeshua themselves, and anyone else who got in their way. Rome, however, will not grant the Jewish dignitaries the authorization they so desperately crave.

By this time, the abject hatred for Yeshua fomenting among the Jewish ruling class will know no boundaries. Getting Him to be sentenced to death will be their ultimate goal—a fact previously settled amongst themselves, long before the meetings begin.

At the end of it all, the Jewish authorities, once again, will begrudgingly bend to the power of Rome. They will reason that "the enemy of my enemy is my friend." So, in these closing hours of Yeshua's life, they will finally succeed in their sinister plan, making Him the supposed enemy of Rome and of a large part of Orthodox Judaism in general.

The empire has continually struggled to keep "peace" in that region of its sacred holdings. Judea is a primarily Jewish province, infamous for spontaneous insurrections. Those melees are usually the result of the religious rantings of extremist rebels, mingled with the hot tempers of the ruling class who relentlessly wields their suffocating authority over the people.

That volatile mixture of power and greed often boil over into the "Jewish" uprisings that cause the empire so much grief. This is why Rome despises the Jews. And the feelings are mutual. Early tomorrow morning, the dreaded scenario of those inflated mood tsunamis will unfurl.

Pontius Pilate, the governor of Judea, will be forced to endure the brunt of the brewing anxiety. But Pilate has been in this position before, several times. So, once more, he'll begrudgingly endure this aggravating inconvenience—and he'll do so with impunity. And that will be that... or so he will assume.

However, what Rome and the Jews cannot have imagined is that all of this has been planned in another realm of cosmic reality. In fact, the Jewish Scriptures contain the prophecies that spell out almost every element of what's about to happen. But most of those Scriptures are an enigma to the Jewish elite. Long ago, those "important ones" made up their minds as to what their Messiah should look like, how He would present Himself, and precisely what He would accomplish. After three years of tedious observation, this fellow, often called "Yeshua of Nazareth," simply does not meet any of their imagined requirements.

Yeshua knows all of these details as well. As a matter of fact, He personally orchestrated the entire affair from eternity past, especially the path leading Him all the way to His own grueling cross of Golgotha.

That's what He has been thinking about as His disciples are now reveling in the midst of the evening meal and high-spirited Passover traditions. The music is playing, and dancing has commenced. Laughter fills the room. Still, no one has any idea of what's ahead.

But nothing of the horror that will soon pounce upon them all will come as a shock to Yeshua. *None of it.*

3

THEY DON'T KNOW

From this point forward, every move He makes, every word He speaks, will matter more than ever—forever.

Yes. Yeshua knows.

Although, at this point, He can't say as much for His disciples. They still don't understand the depths of what they will soon endure. Yet, in the days ahead, after they have observed the fulfillment of a multitude of ancient prophecies, each melding together in all their glorious completion, they will finally begin to get it.

Thereafter, they will proclaim far and wide, and for the rest of their lives, what they will have experienced. Most of them will lose their earthly lives over the affair, solely for being faithful enough to spread the resulting message of the gospel of salvation. In His private prayer hours, Yeshua has often wept about this part of the coming saga.

But there are still a few more vital elements that have yet to be fully accomplished.

The Not-So-Silent Night

So, here He is, the Lamb of God slain before the foundation of the world, sitting at a table with His disciples. At this moment, He is attempting to squeeze a little more enjoyment out of this last meal and the precious few hours He has left with them.

There are so many things He needs to tell these beloved men! Relating those details will be one of the toughest parts of the evening.

The twelve men with Yeshua now are Bartholomew, James the Lesser, James the Greater, Andrew, Peter, Simon, Jude (also known as Judas, the brother of James), Judas Iscariot, John, Thomas, Matthew, and Philip. Most have been with Yeshua since the beginning of His ministry, a journey that began just a little more than three years ago.

None of the wider circle of His disciples are here, including the females; it's only the original twelve who are present. There is a specific reason for this otherwise unusual arrangement. It won't be long, though, when *the twelve* will discover why they are the only ones with Him.

It will also be on this very night that one of them will make his final, slithering exit from the group, thinking that somehow he is doing God a favor. In reality, Judas has already betrayed them all, even before this moment. Unbeknownst to the other disciples, He earlier closed a dark deal with several high-ranking members of the Sanhedrin:[10] He agreed to receive for his act of disloyalty thirty pieces of silver—the equivalent of about six weeks of wages for the working class.[11]

However, the other disciples do not have a clue that Judas' betrayal is even a remote possibility. Only Judas and Yeshua know that detail until the much later hours of the night. However, at this moment, Judas has no idea Yeshua already knows of his treachery.

Omniscient

Not only is Yeshua already aware of the coming betrayal, but He has known it long before anyone else. In fact, He, in reality, *chose* Judas for this very purpose. He knows Judas' heart, and He knew the man would ultimately succumb to his inner demons.[12]

After all, Yeshua is the Word that became flesh. The Creator of the universe is now manifest in human flesh and bone. He knows the hearts of humanity, every single individual.[13]

And that's a huge part of the problem. Because, from this point forward, every move Yeshua makes, every word He speaks, will matter more than ever—*forever*. The fate of the entire fallen humanity hangs in the precarious balance of it all.

THEY DON'T KNOW

The Price

Soon, He will be shoved to the ground and spiked to the beams of a roughly hewn cross. But not before Pilate has sentenced Him to a brutal flogging, a merciless thrashing that will leave Him with great chunks of bloody flesh hanging from His body, from head to feet. Numerous victims don't even survive this preliminary part of the ordeal. Then, after that unspeakable torture, He will be crucified between two common criminals who are already scheduled for execution.[14]

Yeshua will join those sentenced offenders at a place commonly known by the people of that region as Golgotha. This is the place where the deed *must* be done. This, too, was preordained at the throne of Heaven, before earthly time even began.[15]

Each of the two criminals will be crucified on either side of Yeshua. On that inglorious day, He will forevermore be known as "the one in the middle." The resulting iconic symbol of Golgotha's dark day—*three crosses on a hill*—will be emblazoned upon the minds of most of humanity for thousands of years to come.

Yeshua, eons ago, arranged for this imprint to be far more obvious than just an image in the human mind. He has also ensured that the image of Golgotha's groaning would be literal, and then revealed to the world again in the *time of the end*.

But all that will come later. Much later.

Every jot and tittle of this *has* to happen. And each element has to fall into its ordained place in order to be fulfilled to the letter of perfection. He will see to it that all of this comes to pass, exactly as appointed.[16]

This is why He is in *this* room, in *this* place, at *this* very moment... with *these* men. It is also why they will soon make their way to the Garden of Gethsemane, at the foot of the Mount of Olives.

That spot will be exactly where the final hours of His life will quickly unwind.

≡ 4 ≡

A KINGDOM OF PRIESTS

Peter's eyes flood with tears.

As the rest of the men eat and converse among themselves, Yeshua rises from the table, stretches, then moves toward the entrance of the room.

They are in the midst of the first of the Seven Feasts of the Lord given to the Hebrew people at Mt. Sinai almost fourteen hundred years ago.[17] This is the night of the last Passover Yeshua will share with His disciples while He is in this world.

One of the men is strumming away on a lyre. Another joins the tune with his flute. Several others sing the words to the song of celebration, an ancient ballad most have known since they were children; it's a psalm of praise to *Yahweh*. Almost all celebrants are tapping the table or the sides of their thighs and legs to the rhythm of the music.[18]

Amid their loudest crooning, a feral dog just below them on the street gazes up toward their room and howls a mournful protest to their sometimes out-of-tune harmonizing. The men hear it and break into wild laughter, punching the shoulders of those next to them, blaming the others for disturbing the pitiful animal with their off-pitch singing.

Oh, how He loves these men! How He has longed to participate in this night of joyous communion, in spite of the fact that He also knows of the treason that will accompany it…only a few moments from now.[19]

Yeshua's heart aches within the depths of His being. Few things hurt worse than being betrayed by someone to whom one is so intimately connected. Right now, Judas is still among them. The betrayer sways to the music and sings out with the rest of the men, trying not to give any clues about what he's really up to.

Judas' approaching act of betrayal is already welling up within his heart. He knows the moment is close. If only he can find the courage he needs to pull it off! Soon, he will become immersed in the demonic filling of haughtiness that will finally enable him to carry out the deed.

Stunned

Just after Yeshua has risen from the table, He shocks His disciples by removing the top layer of His garments, folding each piece as it is detached, and placing it on a nearby chair. He then moves near the doorway, where he unhooks a towel dangling over the foot-washing basin on the floor. A chair is situated next to the large bowl of water that's been previously muddied by the use of each man entering the room earlier that evening.[20]

An Ordination

"What in the world is Yeshua doing?" Philip mumbles to James under his breath. "Our feet are already clean! He knows that! He watched us as we washed them! And besides that, He is our master, not *our servant*!"

Yeshua ties the towel around His waist and cinches it tight. He opens the door and throws out the old water, then pours fresh water from a nearby pitcher into the basin. He then motions for the men to gather around.

When they're all together, Yeshua points to James the Lesser and beckons him to come forward. He is to be the first one seated in the foot-washing chair. Sheepishly, James complies, while the others look on in astonishment, like a gaggle of curious toddlers. James looks up from his seat at the rest of them, shrugging as if to say, "I don't know either!" No one has a clue what this unusual moment is about.

Yeshua kneels and begins washing James' feet. When He is finished, He wipes them dry with the towel.

GOLGOTHA'S GROANING

Not Me!

As James gets up from the chair to take his place with the others, Yeshua motions for Peter to sit for the next foot washing. To no one's surprise, the generally hot-headed, long-winded disciple objects. "Lord, you're not going to wash *my* feet!" he says. "Are you?" The look on Peter's face reveals his shock at the unfolding events.

"Peter," Yeshua replies, "what I am doing may be difficult for you to understand now. But very soon you will."

None of the disciples realize Yeshua is anointing and preparing them for their coming priesthood. They, and their spiritual lineage, will soon be proclaiming the gospel of Golgotha's Passover sacrifice and the resulting Feast of Firstfruits Resurrection event that will forevermore be associated with it.[21]

It won't be long before that message will commence its centuries-long journey to the entire world. Its spread will not stop until the Son of Man returns to establish His rule and reign over the entire earth. All of this will be started by the men in this room—the first preachers and leaders of the newly born congregation of believers.

Except for one. That man's feet will in fact be washed along with the others, but his heart has already hardened. Although he will go through the ritual of being "ordained," his soul is already blackened, by his own choice. Satan has seen to it. And Judas' pride and greed have obliged him.[22]

It is a well-known and longstanding Levitical law that the bodies, especially the feet, of incoming ordained priests have to be washed by the high priest. In this manner, their entire bodies are symbolically made clean and ceremonially fit for their holy service to the Lord.[23]

They don't know it at this moment, but the Great High Priest of the Universe is now kneeling right in front of them. He is preparing them for their eternal service in the coming Kingdom of God. But of course, Peter has more to say about the matter. He is horrified as Yeshua begins washing his feet, so he pulls them away from Yeshua's hands.

"You will *never* wash my feet!" Peter squares his shoulders as he blurts out his indignant announcement.

A KINGDOM OF PRIESTS

Yeshua replies, "Peter. Please listen carefully. I love you, but if I don't wash your feet, you cannot have a part with me in the Kingdom work that is to come." He patiently searches Peter's expression for a response.

Peter ponders those words for a few moments before a knowing look appears on his face.

While Yeshua continues gazing into His disciple's eyes, waiting, Peter speaks again, his words croaking from his lips like a prepubescent boy's comical changing voice. "Lord, not only my feet then!" He clears his throat and adds, "Please, also wash my hands and my head!"

Peter's eyes flood with tears. Embarrassed by the sudden welling up of emotion, he wipes them dry with the back of his sleeve as he slips his feet back into the basin.

The other disciples remain speechless. Yeshua turns to them and says, "The one who has already bathed does not need to wash, except for his feet," Yeshua explains. "When that last detail is done, however, then that person is completely clean. So, you are now clean, *spiritually*. Fit for Kingdom service."

He hesitates for a moment, then adds, "But not every one of you is clean."

Yeshua lowers His head when He utters these last words. As He speaks, Peter can hear Him groaning, but just barely…as if He is in private agony.

What is it that Yeshua alone seems to know? Who is this mysterious one that is not *clean*?

… 5 …

A TRAITOR IN THE HOUSE

He tells himself that what he is doing will be for the betterment of them all.

When Yeshua has washed the feet of each of the disciples and put His outer garments back on, He urges them to join Him back at the table.

When they're again settled, He says, "Do you understand what I have done for you? You call me 'Teacher' and 'Lord,' and you're right, for that is what I am. If I, then, your Lord and Teacher, have washed your feet, you should wash one another's feet. I've done this for you as an example for you to follow."

Then He speaks again, "A servant isn't greater than his master, and a messenger isn't more important than the one sending the message. If you understand this, you're blessed indeed. I'm not talking about all of you, however; I know the ones I've chosen. I know the hearts of everyone."[24]

As He speaks, a slight groan again emanates from somewhere deep within His chest. This time they all hear it—not just Peter. It is a moment they will talk about for years to come.

Yeshua's cryptic interjections have grown increasingly perplexing. What, and *who*, can He be talking about? Who among them is "unclean"? Why would Yeshua even say such a thing? And why is this cryptic announcement bringing Him such inner turmoil that it's making Him groan?

He lifts His head again and glances around the table, saying, "The Scripture must be fulfilled, 'He who ate my bread has lifted his heel against me.' I am reminding you of this now, before it takes place, so when it does take place, you may believe that I am He."[25]

A TRAITOR IN THE HOUSE

Now they are genuinely shocked and somewhat confused. Each one of them has eaten bread with Him! In fact, He would often, throughout the meal, dip the bread and then pass servings of it to His disciples. At one point He had even declared that the bread represented His own body, and the cup represented His blood—the New Covenant![26] What in the world does He mean by all of this? What is He really about to do?

After a few moments, the bewildered disciples resume eating. They continue for several more minutes, picking around at their food, when Yeshua brings up the mystifying topic once again. "I will tell you the plain truth of the matter. One of you will betray Me, this very night."

When He says this, Peter glances at John and slightly shrugs his shoulders with a look that says, "I don't understand why He's obsessing over this thing—what is it that He's not telling us?"

Do What You Have To Do

The disciples look around at one another, murmuring, still uncertain who He is speaking about. They are floored by His latest—and straightforward—declaration.

The accusation is more than Peter can abide. John, the youngest of the disciples, is seated next to Yeshua, close at His side.

Peter decides this moment is as good as any. Seated on the other side of John, he taps his shoulder to get his attention. John leans back against Peter while Yeshua continues to converse with others at the table.

"What, *Peter*—what do you *want*?" John asks in a hushed tone, indicating his irritation.

In a whisper, Peter pleads, "John! Please ask Yeshua who He's talking about! He'll listen to you. He'll probably tell *you* who it is that He thinks will betray Him! I can't imagine who He's talking about, though, can you? I hope He's not thinking that *I* would betray Him!"[27]

John answers, "I don't know either! I was thinking the same thing about myself. But I'll ask Him as soon as the chance presents itself." Peter, looking a little distraught, asks John, almost with a whimper, "Promise?"

John sighs, "Yes. I promise." *For all of Peter's boldness and courage, he sometimes seems like a little child*, John thinks to himself.

GOLGOTHA'S GROANING

A few moments later, the opportunity comes. John leans and says quietly in Yeshua's ear, "Lord, *who* is going to betray You?"

Yeshua answers, also softly, "It is the one to whom I will give this next morsel of bread, right after I have dipped it. By the way, you can tell Peter it's not him, but say nothing to the others." John gulps. He shakes his head in agreement with Yeshua's instructions.

John watches in stunned silence as Yeshua eventually eases a piece of the Passover bread into the dish. No one thinks a thing about the Teacher's action of dipping the bread and serving it to a disciple.

The piece He has just dipped is then handed to Judas, the son of Simon Iscariot. Judas' eyes meet Yeshua's. A slight grin appears on the disciple's face. There appears to be a visible hint of evil in his eyes. John sees it, and it unnerves him.

Judas turns from Yeshua, avoiding any further discussion with Him, and strikes up a dialogue with one of the men next to him. Judas never engages in a conversation with Yeshua again.[28]

Yeshua knows Satan has entered Judas at that very moment,[29] arming him with a demonic pride and a deranged certainty that somehow he is "doing the right thing." It is the very same look of arrogance Yeshua saw flashing across Satan's face in the Garden of Eden eons ago.

In that moment, Judas thinks to himself, *On balance, who could rightfully blame me? All this talk about being handed over to the Jews, being crucified, but then raised on the third day! Pure madness!*

At any rate, Judas determines that, from this point forward, he will have nothing else to do with this gang of men. Even the authorities in their own synagogues have labeled them all as misfits and blasphemers. He convinces himself that what he is about to do is actually going to be for the betterment of them all. *They will soon see!* he thinks. *Then they will eventually thank me for what I'm doing for them tonight.*

A little while later in the meal, amid Judas' private moment of self-delusion, Yeshua looks right at him. "Judas," He says steadily, "do what you must do, and do it quickly."

None of the rest have any problem with what Yeshua has said to Judas. Some think that because Judas holds the moneybag, perhaps the

A TRAITOR IN THE HOUSE

Lord is simply telling him to buy more food and treats for the feast. Or perhaps He is telling Judas he should go out and give something to the poor, especially on this night of holy celebration. At this moment, not a soul other than John and Peter even considers that Judas might be the betrayer.[30]

But they do know, and they watch, bewildered, as Judas stands. They know this act of betrayal from a man they considered a loyal friend will devastate the rest of their band of brothers. So, as Yeshua instructed, they hold their tongues. Now they understand the reason for Yeshua's earlier moaning—or at least a part of it.

The evening grows darker with each passing moment, and in more ways than one. With the knowledge they now possess, John and Peter sense the doom headed their way. Soon, the fullest horror of Golgotha's groaning will be upon them all.

But not yet.

6

SHOW US THE FATHER

Yeshua motions for the group to move closer to Him, indicating that His next words will be of the utmost importance.

Judas is gone.

He has disappeared into the evening blackness. The scene has been like that of a mongrel dog that had just stolen a succulent piece of lamb trying to hide his prize from the others around him.

Yeshua clears His throat to speak as He finally stands and faces His disciples; His countenance is one of troubled seriousness.

"The time has come," He says, glancing at each of the men. "Now the Son of Man is glorified, and God is glorified in Him. My children! I'll only be with you a little while longer. You will seek Me, and, just as I've said to the Jewish leaders, I say to you, 'Where I am going you cannot come.'"

He has their attention. Not one of them has moved, nor is anyone speaking. They merely sit there, mouths gaping. Peter looks around the room at the rest of his comrades and thinks to himself, *If you men only knew!*

Yeshua continues, "I'm giving you a new commandment: Love one another. Just as I have loved you, I want you also to love one another. By this—by having love for one another—all people will know that you are My disciples."

Where Are You Going?

Peter interjects once again. "But Lord, where are You going?" he asks. "You keep saying this, but we don't understand. At least *I* don't understand!"

SHOW US THE FATHER

Peter looks around the room at the other disciples for confirmation of what he has just said. Philip, Thomas, and James the Lesser immediately nod in agreement.

Yeshua replies, "Peter, where I am going you cannot follow—at least, not now. But you will follow afterward."

"Lord, why can't I follow You *now*?" Peter says. "I will lay down my life for You! You know I will! I would never let anything happen to You!"

Yeshua looks at him with the deepest love Peter has ever seen in their Lord's face.

Through tear-glistened eyes, He asks Peter, "Will you really lay down your life for Me, Peter? *Truly?*"

"I have said it, Lord! And I mean it!" Peter reiterates with a tone of loving annoyance. "You *know* I will! Lord, why do You ask me something like this?"

Yeshua pauses for a moment as He gathers His next words. He takes a long, deep breath. "I tell you the truth, Peter," He replies, "here's what will happen—on this very night. Before you hear the sound of a rooster crowing in the morning, you will have denied three times. When that rooster calls out, you'll remember that I told all of you these things before they happened. When that seemingly impossible thing comes to pass, then you'll know who I am—and where I am going."

By now, the anxiety of those in the room has grown to a much higher level. It is time for Yeshua to soothe the atmosphere. Another "storm in the boat" has erupted. He knows He must once again speak to the "winds" of swirling emotions that now fill the room, and calm them.

Yeshua aligns His gaze as He scans their faces. What He is about to say is directed to the group at large: "Do not let your hearts be troubled over these matters," He says. "You believe in God, so you can believe also in Me. In My Father's house are many dwelling places. If that weren't true, I wouldn't have told you that I go to prepare a place for you." The disciples listen in silence, awaiting more explanation.

"And since I am going to prepare a place for you," Yeshua continues, "I will come again and will take you to Myself, so that where I am you may be also. And, by now, you *know* the way to where I am going."

GOLGOTHA'S GROANING

The Doubter

Now Thomas speaks up. "Lord, we don't know *where* You are going, so how could we possibly know the *way*?"

Yeshua replies, "Thomas. I am the *Way*, and the *Truth*, and the *Life*. No one comes to the Father except through Me. If you had known Me, fully known Me, you would have known My Father also. But from this point forward you *do* know Him, and you have seen Him."

Philip thinks to himself, *Well now. This is odd. Why is Yeshua speaking in these riddles again—and to us, in this place, and in this moment?*

Philip to the Rescue

Then Philip has an idea. It comes to him suddenly. Surely, *this* will solve everything!

He blurts out, "Lord, just show us the Father and it will be enough for us!" Philip sits up a little straighter as he glances at the others. He has just offered a way to clear up the hidden meanings of this conversation. At least that's what he thinks.

In reality, this request from Philip stabs at Yeshua's heart. Similar words, expressing the very same request, have often been spoken by the Pharisees and Sadducees during the last three years. And now one of His dearest disciples is asking Him the same thing: *Show us the Father! Give us a sign from Heaven!* Yeshua sighs. When will they finally see?[31]

He motions for the group to move closer to Him, indicating that His next words are of the utmost importance. His answer will serve as a lesson for them all.

Once they have gathered in front of Him, He begins explaining, "Have I been with you so long, and you still do not know Me, Philip? Whoever has seen Me has seen the Father! How can you say, 'Show us the Father'? Do you not believe that I am in the Father and the Father is in Me? The words I say to you I don't speak on My own authority, but the Father who dwells in Me does His works. Believe Me that I am in the Father and the Father is in Me, or else believe on account of the works themselves."

It's now become obvious that Yeshua is about to say something that will prove to be eternally important.

They will not be disappointed.

≡ 7 ≡

ONLY GOD

I did not come to merely pronounce who I Am, but to actually demonstrate who *I Am.*

No one has moved.

The men are absorbed in His words. Their souls are open. Now is the time for them to *see.*

Yeshua continues, "Let Me remind you of just a few things you've already witnessed. And, let Me remind you of why it was important that you experienced those events! When I do this, you will all possess the answer to Philip's request."[32]

The majesty with which Yeshua's voice resonates through His next words floors them all. Yeshua begins, "Do you not know? Do you not remember? Even after all this time, and in light of everything you've seen? The miracles that have been done, right before your eyes...each one was showing you things that only the Father Himself can do! That was the point of every one of them!"

Yeshua continues, "Think of it! Only God can walk on water! And only He can speak to the wind and waves of a storm...and by His command they are stilled. The powers of the universe obey only Him! Those very facts are proclaimed throughout the Tanakh." He then recites several of the passages.

Yes! Now they are remembering![33]

"Each of you has seen me accomplish all of those works. *Peter—you remember, don't you?*" Yeshua winks at the outspoken disciple, whose face explodes in a blush, then a huge smile. Of course he remembers! He walked on the water himself—but only at Yeshua's command!

ONLY GOD

"Oh!" Peter bellows. "How could I ever forget that night?"

"Philip," Yeshua continues, "You were there also, and *I know* you remember! You were among those who asked, 'Who is this that commands the wind and the waves, and they obey Him'? Well, there's your answer, Philip. Now *you know* who it is that you have seen."[34]

Philip drops his head in silent embarrassment. How could he have been so dull as to have demanded a "sign" from their Lord? His eyes had beheld multiplied dozens of signs, just like the ones Yeshua is now describing. He had begun seeing those miracles on his very first day with the Lord!

Yeshua goes on, "And this is not the end of what you've seen, Philip! Only God Himself can create something out of *nothing*. Do you remember when we fed the ten thousand with nothing but My Word and a few borrowed fish and chunks of bread offered by a little boy?"

Philip nods in acknowledgment. After a brief pause, Yeshua continues, "Or, how about forming perfectly working eyeballs inside the completely healed sockets of the man born blind? That was just a few months back. Remember?" All the men are showing their agreement now—some with huge grins.

"And what about raising the dead," Yeshua continues, "with only My command? Do you not remember that I alone commanded life to enter again into three different people who had died? And life *did* return to them, *instantly*! Who can do such a thing as this, but the Father alone?[35] And who is it that creates and heals body parts—only at a Word![36]

He looks around the room. They are remembering everything now, in vivid detail. He can see it in their eyes. He knows it in their thoughts.

"These things make up just a very short list of all that you've seen," He says. "But I will continue. How about knowing exactly what people were thinking, and what they were going to say before it even happened? Did you not also see demons exiting a person immediately, only upon My Word? I did not plead with those demons; no tricks, convoluted religious rituals, or dark potions of any kind were involved. I only gave a simple command, and those evil ones fled, shrieking as they left!

GOLGOTHA'S GROANING

Only the Father can do these things. The Scriptures plainly declare this truth! Yet, you've witnessed all of this, and so much more!".

The disciples remain quiet, clearly in a state of rapt attention. "Again I ask you," Yeshua prompts, "how can any of you say to Me, 'Show us the Father?' Here is the truth of the matter...if you've seen Me, you've seen the Father!"

He turns to Philip. "Do you know who I am *now*, Philip?'

Philip answers with a choked, trembling voice, "Forgive me Lord, I've spoken too soon, and in ignorance." The look on Yeshua's face affirms His forgiveness.

Then Yeshua says to all, "Please understand this, I did not come to simply *pronounce* who I am, rather, I came to *demonstrate* who I am—but only for those with eyes to see. Anyone can appear among the crowds and proclaim to be God! And there will be many in the last days who will do that very thing! But only one can do what God alone can do, and do it time and time again in your presence. You have now seen Him. If you've seen Me, you've seen the Father."[37]

Departure to Gethsemane

Yeshua rises as He stops teaching. The disciples sense it is nearing time to depart from their borrowed room of Passover celebration. They begin to gather their belongings. They aren't quite sure what will happen next, but only a few hours from now they will know the full and ugly truth.

Yeshua speaks again while they prepare to leave; the men stop what they're doing to focus on Him.

"All these things I tell you while I am still with you," He says, "but the Holy Spirit, whom the Father will soon send in My name, He will teach you all things and bring to your remembrance all that I have said to you this evening, and even before.

"Peace I am leaving with you; *My peace* I give to you. So let not your hearts be troubled, nor let them be afraid. You heard Me say to you, 'I am going away, and then I will come back to you.' I have told you before it takes place, so that when I return you may believe.

"I will speak to you very little from this point forward, for the ruler of this world is coming. He has no claim on Me, but I do as the Father has commanded Me, so that the world may know that I love the Father."

Yeshua leads them in singing a psalm of praise, a traditional part of the final closing of the Passover meal and evening activities known to all the disciples.[38]

When they finish the song, Yeshua walks to the entrance of the room, to the same door Judas exited through not long ago. With a calm, matter-of-fact voice, He turns to His disciples and says, "Let us leave from this place. Follow Me. And stay close."

… 8 …

A GARDEN

Yeshua senses the presence. It is as evil as evil gets.

Yeshua and the disciples slip through the shadows, careful not to make a ruckus as they go.

After Yeshua's stern warnings, the disciples are feeling a heavy atmosphere of impending danger wafting among them. This is *the day*—the one planned before the dawn of time itself. Its secret has been sealed at Heaven's throne for eons. Now the night hours of that ominous day have arrived. Yeshua is perfectly positioned in the middle of it all. So far, so good.

As the men walk on, an owl hoots its mournful notes from a nearby tree limb. The sounds of people scurrying about, bolting their doors and shuttering their windows, can still be heard in the distance. Various other echoes of a large city closing down its activities and preparing for a new day continue to punctuate the night air.

The evening is much cooler now. Against the dropping temperature and the increasing breeze, several of the disciples pull tighter their outer clothing. Soon, they exit the city by way of the East Gate, not far from where they just celebrated the Passover. From there, they cross over the Kidron brook on a small footbridge and head back up the western slope of the Mount of Olives, an area they're intimately familiar with.

Just on the other side of the brook is the Garden of Gethsemane, which they enter within a few minutes and slip among the vast grove of ancient olive trees. The group is now secreted away under the lengthening nighttime shadows. The trees surround the men like mighty sentinels in the cloud-covered night. Yeshua instructs His disciples to watch and

A GARDEN

pray, and to remain where they are in the Garden while He retreats to a place about a stone's throw away in order to pray.

From this point forward, Yeshua will never again close His eyes in earthly sleep. This is going to be a long night, and an even longer day tomorrow. This is what He has come for, and in His human flesh He dreads every minute of what is to come. But He will endure it anyway... all the way to Golgotha.

During the next few hours, He occasionally rises from prayer to check on His disciples. It saddens Him to find them sleeping. They're not keeping a vigilant lookout, nor are they fervently praying, as He has instructed. How can one be surrounded by a group of such true friends, but at the same time feel so very alone?

Yeshua sighs. As He watches the slumbering men, several tears escape from His eyes and splat into the dust at His feet. He shakes His head and groans slightly as, once again, He turns to walk back to His place of prayer.

But deep into the blackness of the thickly clouded, earliest hours of the morning, Yeshua senses a presence. Even the air around Him takes on an oppressive feel. This is it. *They* are coming!

The Gang

He can hear them talking as they swish their torches back and forth, attempting to bring light into the darkness that secludes Yeshua and His men. The formerly gleaming Passover moon has now been completely obscured by the heavy cloud cover. The approaching entourage continues to close in, having just left the city through the East Gate.

It won't be long.

Judas knows where he thinks Yeshua is, or at least close to it. Yeshua often met with His disciples in the same vicinity. At this moment, the traitor is leading a company of Temple guards who have been sent by the Sanhedrin officials.

At first, their torches and lanterns had looked like a whirlwind of fireflies in the distant night. Soon, however, they appear more like the harbingers they are: sizzling, roaring flames of evil intensity being used to search frantically through the darkness for the men's whereabouts.

GOLGOTHA'S GROANING

The closer they come, the more the visages of their swords, spears, and clubs become apparent. Yeshua, knowing what is about to happen, rushes to His disciples and shakes them from their slumber. They awaken with a jolt as the invaders step from the shadows and right into their midst.

Yeshua comes forward from the group of drowsy disciples. "Who is it that you seek?"

"Yeshua of Nazareth!"

"I am He. I am the one you seek."

Yeshua sees Judas in the group. The traitor steps forward; a stride of arrogance seems to propel him toward Yeshua. Judas grabs Yeshua in an embrace, greeting Him with a kiss on the cheek. "Rabbi!" he exclaims, loudly enough that his entourage can hear. The kiss and the spoken identification had been prearranged signs indicating Yeshua's identity to the Sanhedrin. This would be their assurance that they are taking into custody the correct man from among the bunch.

Yeshua pulls Judas close to His face and whispers, "You would betray Me with a kiss, Judas? A kiss of *friendship*?" Judas returns the question with a blank, cold stare. He huffs under his breath as he turns his back to Yeshua and walks away, shaking his head as though he is the sane one and Yeshua is the one who has finally gone mad. Satan's vile spirit of deception has its talons deeply embedded in the traitor-puppet.

Suddenly, the arresting officers dart toward Yeshua. Here He stands! Here is their prize! They are just about to seize Him...*when it happens*.

The Crime

Peter. Hot-headed, loud-mouthed Peter, who just a few moments ago was startled awake, pulls his sword out of its leather sheath. It exits the scabbard with a *pop*. Without another thought, he swings the weapon at the head of the high priest's servant, Malchus, the nearest figure in the invading entourage.

In the heat of the moment, Peter reasons that he is keeping his word to Yeshua. Back at the Passover meal celebration, he had promised Yeshua that he would die for Him—he would even die *with Him*, if

A GARDEN

necessary. As far as Peter is concerned, the time to make good on that promise has just arrived. But it is a vow Yeshua never asked Peter to make. In fact, He had actually forbidden it.

But Peter is having none of this unwelcomed *garden invasion*, much less will he tolerate the obvious fact that they are here to lay hands on his Lord. If it is violence they want, Peter will give it to them. He is no stranger to it.

With all his might, fueled by his brewing anger…Peter swings his blade at Malchus' head.

9

A RECTIFIED CRIME

What is already a long night has just gotten much longer.

Peter slashes his sword through the air, murderous rage etched in the contortions of his face. His pent-up anger has finally exploded.

Fortunately for him, Malchus actually sees the uncaged fury coming just in time. As soon as he hears the swish of Peter's sword and sees that it's on the way to his head, he jerks aside.

The sword barely misses his skull, but it catches Malchus' right ear and severs it clean away. The appendage lands at his feet in the darkness of the night, in the dirt of the garden. A collective gasp of shock shoots forth from the members of the stunned mob now moving toward the disciples, swords drawn.

In the same instance that his ear goes flying from his head, Malchus falls to the ground, crumples up, and screams the most horrific sounds of pain one can imagine. He wallows on the ground sounding like a mortally wounded animal.

Yeshua scolds Peter. "Put your sword away! *Now!* Will you keep Me from drinking the cup the Father has given Me to drink? After everything I've shown you, and all that I've taught you, you would still do something like *this*?"

Malchus continues to writhe in the dirt in torturous pain, bleeding profusely. If the gaping wound isn't quickly attended to, there is a good chance he will bleed to death in just a few more minutes. This is the last thing Yeshua needs.

Yeshua looks at the chief officer among the Sanhedrin consort and pleads, "Please. Let Me attend to Malchus! Give Me less than five

A RECTIFIED CRIME

minutes, then I will go peacefully, even quietly, with no more words or resistance. You have My word. I can help him. May I please do so?"

The officer, seeing no danger in letting Yeshua kneel beside Malchus for a short while, grants permission. After all, armed soldiers and temple guards now surround Yeshua. Also, He has just been abandoned by His disciples who, at their first opportunity, scampered away into the shadows, like panicking deer hiding from a pride of hungry lions.

Because of what's happened to Malchus, the band of officers occupying the garden with swords and torches isn't pursuing the fleeing disciples. They will deal with Peter later, and he *will* go to prison for his crime! Of that fact, they are certain. He might even be put to death. They had all witnessed an attempted murder with their own eyes.

The main reason Peter's action has been deemed such a serious offense is because there is no more important man in all Judea, outside of the Roman officials themselves, than the high priest of the Sanhedrin Council. And there is no one more important to the high priest than his personal assistant.

That's why Malchus is in the garden now—possibly dying. He was sent here to represent the high priest. If Caiaphas hears of this atrocity wrought by the edge of Peter's sword, news of it will most likely be followed by the steepest penalty possible.

Yeshua knows all of this. By now, these truths have finally come to Peter's mind as well. But Peter and John are now deep within the darkness...hiding, huddled close together, praying...and planning their next moves.

Yeshua drops to the ground, lying face down beside Malchus, who is moving in and out of consciousness. His life hangs by a very short thread. Blood continues to spurt from the gaping, ragged cavity on the side of his head where his ear should be.

Yeshua sweeps up the mangled ear from the ground. He pulls Himself closer to Malchus, and embraces him as He eases what is left of the ear directly over the place where it was severed. The Jerusalem gang looks on with stunned curiosity. All torches are illuminating the grisly scene on the ground in front of them.

GOLGOTHA'S GROANING

Yeshua whispers something Malchus alone can hear: "Peace Malchus! All is well. You can trust Me. Soon, you'll have your ear restored."

In that very moment, not only can Malchus hear out of that ear again, but it is no longer mangled! It is attached and whole, as though the entire affair never happened! Not a scar is seen, and not one drop of blood is on the ground or anywhere else. And the pain has instantly vanished—at Yeshua's word!

Malchus sits up and weeps, clutching Yeshua and thanking Him with pitiful sobs accompanied by a tinge of remorse for even being there to arrest Him. *Almost.*

The onlooking men stand speechless. What have they just seen? This is no trick! What they've witnessed didn't occur at the hands of a deceiving magician or a demon-possessed sorcerer, as many of the rabbis, priests, and Pharisees often accuse Yeshua of being.

This! This had been something *miraculous*. And somehow the entire dramatic affair had seemed like some kind of mere cosmic inconvenience to Yeshua—like a thing that simply had to be quickly cleaned up so He could submit Himself to arrest! They have never experienced *anything* like this before!

And now, the officially dispatched band of officers finally arrests and binds Him. Yeshua keeps His promise; He does not resist. From this point on, He will say little else—*to anyone.*

Night of Sedition

The brigade embarks on their trek of leading Yeshua back through the city gates and up to the house of Annas, the father-in-law of Caiaphas and a former high priest himself. This is the first part of Yeshua's illegal seizure. Later in the night, however, Annas will send them off to Caiaphas' house, where the trial will take place. From there, early in the morning daylight hours, they will take Yeshua before Pontius Pilate, the Roman governor of Judea.

Peering from the Shadows

But, just now, still in the darkness of the night, two men appear in the Garden of Gethsemane. They emerge like apparitions from deep within

A RECTIFIED CRIME

the foliage as the armed men from the Temple are leaving with Yeshua. The two have concealed themselves as they make plans to try to help Yeshua. Each has fairly warm clothing, with attached hoods, to protect them from the deep chill of the spring evening.[39]

They pull their hoods low, cinch them tightly, and trail far behind the crowd that leads Yeshua back into Jerusalem. What has already been a long night is quickly growing much longer. It is bizarre to think that they, just a few hours ago, were celebrating the Passover meal together by singing, dancing, and reciting Scripture. That's when John thinks to himself: *And look where we are now!*

When the officials escorting the "criminal" Yeshua to Annas' house arrive, John decides to take a chance. He enters through the courtyard door with them. John is personally known to the former high priest. The servant girl guarding the door also knows him. For this reason, she allows John to enter with the rest of the entourage. Peter, however, remains outside the door with his hood pulled low over his head, hiding a good portion of his face.

Once John is secure inside the courtyard, he sees Yeshua's arrestors escort Him into Annas' house. He mumbles under his breath, "This is not going to be good, not at all!"

John then goes back to the courtyard gates and asks the servant girl if he can bring Peter inside with him. She agrees.

Peter is hesitant to enter. But, by now, he feels a bit more certain he won't be recognized, especially if he takes cover within the pockets of the large group of men standing around the charcoal fires, warming themselves. The men are mingling in casual conversation as the dancing sparks pop and glitter in the frigid night air.

For now, everything appears to be under control. Peter finally breathes in, then exhales a long, relaxing breath as he steps through the gate and into the courtyard.

But very soon all that will change.

≡ 10 ≡

THE DENIAL

As He is soaked in the dark grip of indescribable grief, the door to Caiaphas' house opens.

As Peter enters the courtyard with John, the servant girl addresses him in an almost-panicked tone. "Oh!" she accuses. "I think I recognize you! You are also one of that man's disciples, *aren't you?*" She expresses her suspicions much louder than Peter likes. All eyes are now on him! John's eyes widen with anxiety, but he remains silent.

"I am not!" Peter insists. "In fact, I don't know Him at all!"

The answer satisfies her, at least for now. Just then, a cold chill runs up Peter's spine. His immediate thoughts are thick with panic. *Should I run, and certainly look guilty? Or should I just stay here and hope for the best?*

The other servants and several of the officers return to their casual banter and gather closer to the crackling fires. The night is quickly slipping into a bitter chill. And it will get even colder toward the dawn. So Peter eases up to the men and stands among the fires with them, warming his hands.

Perhaps I am safe, Peter reasons. He decides to stay put a little longer. John has already left Peter and is milling about. He is on the lookout for any tidbit of information concerning Yeshua.

Peter chats with the men beside him around the fire making as much small talk as possible. Suddenly, one of the men says, "Hey! You *are* one of His disciples, aren't you? I recognize you! Yes! *You're one of them!*"

Again, Peter denies the accusation. "Man! You don't even know what you're talking about! I am not one of His disciples. In fact, I don't even *know* the man! I'm just here to see what all the fuss is about—just like you!"

THE DENIAL

But, about an hour later, one of the personal servants of the high priest, a relative of the man whose ear Peter cut off, also eases up to the fire. He asks Peter, "Did I not see you in the garden with Him tonight? You look just like one of them! I'm not going to make an accusation about *which* man you look like, but that disciple is in big trouble! This fact I know!" The man turns to the others and exclaims, "This man was in the garden with Yeshua, I'm almost certain of it! He, too, is a Galilean!"

Peter is more frightened than ever, thinking that he may soon go to prison, *or worse*. So he answers the man with the most sincere-sounding response he can muster. "You have no idea what you're saying, sir!" he insists. "I've never met the man—I have never even known this Yeshua you're speaking of! I was not with Him, and I would have no reason to have been with Him!"

At the moment Peter denies having any connections to Yeshua, a rooster crows a long, throaty call. No one is startled by the obnoxious noise except Peter. He recoils at the sound, terrified beyond words. His stomach becomes sick, and he looks for a shadowy corner where he can relieve the contents of his souring belly.

As he flounders in the grip of indescribable grief, the door to Annas' house opens. Yeshua is being escorted outside! The word spreading among the crowd is that they are headed to Caiaphas' home—the residence of the high priest of the Sanhedrin.

John has just drawn near the departing entourage. The look of utter despair on John's face unnerves Peter to the core. Peter leaves the warmth of the fires and stumbles up to him.

John whimpers to Peter, "I don't like this! This is not going well at all!"

Just then, the entourage of officials, with Yeshua in tow, passes by them. Yeshua's hands are bound, and His face is badly bruised. Someone had struck him! Peter's pent-up fury swells to a new level. He tells himself, "You've got to get a *grip* on this!"

Yeshua is quickly moving nearer to Peter, shoved along by His captors as though He were a violent criminal. As Yeshua draws almost next to where Peter stands, He turns and knowingly looks straight into the eyes of His beloved disciple. The rooster crows again at that very second.

GOLGOTHA'S GROANING

Yeshua groans in pain as He is snatched along like a chained animal. Peter ponders to himself as he watches Yeshua and His captors, and John following them all, disappear into the night. *This is so obvious—they have an execution in mind!*

The rooster continues its crowing. Peter falls to his knees, then crumples onto the dirt and curls up like an infant. He groans in heart-wrenching heaves of anguish. Yeshua's earlier prophecy about the events of this very night come pouring back into his memory. He has betrayed Yeshua precisely three times, just as He said!

As soon as Peter finishes that thought, the rooster crows again, as if cruelly mocking him in the midst of his grief.

Before he can stop himself from sobbing, he blurts out, "How can I be so horribly stupid! *So stupid! So incredibly stupid!*" He pounds the ground with balled-up fists.

Peter doesn't yet know that Yeshua has already removed all evidence of his earlier assault of Malchus. While Peter had been running away with the rest of the disciples, Yeshua had restored the man's ear, leaving behind no scars, hearing loss, blood, or pain.

Now, there is no way anyone could convict Peter of a crime. Even the man whose ear had been severed won't press charges because there simply is no evidence that the deed occurred. And besides, if anyone speaks of yet another miracle wrought by Yeshua, the elders will most likely unleash their maddening fury upon them!

Peter has been spared the wrath of Rome and the Sanhedrin, and of the victim himself...by the power and grace of Yeshua HaMashiach.

On the other hand, Yeshua Himself *has not* been spared the wrath of Rome, or of the Sanhedrin. Every bit of that madness, and much more, will soon pour down upon Him like a cauldron of fiery, hot liquid.

Golgotha's horrific groaning is right around the corner. Not a soul on the planet can fathom just how horrid this will be.

But Yeshua knows; He always has.

≡ 11 ≡

PETER AND JOHN

John names Peter as the one who has done the deed.

Peter doesn't know it yet, but after Yeshua's crucifixion and resurrection, he will become the lead pastor of the first congregation of true followers of Christ. In that position, he will become friends, and a gospel co-laborer, with the Apostle Paul, the man whom the Holy Spirit of God will inspire to eventually write half of the material in the New Testament.

Several decades later, in AD 64, Peter will go to his own death under the hand of the demonically deranged Roman emperor Nero. As Peter is dying by an upside-down crucifixion, the effigy of three crosses on Golgotha's hill is still etched in his mind's eye.[40] That image will have haunted him since the day it happened.

But, before his death, Peter will write two Holy Spirit-anointed letters that will forevermore become cherished books among the New Testament churches of his day—and forever thereafter.

But, again, he knows nothing about any of that right now. All he knows is that Yeshua is headed to a Roman cross—where He will undergo the most terrifying, humiliating, and excruciating way a person can die.

In the midst of his grief, as Peter begins to compose himself, he lifts his head just in time to see Yeshua completely disappear into the early morning hours of darkness. To Peter, it seems as though Yeshua is already dead.

The Reason

When the four Gospels were finally written and dispersed among the churches, the writers of the first three—Matthew, Mark, and Luke—left out Peter's name as the one who committed the garden crime. Two of those three—Matthew and Mark—didn't even mention the name of the victim, most likely in an effort to protect Peter against any attempts at retribution. Peter not only was still alive when those books were written and widely distributed, he was the lead pastor of the first body of believers. If the details of what had happened in the garden were circulated throughout the Roman Empire, the crime easily could have cost Peter his life.

The Gospel of Luke was written shortly *after* Peter's death. Though he named Malchus as the victim, Luke did not mention that Peter had been the one to cut off the man's ear.

John, however, wrote his Gospel account almost three decades after Peter's execution and provided more details of the incident, even naming Peter as the one who did the deed. Thus John's narrative proved to be an indispensable tool in understanding the events of that night—for generations to come.

If Peter had any excuse at all for denying Yeshua, he wouldn't be vindicated until his dear friend John revealed the details of that night. Peter, a *man's man* otherwise, had been terrified that his arrest would happen at any moment. So, he had denied being with Yeshua at Gethsemane three times.

In revealing that information, John disclosed why Peter did such a seemingly underhanded thing. But Peter's betrayal of Yeshua wasn't nefarious, as was Judas'. His was merely a desperate attempt to save his own life in the face of everything that was rapidly unfolding that night. Many things transpired during those hours that were unknown to Peter until much later.

In Pilate's Hands

Now, back to the early daylight hours of the morning when Yeshua is taken before Pilate. The Sanhedrin council finally has Him in custody and under official arrest. Several of their most prestigious representatives have just delivered Him into Pilate's hands, and they're now in the process of working their prearranged plan…to kill Yeshua.

Eventually, the Roman governor orders his men to flog Yeshua, a vain attempt to satiate the obvious bloodlust of the Jewish elite and perhaps calm the burgeoning storm that seems to be engulfing the people of Jerusalem. But that objective is not to be satisfied. Pilate reasons that the already languishing Yeshua must die…in order to "keep the peace" in the vast Roman region. At this point, He sees no other way to resolve the matter. So he washes his hands of the entire affair, in front of a large crowd of onlookers, and summarily orders Yeshua's crucifixion.[41] Pilate turns and goes back to his office, under heavy guard. He has more important affairs upon which to direct his attention and time.

Or so he thinks…

At Golgotha

Yeshua is taken to Golgotha's hill, along with two criminals who have also been sentenced to crucifixion that day. In the midmorning, rough iron spikes are hammered into Yeshua's hands and feet. He is then suspended between heaven and earth…between the two criminals. Peter and most of the other disciples once again go into hiding.[42]

However, John is there, at the foot of Yeshua's cross. Not afraid to be seen supporting his Lord, he stands embracing Mary, the mother of Yeshua. Six grueling hours later, John is still there when Yeshua takes His last breath. The "disciple whom Yeshua loved" has never left His side throughout the entire horrid ordeal. He had planted himself there until the groanings of Golgotha had mercifully ceased, and until he could collect himself after his almost inconsolable weeping and smothering grief.[43]

On The Third Day

Three days later, after Yeshua's burial in the borrowed tomb of one of the richest men of the Sanhedrin (one who had not approved of Yeshua's execution),[44] the world is forever changed. Unbridled panic ensues, both on earth and deep within Satan's vast lairs. *It has begun.*

Yeshua has indeed risen from the dead, just as He has promised. His body is gone…but *He is alive!* He will soon be seen by many of His disciples, in the flesh, glorified and whole. He will show Himself to them for a full forty days. Eventually, hundreds—perhaps thousands—will see Him in person and even talk with Him.[45]

GOLGOTHA'S GROANING

It is now Satan's time to groan in insatiable agony. His diabolic wailing and vile cursing reverberate throughout the corridors of the cosmos of darkness. The "shame" of Golgotha has turned him into a universal spectacle of defeat and humiliation.[46]

To this day, that ancient serpent continues to drown in a cauldron of desperation and unbridled fury, because now he knows his time is short, *desperately short.*[47]

He also knows there's nothing he can do about it. Only Heaven's throne knows the day and the hour of Yahweh's coming judgment.

But that day is coming soon…very soon.

12

THE JOURNEY

Therefore every scribe who has been trained for the kingdom of heaven is like a master of a house, who brings out of his treasure what is new and what is old. (Matthew 13:52)

The exploration you're about to embark upon arose largely from the extensive research that went into my previous two books, *Yeshua Protocol* and *Eyes to See*. Both, published by Defender Publishing, have been featured in major Christian media outlets, as well as in a few popular secular sources—all of which have broadcast the message of those books to the world.

This book, however, will continue to build upon several vital facts I revealed in those previous works. I've included a review of those books in case you're not familiar with that material. The details of those included sections are found in part three. So, if you've recently read the two previous books and are familiar with the material in each of them, you might wish to simply skip to part four to unfurl the latest revelations that are the focus of the rest of this book.

However, if you haven't read those books, don't worry; it isn't necessary for you to do so in order to fully understand this one. You can simply continue reading into part two all the way through to the end.

That way, you'll have all the information you need to completely experience and understand the newest disclosures you'll soon see.

Part Two

THE INVISIBLE BECOMES VISIBLE

Forever, O LORD, your word is firmly fixed in the heavens. Your faithfulness endures to all generations; you have established the earth, and it stands fast.
(Psalm 119:89–90)

But we impart a secret and hidden wisdom of God, which God decreed before the ages for our glory. None of the rulers of this age understood this, for if they had, they would not have crucified the Lord of glory.
(1 Corinthians 2:7–8)

☰ 13 ☰

FROM THE BEGINNING

From now on I will tell you of new things, of hidden things unknown to you. They are created now, and not long ago; you have not heard of them before today. So you cannot say, "Yes, I knew of them." (Isaiah 48:6–7, NIV)

The first ten English words of Genesis 1:1 are some of the most recognized in the Bible: "In the beginning, God created the heavens and the earth." However, in its original language, there are *seven* Hebrew terms.

Now, consider these intriguing questions: What mysterious links do the first Hebrew letter (*bet*) and the first Hebrew word (*bereshith*) share? How are those links in direct relationship with *all seven* of the Hebrew words that make up Genesis 1:1? And, maybe most importantly, how do the answers to those two questions link to several dozen passages found in both the Old and New Testaments?

The answers to these questions are the core subjects of our journey. This quest will uncover the undeniably supernatural message encoded throughout Scripture, in both the Testaments—from Genesis to Malachi in the Old and from Matthew to the final paragraphs of Revelation in the New.

Genesis 1:1

haaretz	va-et	hashamayim	et	Elohim	bara	Bereshith
הָאָרֶץ	וְאֵת	הַשָּׁמַיִם	אֵת	אֱלֹהִים	בָּרָא	בְּרֵאשִׁית
the earth	and	the heavens	eth	God	created	In the beginning

GOLGOTHA'S GROANING

The truth is that all these revelations have been hiding in "plain sight" since the first divine inscription of the First Covenant at Mt. Sinai. But until fairly recent history, no one could have known they were there, in accordance with God's promises.

> I will give you the treasures of darkness, riches stored in secret places, so that you may know that I am the Lord, the God of Israel, who summons you by name. (Isaiah 45:3, NIV)

The supernatural message I'm speaking of is an eternal association that ties together the Word of God in a sensational manner. It's a relationship that is out-and-out, humanly impossible to exist—yet, it is certainly there! And that enigmatic cipher thoroughly punctuates what is emphasized in black and white throughout the *surface text* of the totality of God's Word.

Once you've seen this phenomenon for yourself, it's possible that you'll never again take the inspired message of God's Word for granted. Every time you read the Bible, from this day forward, the underlying images found in the passages that speak this biblical truth will probably remain in your mind's eye.

The unquestionably significant iconic figures all point to the same biblical event. That particular day was a sacred affair, decreed from the throne of God before the universe was created.

It is also the overriding message of the pounding heart of God's Word itself.

14

THE SCARLET THREAD

> *Then the soldiers of the governor took Jesus into the governor's headquarters, and they gathered the whole battalion before him. And they stripped him and put a scarlet robe on him.* (Matthew 27:27–28)

The unspeakable suffering that surrounded the darkness of Golgotha's cross was the preordained instrument of God's plan for providing our eternal salvation.

Even according to the secular National Institutes of Health (NIH), that first-century horror was one of the most brutal and humiliating forms of execution known to humanity's entire storied history. A number of experts maintain that this gruesome fact holds true to this day.[48]

However, that same cruel cross also proved to be the death knell of Satan's stolen kingdom, dating at least back to the Garden of Eden. It was at Golgotha where the "Lamb slain before the foundation of the world" was offered for our redemption, releasing those who are born again in Yeshua from Satan's otherwise eternal grip (see Revelation 5:9; Revelation 5:12; Revelation 13:8; Isaiah 53:7; John 1:29; John 1:36; Galatians 4:4; 1 Peter 1:19–21).

At the end of it all, the crucifixion turned out to be Heaven's preplanned victory lap around the cosmos.

> And having disarmed the powers and authorities, He made a public spectacle of them, triumphing over them by the cross. (Colossians 2:15, NIV)

GOLGOTHA'S GROANING

Because of Golgotha's victory, Satan is filled with unmitigated rage. That demonic fury is sloshing over the edges like a boiling pot of oil, right in the middle of our day…the most prophetic days since the first coming of Yeshua HaMashiach.[49]

> And I heard a loud voice in heaven, saying, "Now **the salvation and the power** and the kingdom of our God and the authority of his Christ **have come**, for the accuser of our brothers has been thrown down, who accuses them day and night before our God. And they have conquered him **by the blood of the Lamb** and by the word of their testimony, for they loved not their lives even unto death. Therefore, rejoice, O heavens and you who dwell in them! **But woe to you**, O earth and sea, for the **devil has come down** to you **in great wrath**, because he **knows that his time is short!**" (Revelation 12:10–12, emphasis added)

There can be no doubt: Two thousand years ago, Satan walked right into Heaven's divine trap.

> **None** of the rulers of this age **understood** this, for if they had, they **would not have crucified** the Lord of glory. (1 Corinthians 2:8, emphasis added)[50]

However, that snare *was* set at a terrible sacrificial price to Heaven's throne.

And it was laden with the cavernous groanings of Golgotha.

≡ 15 ≡

INDISPUTABLY UNIQUE

See, the former things have taken place, and new things I declare; before they spring into being I announce them to you.
(Isaiah 42:9, NIV)

The images in the pages that follow shout the affirmation, "Only the Word of God possesses such a supernaturally coded revelation!"[51]

Once I reveal the abundant connections of this *scarlet thread*[52] of redemption's plan, I pray that your soul will be overwhelmed by the unexplainable intricacy with which the Word of God has been encoded. Even if we only consider the prophetic revelations of Scripture's *plain surface text*, there are still no other books known to humanity that are anything like it.

For example, no historical piece of literature comes close to proclaiming the many detailed prophecies concerning the coming Messiah. Each prophecy was fulfilled in Yeshua and no one else.[53] At the time of Yeshua's resurrection alone, at least *twenty Old Testament predictions* were fulfilled within a twenty-four-hour period.[54]

Added to this truth is the fact that there are eight times more prophecies of His Second Coming than of His First Coming. Several distinguished biblical scholars have isolated as many as 1,845 different references to the Second Coming. In the Old Testament alone, seventeen books refer to Yeshua's return to the earth in the last days. The New Testament speaks of that same event in twenty-three of its twenty-seven books.[55]

The truth of the uniqueness of God's Word also includes more than fifty prophecies, from Deuteronomy to Zechariah, that speak of an eventually returned nation of Israel to the Middle East in the very last days. That rather recently fulfilled prophecy is still shaking the planet to this day.[56]

This is also true of the prophecies telling of the resultant international attack that would, in time, be leveled upon the returned nation of Israel. One of the main actors in that attack is prophesied to be Persia/Iran, as well as a consortium of other nations that will eventually be in alliance with Iran (Ezekiel 38). The world undoubtedly witnessed the beginning stages of this exact prophecy on October 7, 2023.[57]

Of course, we must not forget that those last-days prophecies, found only in God's Word, also include the now-fulfilled and continuous fulfillment of exponential explosions in the unprecedented technological advancements of our own generation. No other writing has ever attempted to explicitly predict such events, and in such unexplainable detail, thousands of years before they would happen. This fact alone is a staggering consideration.[58]

Yet, we are now the first generation to actually see them completely fulfilled, or at least in the undeniable process of *being* fulfilled.[59]

Spiritual DNA

The exploration we're embarking on will illuminate the even more obvious fact that God's Holy Word was given to humanity directly from Heaven's throne. The matters we're about to look at make the various arguments that constantly emanate from the "Bible attackers" increasingly difficult to defend. Those protests can be summed up in these words: "The Bible can't be the Word of God! It obviously was *written by mere men*!"

Yes! It *was* written by mere men. That's the point!

How could "mere men" have written, thousands of years ago, about what we're currently living in the middle of, and in *only* our generation, right down to the nth detail? The answer is that without supernatural intervention, they simply couldn't have done so.

I'm convinced that the images you'll see within the following pages of this book were also supernaturally encoded within the Word. It's the

INDISPUTABLY UNIQUE

only logical explanation for their presence in the precise places they *need* to be. They simply could not have been placed there by "mere men." The Golgotha likenesses begin with the first letter of the first word and continue to some of the very last words of the book of Revelation. I am convinced they stand as God's divinely inserted "proof" for people who are living in the final days of human history just before the return of Yeshua HaMashiach.[60]

The *Golgotha trail* melds the entire Word of God into its single, cohesive message, and at a (metaphorically) *microscopic* level. It will be as though we are examining what could be described as the "spiritual DNA code" of the Bible itself—a strand of letters forming a supernaturally coded language—over and over again. And, just like DNA, that language ties everything into a properly functioning whole.

Now, let's peer through that microscope of revelation so you can examine the evidence yourself.

Part Three

FOUNDATIONS

…like that of a lamb without blemish or spot. He was foreknown before the foundation of the world but was made manifest in the last times for the sake of you. (1 Peter 1:19–20)

≡ 16 ≡

LETTERS THAT BECOME IDEAS

> *The secret things belong to the Lord our God, but the things that are revealed belong to us and to our children forever, that we may do all the words of this law.* (Deuteronomy 29:29)

As stated earlier, in my previous books, *Yeshua Protocol* and *Eyes to See*, I presented an assortment of truths that strengthen the overall message of this one. But let me assure you again, *it isn't necessary* to study either of those books to understand the revelations disclosed within this one's pages.

If you have read *Yeshua Protocol* and *Eyes to See,* you may wish to jump to part four. However, if you haven't read them, I will summarize, in the next several chapters, the key features of those foundational truths.

The Astonishing Hebrew Language

In 2013, *Haaretz*, one of Israel's most prominent and internationally circulated news organizations (often compared to the *New York Times*) published an article titled, "In the Beginning: The Origins of the Hebrew Alphabet."

That article spoke of the Hebrew "ideograms"—specific *ideas* represented by each letter of the ancient Hebrew alphabet. Those same ideograms continue to be intimately associated with the modern alphabet. The following excerpt from that *Haaretz* article confirms the truth:

> Four elements distinguish the Hebrew alphabet from others....
> **Third**, the names of **the Hebrew letters have meaning** [ideas] in

the Hebrew language. That doesn't actually matter when writing or reading, but it is nice to know.⁶¹ (emphasis added)

Another expert source supporting this vital truth comes from *Hebrew Today*, a publication from a renowned Israeli organization that describes itself as a professional Hebrew language learning institution. *Hebrew Today* offers support in line with the assessment of *Haaretz* concerning the alphabet ideograms.⁶²

Each letter in the Hebrew alphabet has both a literal and mystical **meaning**. This means that each name **has a mystical significance**, based **on the letters** which form the name.⁶³ (emphasis added)

Undeniable

Regardless of what a handful of naysayers might claim about the phenomenon, this widely acknowledged ideographic element of the Hebrew alphabet is also *universally demonstrated:* Affixed on the doorposts of almost every Jewish household and/or business around the world is the Hebrew *mezuzah*.⁶⁴ On practically every one of those *mezuzahs* is emblazoned the single Hebrew letter "*shin/sin*" (pronounced *sheen or seen*).⁶⁵

The *shin* is found on the *mezuzah* precisely because of its symbolic ideographic meaning. The *shin* stands for *El Shaddai*, the Hebrew phrase translating to "God Almighty."⁶⁶

The *shin*, used in this way, is a prime example of an ancient ideogram in the Hebrew alphabet that's still in use today. That letter is meant to deliver a "message" that attests to the blessings of Almighty God upon the home or business to which the mezuzah is attached.

LETTERS THAT BECOME IDEAS

The Most Foundational Word in the Bible

Now that we have the historical *fact* of the ancient ideograms settled, let's continue by developing the ideographic meanings of two of the most prominent letters in the Hebrew alphabet. Our understanding of the significance of those two letters and the Hebrew word they spell will open up a floodgate of discoveries.

They will help lay out the path to exploring the very latest revelations illustrated in this book.

≡ 17 ≡

THE FIRST

I am the Alpha and the Omega, the First and the Last, the Beginning and the End. (Revelation 22:13)

Yeshua declares in the book of Revelation that He alone is the *Alpha* and the *Omega*. However, if He had used the Hebrew language as He spoke the words of Revelation to John, He would have actually said, "I am the *Aleph* and the *Tav*." This is because the letters *aleph* and *tav* are the first and last letters of the Hebrew alphabet.

Aleph-Tav

The Hebrew *aleph-tav* carries the same message used by Yahweh in the Old Testament as He used in the New. Yahweh declares Himself to be the "First and the Last" in three different Old Testament passages. In each of those passages, all of which are found in the book of Isaiah, Yahweh also calls Himself "the Redeemer" in conjunction with being the "First and the Last," or the *Aleph-Tav*.[67]

As a matter of fact, Yahweh identifies Himself as our "Redeemer," "Savior," or "Salvation" seventeen times in the Old Testament. And, of course, there is simply no question concerning the New Testament affirmation that the only One exalted as the ultimate manifestation of our eternal Redeemer is Yeshua/Jesus Himself.[68]

The Aleph

Like the *shin*, God Almighty, the first letter—*aleph*—also denotes a specific name for God. The *Harvard Theological Review*, in a publication titled "Yahweh and the God of the Patriarchs," asserts that since the

THE FIRST

most ancient days, the *aleph* represented God Himself.[69] We also know the *aleph* was pronounced "El."[70]

In the Proto-Sinaitic alphabet (the immediate precursor to the ancient Hebrew in which the Tanakh was written), the first letter of the alphabet was originally represented by the pictographic form of an ox head. That symbol meant the "leader," or the one who is "most powerful." The following illustration shows the development of the shape of that first letter.

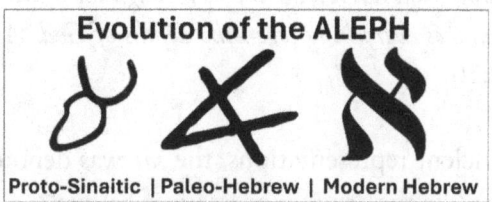

The Proto-Sinaitic alphabet is thought by a majority of archeologists to have preceded the Paleo-Hebrew alphabet. But it was the Paleo-Hebrew alphabet that was used in the original Hebrew documents of the Tanakh.

Since the Word of God was ultimately delivered in that alphabet, this is the one we'll examine to discover the original biblical DNA message that is the focus of this book.

The Tav

It is the *last* letter of the Hebrew alphabet, the *tav*, that may hold the most significance for our current study. In the next chapter, I'll summarize its foundational importance.

In the *tav*, the supernaturally coded message of Golgotha's "groanings" will begin to take shape as seemingly living pictures. They create images that leave a thoroughly unforgettable and supernatural impression.

18

THE LAST

These things God has revealed to us through the Spirit. For the Spirit searches everything, even the depths of God. (1 Corinthians 2:10)

In the most ancient representations, the *tav* was denoted by a symbol that looks just like the crucifixion cross of Yeshua.

Down through the ages, the *tav* has retained a similar appearance, especially in the Paleo-Hebrew, the original script of the Hebrew Scriptures. That ancient Hebrew script remained in use until nearly the second century BC.[71]

Interestingly, the Paleo *tav* looks like a crucifixion cross under a load, as though a person might be impaled upon it!

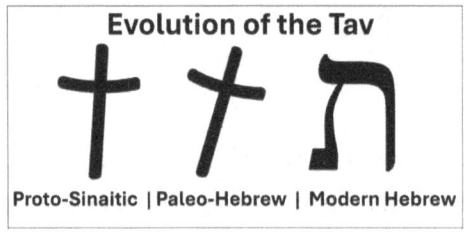

The ideographic meaning of the letter *tav* is "the mark," "the sign," or "the covenant."[72]

By declaring that He is both the *aleph* and the *tav*, Yeshua affirmed that He is actually "God with us" and completely one with the Father. That designation also indicates that Yeshua is the Living Word of God, who became flesh in order to become our Savior through His sacrifice on the cross. Therefore, He is God's "sign" to the world that His New Covenant would be culminated on Golgotha's sacred ground.[73]

A Startling Connection

For several years, my aforementioned ministry associate, Messianic Rabbi Porat of Tel Aviv, Israel, has been using the teaching of the Paleo-Hebrew *aleph* and *tav* symbols among the Orthodox Jewish people in Israel. He employs this technique to lead them to Yeshua as Messiah. Following is what he has to say about this phenomenon:

> What's really disturbing about this, though, is that Israel is the only nation that has ever tried to eliminate and cover up its own alphabet![74] Especially the teaching of the ideographic meanings, and the symbols for each of the letters.
>
> Before Yeshua was crucified, the rabbis didn't understand the sign of the cross—*the tav*—as being directly related to Messiah. However, *after* the crucifixion, they *all* saw it! They stopped teaching about the symbols that represented each Hebrew letter within a few decades of the crucifixion of Yeshua, because they knew it matched Yeshua's *aleph-tav* statements. This fact is verified in our own history. And we all know that the cross is the greatest symbol by which Yeshua is known today throughout the world.
>
> I have used this information about the ancient Hebrew alphabet in our ministry's witnessing outreach in Israel, on many occasions and in various important venues. Teaching these symbols and their meanings to today's Jewish people is such a powerful way to open their eyes to the truth of Yeshua as Messiah.[75]

Stop This!

"In fact," Zev revealed, "teaching the *aleph-tav* is so effective that not too long ago I actually had two prominent Israeli rabbis contact me about what I was doing. They pleaded with me to *not teach* these ancient symbols to Jews in my outreach presentations. They claimed that it might 'confuse' the people." He continued:

GOLGOTHA'S GROANING

One of the rabbis contacted me by email, the other one called me on the phone. It's a fact that for thousands of years these symbols were not confusing at all—that is, until after Jesus was crucified on a cross and fulfilled every prophecy of the coming Messiah!

After speaking with those concerned rabbis, it became apparent to me that this one tremendous truth alone, *the ancient Hebrew pictographs and their letter-meanings*, was having a much larger impact in witnessing to the Jewish people about Yeshua than I had imagined. I politely told them that I would continue to use the teaching—after all, it is a historical fact of our own language, dating back thousands of years!

Zev asked, "Why should our people not know these eternal truths? But I can tell you—the rabbis clearly don't want this truth taught anymore, because it points directly to *Yeshua HaMashiach*!"[76]

Entwined

As you're about to discover, this understanding about the "picture" of the *aleph* and the *tav* will also help us unveil the brand-new revelations laid out in the coming chapters.

≡ 19 ≡

THE ETH

Now to Him who is able to strengthen you according to my gospel and the preaching of Jesus Christ, according to the revelation of the mystery that was kept secret for long ages. (Romans 16:25)

When the *aleph* and the *tav* are joined as a single Hebrew word unto itself, it is written in English as *eth* or sometimes as *et*. It is phonetically pronounced "et."

The *eth* is represented in the Paleo-Hebrew and the Modern Hebrew—reading right to left—as shown in the following illustrations.[77]

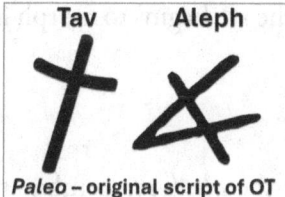

The English language has no equivalent to the Hebrew *eth*; therefore, it remains unwritten and unpronounced in English translations of the Old Testament Scriptures.[78]

So, exactly what is the mystery behind this otherwise strange word, *eth*?

In its strictest Hebrew literary sense, *eth* is what is known as an "accusative case grammar marker." This Hebrew marker points the action word (verb) to the outcome (object) of that verb. The *eth* is found in about eleven thousand instances in the Old Testament. Therefore, on average, it appears more than ten times on each page of the Tanakh![79]

GOLGOTHA'S GROANING

Premiere of the Eth

The first time *eth* is used in the Scriptures is in the very first sentence of the book of Genesis. As it is written in Hebrew, we find it right in the middle of that seven-word sentence.

The *eth* comes immediately after the word *Elohim* ("God"). However, it is pointing the verb *bara* ("created") to the outcome of the verb—"the heavens and the earth." This indicates that God created the heavens and earth in the beginning—not that the beginning somehow "created" God.

There is no equivalent grammar marker in English. The way the English language is constructed, we have no need of such a grammar pointer.

However, the preceding material prepares us for what comes next. And it's from this point forward that the *eth* begins to morph into something supernaturally revelatory.

The Mark

You've probably noticed by now that the *aleph-tav* combination, in its ideographic format, holds quite a shocking message. Remember, the *aleph* means God Himself. The *tav* means the sign, the mark, or the covenant. When those letters are joined, the ideographic meaning of that combination translates to something like this: "God Himself (in human flesh) will go to the cross for us in order to establish His new covenant. The cross itself will be the sign/mark of that covenant."

The prophet Zechariah plainly states the meaning of the *aleph-tav*:

> And I will pour out on the house of David and the inhabitants of Jerusalem a spirit of grace and pleas for mercy, so that, **when they**

THE ETH

look on me, on him **whom they have pierced**, they shall **mourn** for him, as one **mourns** for an only child, and weep bitterly over him, **as one weeps over a firstborn**. (Zechariah 12:10, emphasis added)

From *Dr. Constable's Expository Notes:*

The unusual combination "they will look to *Me* whom they have pierced" and "they will mourn for *Him*" suggests two different individuals, but **the deity of the Messiah solves this problem. Yahweh Himself would suffer** for the people **in the person of Messiah** [**on Golgotha's cross**]. Other references to this text point to a substitute suffering (e.g., John 19:37; Revelation 1:7; cf. Isaiah 53:5; Isaiah 53:8).[80] (emphasis added)

Hebrew Scholars Speak

It's important to note that the *eth*, in a relatively significant number of its appearances in the Tanakh, doesn't seem to have a discernable "grammar-marking" purpose at all.[81]

A number of Orthodox Hebrew scholars assert that there are, therefore, certain "mystical" interpretations of the *eth* as well as its usual relevance as a grammar marker. Those understandings are in regard to several unique Scriptures wherein the more *mystical meanings* exist. Orthodox Rabbi Eli Brackman says the *mystical-meaning* proposition is "ultimately…the most satisfactory explanation" of the presence of the *aleph-tav*.[82]

When we consider that the undeniable message of the *aleph-tav* speaks of God Himself going to the covenant cross of Golgotha…well then, we begin to see a clear punctuation of the central message of the entire Word of God! And that message is imprinted on almost every single page of the Old Testament within the original Hebrew text.

It seems Rabbi Brackman and others who believe, as he does, that the *eth* holds a deeper meaning have hit the proverbial nail on the head.

However, as unbelievable as all of this may seem, even that singular revelation ultimately pales in comparison to what we will soon discover in the chapters to come.

20

WORDS THAT ARE PICTURES

> *But when the fullness of time had come, God sent forth his Son, born of woman, born under the law, to redeem those who were under the law, so that we might receive adoption as sons.* (Galatians 4:4–5)

In my first book on this topic, *Yeshua Protocol,* I introduced several of the following supernatural revelations. As stated earlier, I'm briefly repeating a portion of that teaching here. I do this because the earth-shattering images the Paleo-Hebrew creates form the basis for the disclosures you'll soon observe throughout the Word of God.

From the Beginning

Have a look at Genesis 1:1, where we see the seven Hebrew words that make up that verse: *Bereshith bara Elohim et hashamayim va-et haaretz.* Also notice that the *aleph-tav* is found in the exact middle of the seven.

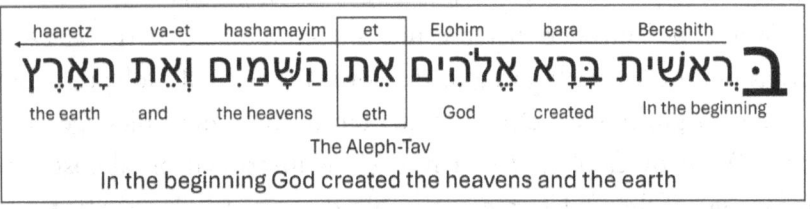

Following is an image of the oldest archeological evidence in existence of the Paleo-Hebrew. This artifact demonstrates the undeniable truth of the *tav's* earliest shape. The relic dates from the 800s BC, making it about three thousand years old. In it, you can see the distinctive shape of a cross in the *tav*. The similarity is unmistakable.[83]

WORDS THAT ARE PICTURES

SILOAM INSCRIPTION - Dr. David Graves
https://biblicalarchaeologygraves.blogspot.com/2014/12/figure-19.html

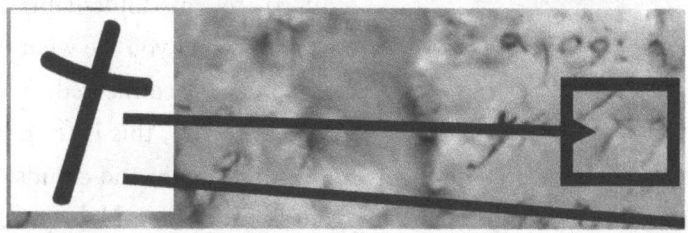

Now that we know what the *tav* looks like in both the Paleo and Modern Hebrew scripts, we can also see that there are three *tavs* in the first verse. The first is in the word *bereshith*, the second is in the *aleph-tav*, and the third is in the word "and" (*va-et*).

The First Golgotha Image

When we drop those three Paleo *tavs* (crosses) and locate them directly under the Modern Hebrew script of the *tav*, the imagery in the first verse of the Bible displays a stunning picture. It is the likeness of Golgotha! Three crosses, with Yeshua (the *Aleph-Tav*) in the middle—a depiction of the "Lamb slain before the foundation of the world."

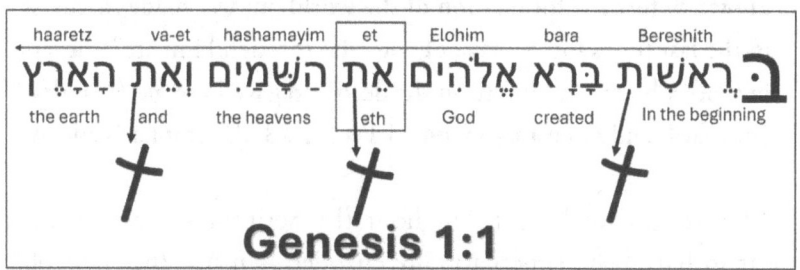

GOLGOTHA'S GROANING

What are the chances of this iconic image being present in the verse that speaks of laying the world's foundations? The probability would be highly unlikely. However, by the time you've finished reading this book, I believe you'll agree that the likelihood of this phenomenon being mere happenstance will have been reduced to an undeniable zero—especially when you see what else this iconic image is connected to.[84]

I assure you, this isn't an exercise in looking for shadowy figures of bunny rabbits in the clouds. To the contrary, we also find the same imageries of the Paleo-Hebrew "crosses" of Genesis 1:1 in other relevant Golgotha passages throughout the entirety of God's Word!

The New Testament

Amazingly, even the New Testament Scriptures that speak of Golgotha contain these same hidden pictures when they are translated to Hebrew. They, too, appear to attest to the historical veracity of Yeshua's crucifixion, as well as to the fact that Golgotha was planned before the foundation of the universe.

> Knowing that you were ransomed…with the precious blood of Christ, **like that of a lamb** without blemish or spot. He was **foreknown before the foundation of the world** but was **made manifest in the last times for the sake of you** who through Him are believers in God, who raised Him from the dead and gave Him glory, **so that your faith and hope are in God.** (1 Peter 1:18–21, emphasis added)

The images we'll see throughout the Scriptures most reasonably appear to have been supernaturally encoded—in just the right places.

WORDS THAT ARE PICTURES

Also consider that the iconic nature of the three crosses of Golgotha was entirely unknown to the various men the Holy Spirit anointed to write those passages. So, they could not have come close to *purposely* encrypting the images (1 Peter 1:10–12).

Next, we'll explore how this phenomenon is punctuated in yet another mysterious way. That revelation is tied to the first Hebrew word of the first verse of Genesis 1, and is translated into English as "in the beginning."

≡ 21 ≡

MAGNIFIED

In My Father's house are many dwelling places; if not, I would have told you. I am going away to prepare a place for you.
(John 14:2, HCSB)

The first Hebrew word of Genesis 1:1, *Bereshith* (pronounced "beh-rah-sheet"), is translated into the three English words "in the beginning."

Bereshith is spelled with only six Hebrew letters. As explained earlier, Hebrew reads from right to left, so the six letters comprising the first Hebrew word in the Bible are *bet, resh, aleph, shin, yud,* and *tav.*

One oddity you might have already noticed is that *bet,* the first letter, is much larger than the remaining letters. The ancient Hebrew script has no capital letters, so the *bet* is not larger because it is capitalized, as would be understood in English. Rather, the *bet* is said to have been *magnified*—an ancient Hebrew term for the original Paleo letters that are occasionally scripted as larger than normal.[85]

There are seventeen places in the first five books of the Old Testament—often referred to as the Torah[86]—wherein a letter is magnified. A number of Orthodox Hebrew scholars agree that the enlargement of those letters is meant to signal readers to take a deeper look at that letter and/or the words associated with it, as there is often a hidden mystery to be discovered.[87] This is most noticeably true of the *first* letter of the *first* verse, on the *first* page of Scripture!

MAGNIFIED

The House of God

The Hebrew word *bereshith* comes from the word *reshith*, which simply means "the beginning." In the word *bereshith*, the first letter, *bet*, serves as the preposition "in." Thus, *bereshith* is actually a sort of compound Hebrew word meaning "in the beginning."

Also, since the *bet* of *bereshith* in Genesis 1:1 is magnified, and the Hebrew ideogram of that letter means "house or dwelling," then the magnification of *bet* in this case can reasonably signify the "House of God" rather than just *any* house.[88]

But is this the only meaning of that enlarged letter? Or does the magnification perhaps speak to something hidden within the entire word that it's emphasizing? In this case, the answer is a resounding "yes."

The Message of Bereshith

Now comes the first major revelation about the first word of Genesis 1:1. When we take each letter of *bereshith* and assign those letters to their ancient ideographic meanings, here's what we discover.

- *Bet:* (magnified) "the house of God"[89]
- *Resh:* "the head, the leader"[90]
- *Aleph:* "the first; the Creator, God Himself"[91]
- *Shin:* "God Almighty"[92]
- *Yod:* "the hand of God"[93]
- *Tav:* "the covenant, the sign" (the shape of a cross)[94]

From the ideogram meanings of the Hebrew letters in *bereshith*, we see the following potential missive:

> From the **House of God**...the **Head**, who is the **Creator** Himself, **God Almighty**, stretches out His **own Hands** to make His **Covenant** with us...the **Sign** of that covenant is the **Cross**! (emphasis added)

If you think that revelation is something to behold, and perhaps even humanly impossible, *hang on!* The disclosures we'll explore next are exponentially astonishing.

22

TWELVE SUPERNATURAL WORDS

It is the glory of God to conceal things, but the glory of kings is to search things out. (Proverbs 25:2)

Here is yet another unexpected fact concerning the first word of Genesis 1:1: Within the Hebrew word *bereshith*, there are at least *twelve* other Hebrew words.

Please understand—this isn't a simple "letter scramble" game. I'm not merely taking a random selection of letters from the word and rearranging them to "coincidentally" create other words. Rather, all six letters of the first word, when placed in consecutive and/or symmetrically connecting patterns, form twelve distinctive Hebrew words out of that one word…*bereshith*.

In the following images, you can see those twelve words and the symmetrical manner in which they're formulated from the six letters of *bereshith*. Accompanying each word is an example of its actual use in the Hebrew Scriptures. I have highlighted the words by underlining the corresponding letters that form them.[95]

TWELVE SUPERNATURAL WORDS

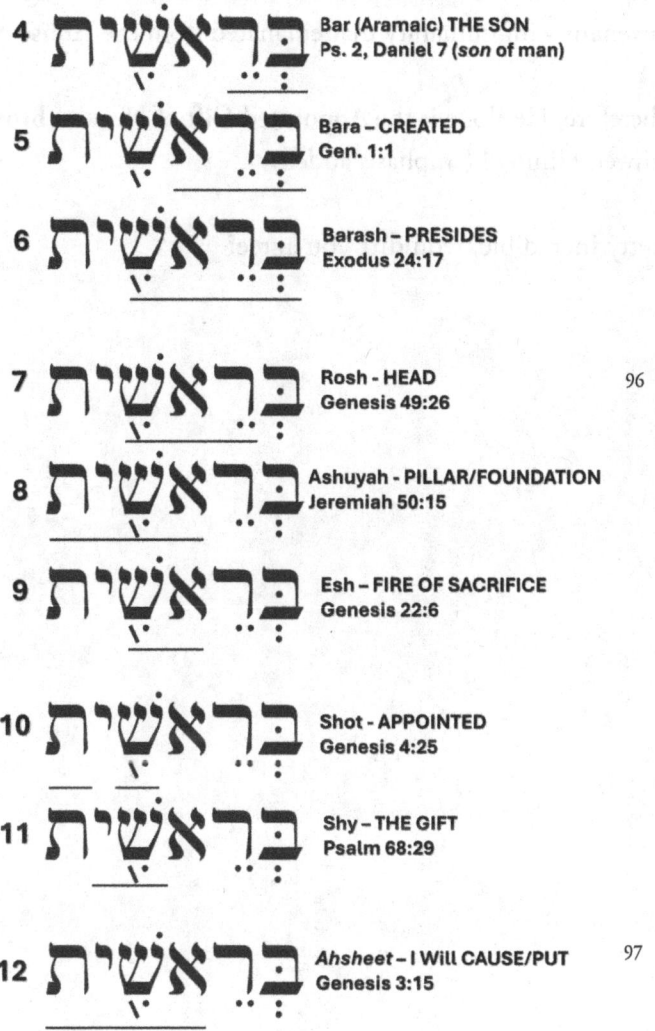

Here is an example of how the *message* of the twelve words (in order) found within the first Hebrew word of Genesis 1:1 can be contextually laid out:

From the Beginning, from the **Covenant House** of God, the **Son Created** everything. He **Presides** as the **Head** of it all.

He is the **Pillar and Foundation.** He **holds all things together.** He also willingly became the **Fire of Sacrifice** [depicting the imagery

GOLGOTHA'S GROANING

of the "Burnt Offering" in the Old Testament]—securing that final **Covenant** with humanity that emanated from the **House of God**.

Therefore, He alone is the **Appointed Gift** of Heaven, **brought by** Yahweh Himself! (emphasis added)

Pretty incredible, wouldn't you agree?

≡ 23 ≡

THE MIRROR IMAGE AND THE GIFT

[This is] the mystery hidden for ages and generations but now revealed to his saints. To them God chose to make known how great among the Gentiles are the riches of the glory of this mystery, which is Christ in you, the hope of glory. (Colossians 1:26–27)

Unbeknownst to most of today's theological world, the Apostle Paul actually included the message of the *bereshith* phenomenon in his letter to the church at Colossi. His words form a replica of the message we saw in the last chapter. Paul used *all twelve* words, or at least their undeniable concepts and synonyms, in a single, complete thought. Take a look at the following passage, in which I've added the words in emphasis and brackets to make it easier to follow the distinct synonym connections to the *bereshith* message:

He is the image of the **invisible God**, the **firstborn** of all creation. For by him [in the beginning] **all things were created**, in heaven and on earth, visible and invisible, whether thrones or dominions or rulers or authorities—**all things** were **created through him and for him**. And he is **before all things**, and in Him **all things hold together** [pillar/foundation]. And He is the **head of the body**, the **church** [the Covenant House of God—the family of God—the Body of Christ—the *Ecclesia*]. He is **the beginning**, the **firstborn** from the dead, that in **everything** He might be **preeminent**. For in Him **all the fullness of God** was pleased to dwell, **and through Him** [caused by God Himself] **to reconcile** to Himself all things, whether on earth or in heaven, **making peace by the blood of His cross** [**by the fire** of the burnt offering of sacrifice at Golgotha]. (Colossians 1:15–20, emphasis added)

Here is yet another awe-inspiring revelation: Either Paul knew about the *bereshith* phenomenon and its message or the Holy Spirit directed the writing of those words of biblical truth. Or both! Because it's there, for the whole world to see!

Then, consider this: The last declaration of that passage is a *direct reference* to Golgotha. The King James Version translates those Greek words into English like this:[98]

And, having made peace **through the blood of His cross**, by Him to reconcile all things unto Himself; by Him, I say, whether they be things in earth, or things in heaven. (Colossians 1:20, KJV, emphasis added)

When translated into Hebrew, that verse also includes the imagery of the three *tav* crosses of Golgotha, with the middle cross represented by the *aleph-tav*. How humanly improbable might it be that this specific image would be hidden within *that* particular verse? It would be very close to impossible! So, once again, we see the apparent mark of the supernatural.

COLOSSIANS 1:20

וּלְרַצּוֹת לְעַצְמוֹ אֶת־הַכֹּל עַל־יָדוֹ בַּעֲשׂוֹתוֹ שָׁלוֹם בְּדַם־צְלוּבוֹ עַל־יָדוֹ הֵן

✝ ✝ ✝

אֲשֶׁר בָּאָרֶץ הֵן אֲשֶׁר בַּשָּׁמָיִם

The Gift That Was Preordained

As demonstrated in the last chapter's list of the twelve supernatural words, the letters *aleph* and *tav* are also found in the word *bereshith*.

In the middle of those two biblically ominous letters is another

THE MIRROR IMAGE AND THE GIFT

Hebrew word we've already noted: the word that spells "the gift." We also know that the word spelled *aleph-shin-yud-tav* is the Hebrew word for "I will cause it." That word is used nine times in the Tanakh.[99]

The message of this remarkable connection is utterly majestic. Buried within the heart of the *aleph-tav* is the disclosure of the greatest gift ever given to humanity. This is "the gift" appointed eons ago. It is the gift that Yahweh/Yeshua Himself would *cause to happen*. In other words, Golgotha was no accident. It was planned from the beginning—and the twelve words found in the *first word* of the Bible scream that fact:

> [Yeshua said,] No one takes my life from me. I give it up willingly! I have the power to give it up and the power to receive it back again, just as my Father commanded me to do. (John 10:18, CEV)[100]

Golgotha was the gift of Heaven to a totally fallen world, a gift Yahweh knew would come at the price of untold agony and the heartbreaking groaning of Heaven's Only Son. But He sent that gift anyway—to us!

The Impossible Word

What six-letter English word contains at least twelve other symmetrically located English words, without invoking a merely random letter-scramble upon that word? None, I dare say.

Even if we *did* find a six-letter English word encompassing twelve other proportionately placed English words, how could those words form a synopsis of the story of the Gospel of Yeshua and *our* connection to it? That would be impossible in the English language, or in *any* other language, for that matter. That is, except Hebrew, apparently.

Simply put, the Word of God is unequaled. There is no other volume like it on the planet. It is supernatural, from the beginning to the end.

Part Four

PILLARS OF THE TEMPLE

He gives wisdom to the wise and knowledge to the discerning. He reveals deep and hidden things.
(Daniel 2:21–22)

≡ 24 ≡

PROPHESYING PILLARS

The mystery of the names given to the Temple pillars no longer has to remain an enigma.

In the last several chapters we've explored the twelve Hebrew words encoded within the very first word of Genesis 1:1, *bereshith*, forming a straight-line message that seems to have been supernaturally inserted.

I've also demonstrated how the entire supernatural *bereshith* message of Genesis 1:1 perfectly corresponds to the words Paul wrote in Colossians 1:15–20.

Ashuyah

As we've seen, the eighth word of the twelve is *ashuyah*, the Hebrew word that means "pillars" or "foundations." Most specifically, according to the *Brown-Driver-Briggs Hebrew Lexicon*, *ashuyah* means "columns, supports, or buttresses."[101] Of course, a column and a pillar are essentially the same thing, and they're often used as synonyms in both English and Hebrew.[102] The word *ashuyah* is found in the Hebrew text in Jeremiah 50:15.[103]

Paul alluded to the meaning of *ashuyah* in Colossians 1:17 when he declared that in Yeshua "all things hold together." He used that phrase because that's exactly what a pillar/column or a foundation does—hold things together. With this in mind, consider the following passage from 1 Kings 7:

> **Huram set the pillars at the entrance of the Temple,** one toward the south and one toward the north. **He named** the one on the

south **Jakin**, and the one on the north **Boaz**. (1 Kings 7:21, NLT; emphasis added)[104]

In this passage, we immediately notice the word "pillar." In the 1 Kings 7:21 reference, the Hebrew word used is not *ashuyah*, but *ammud*. However, *ammud* is a synonym of *ashuyah*, possessing virtually the same nuance of meaning. Both of those Hebrew words are translated throughout the Old Testament as "pillars," or a corresponding synonym.[105]

Also in that 1 Kings passage, we discover that the grandiose pillars of the Temple were given names: *Jachin* and *Boaz*. The naming of those pillars has been somewhat puzzling to many Bible readers, both ancient and modern. Why would they be given names, and what's the message they are meant to communicate?

However, the conglomerate message of the pillars is no longer an enigma. This is because many Hebrew names have distinctive meanings, and the deeper meanings of certain names, when connected, often carry a biblical message. Such is the case with the pillars that stood like ominous sentinels at the entrance to the original Temple of God on the Temple Mount.

And, as you've already seen, some of those *word/name messages* contain very important illustrations, now disclosed as iconic images made by the ancient Hebrew script in which the messages were written.

Namely, the picture of Golgotha.

25

WHAT'S IN A NAME?

As it turns out, the names were rich with the deepest of prophetic meanings.

It isn't difficult to discover that the names of the Temple pillars, Jachin and Boaz, have distinctive Hebrew meanings attached. Here's where this seemingly odd passage of Scripture gets really interesting!

The Hebrew name *Jachin* (pronounced "Yah-keen") means "He will establish it."[106] On the other hand, *Boaz* means "strength/power" and/or "swift."[107]

So the ancient Hebrews generally agreed upon the meaning of the names of the two pillars. They understood the message to mean something like: "Yahweh Himself will swiftly establish the power of His presence among His people, beginning in this place—the Temple of God."

Benson Commentary (1 Kings 7:21):

> So these pillars, being eminently **strong and stable, were types of that strength,** which was in God, and would be put forth by God for the **defending and establishing of his temple and people,** if they were careful to observe the conditions required by him on their parts.[108] (emphasis added)

The message proclaimed by the two pillars was a powerful declaration of promise and encouragement to God's people. But what they could not have known at the time was that the Temple itself would have its ultimate fulfillment in Yeshua HaMashiach. (Ezekiel 43:7;

GOLGOTHA'S GROANING

Zechariah 2:10; John 1:14; John 2:19, 21–22; Ephesians 2:19–22; and almost the entire book of Hebrews)[109]

Nor would they understand that each of the two Hebrew names on the Temple pillars carried more weight than they imagined. As it turns out, the names were rich with the deepest mystery of Messianic prophetic meanings—and they pointed to a coming event that would be even greater than the presence of the Temple itself.

The Priestly Redeemer

According to *Nave's Topical Encyclopedia,* Jachin is a "notable figure in the Old Testament, *recognized as a priest* and the head of one of the twenty-four divisions of priests established by King David"[110] (emphasis added; also see 1 Chronicles 24 for the list of the priestly divisions).

On the other hand, Boaz is best known from the Old Testament book of Ruth as a *redeemer.* In that book, Boaz is called a "kinsman redeemer" (Hebrew—*Goel*). He served in that capacity for the family of Naomi, Ruth's mother-in-law, the main people of the book of Ruth. As that redeemer, Boaz wound up saving the lives of Naomi's entire family.[111]

In addition, Boaz eventually married Ruth, and they went on to become the great-grandparents of King David, as listed at the end of the book of Ruth and in the Gospels of Luke and Matthew. Through that human lineage, Yeshua HaMashiach, the son of David and the *ultimate Redeemer,* came into the world—and went to Golgotha.

The Gospel of Golgotha

Now consider the greater implication of the two pillars at the entrance to the Temple of God. It emanates from the root meaning of their names, as well as from their biblical stations in life. Therefore, the complete message of the pillars, as it might be spoken by Yahweh Himself, would actually declare something more like the following:

> This Temple is where my people will meet with Me and see My power in their lives! But one day in the future, this entire Temple will eventually be fulfilled in a Person (Hebrews 9).

WHAT'S IN A NAME?

He is the **Great High Priest** of eternity—the **mediator** between mankind and the Throne of God. He will also prove to be the ultimate **Kinsman Redeemer** of all who will come to Him! (emphasis added)

There's an abundance of meaning in the names of those two pillars. They stood before the priests and people with their greatest and temporarily hidden meanings staring right at them for centuries.

Redeemer

As noted in an earlier chapter, seventeen times in the Old Testament—from Job to Jeremiah—Yahweh is called our Redeemer. And most of those times, Yahweh speaks of *Himself* as the Redeemer of humanity. Therefore, one of those pillars represented the deeper biblical meaning of *Goel*—the Redeemer![112]

The bottom line is this: From the time the Temple was built and began to operate on the Temple Mount, the pillars stood as a message of promise. That promise was, "The Golgotha of your Salvation is coming!"

At this point, what image do you think might be embedded in the words emphasized below? Those words hold the hidden message of the pillars.

Huram set the pillars at the entrance of the Temple, one toward the south and one toward the north. **He named the one on the south Jakin, and the one on the north Boaz.** (1 Kings 7:21, NLT; emphasis added)

If you guessed it would be the image of Golgotha, you're correct. The boldfaced words display three *tav* crosses. And the middle one is under an *aleph-tav*.

GOLGOTHA'S GROANING

Job's Revelation

This isn't the only connection to the Redeemer who goes to Golgotha. The first of the seventeen times Yahweh is called the Redeemer in the Old Testament is found in Job 19. Job is the oldest book in the Bible, and it also happens to be one of the very oldest books in history.[113]

Job's words about the Redeemer also contain the same iconic imagery of Golgotha! Could this be a mere coincidence? It's highly doubtful!

Have a look at Job's prophetic words:

> For I know that my Redeemer lives, and at the last he will stand upon the earth. And after my skin has been thus destroyed, yet in my flesh I shall see God, whom I shall see for myself, and my eyes shall behold, and not another. My heart faints within me! (Job 19:25–27)

These three verses make up Job's declaration regarding his supernatural revelation of the coming Redeemer/Messiah. Each verse contains only one *tav* cross, for a total of only three *tav* crosses in Job's entire statement. The middle cross is the *aleph-tav*. Once again, it presents the picture of Golgotha.

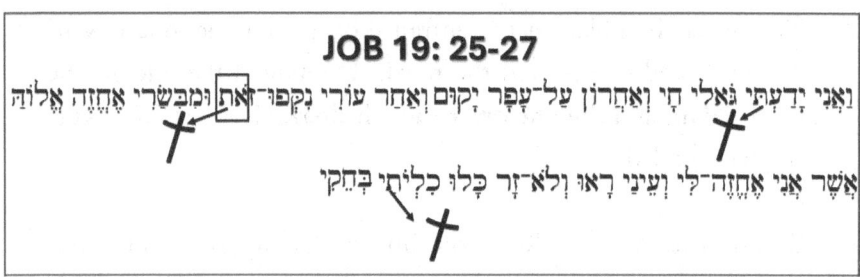

The bottom line is this. One of the very oldest books known to humanity also has the iconic image of the coming Golgotha of our salvation hidden within the letters of the language in which it was written. And that book is found right in the center of the Word of God. Also, that image just happens to be seen in the precise place it *ought* to be found, if in fact it truly is a supernatural code. Imagine that!

The "pillars and foundation" of our journey are now solidly laid.

Part Five

THE PATH OF GROANING

My God, my God, why have you forsaken me? Why are you so far from saving me, from the words of my groaning? (Psalm 22:1)

Kings shall shut their mouths because of Him, for that which has not been told them they see, and that which they have not heard they understand. (Isaiah 52:15)

26

THE TRAIL OF TEARS

The LORD looked down from his sanctuary on high, from heaven he viewed the earth, to hear the groans of the prisoners and release those condemned to death. (Psalm 102:19–20, NIV)

To reliably examine the possibility of three *tavs* also being present in specific New Testament passages, I used the most widely and academically revered Hebrew translation of the New Testament—*The Hebrew New Testament of the British and Foreign Bible Society* (1883).[114]

The work was produced by biblical scholar Franz Julius Delitzsch, along with a hand-picked staff of expert assistants.[115] Delitzsch also co-wrote the *Keil & Delitzsch Old Testament Commentary*, a scholastically acclaimed set of commentaries still in use by practically every seminary, Bible college, and serious Bible scholar around the world.[116]

The Path of Groaning Begins

In the New Testament book of Romans, the Apostle Paul penned some eerily insightful words concerning the goal of our exploration of the Golgotha Paleo-Hebrew likenesses found throughout the Scriptures.

> For we know that **the whole creation has been groaning** together in the **pains of childbirth** until **now**. And not only the creation, but **we ourselves**, who have the firstfruits of the Spirit, **groan inwardly** as **we wait eagerly for adoption** as sons, **the redemption** of our bodies. For in this hope **we were saved**. (Romans 8:22–24, emphasis added)

GOLGOTHA'S GROANING

In this passage, Paul speaks of the entire creation existing in a state of *groaning* since the fall of humanity in the Garden of Eden. And, of all things, Paul cryptically states that the curse of that globally pervasive *groaning* was also wrapped up in the metaphorical illustration of the anticipation of the birth of a child.

We now know it would take the "earthly" birth of Heaven's Divine Son to eventually bring about our redemption. This truth not only involves our personal salvation, but also the restoration of our divinely planned state of being reunited with our Creator as His eternal children, as well as becoming co-heirs with Yeshua—in the coming Kingdom (Romans 8:17).

That eternal reunion promises to be the ultimate obliteration of our own earthly groanings (Revelation 21:1–8). The following are only a few from among a sizable number of other commentary entries for Romans 8:22–24 that verify my assessment of those connections.

Ellicott's Commentary for English Readers:

[**Groans and Travails**]…The idea of travailing [groaning], as **in childbirth**, has reference to the **future prospect of joyful delivery** [only affected by Yeshua HaMashiach!]. Until now.—This consciousness of pain and imperfection has been continuous and unbroken (nor will it cease until an end is put to it by the **Coming of Christ**). (emphasis added; parentheses in original)[117]

Barclay's Daily Study Bible Commentary:

The more a Christian thinks of his [born again] experience the more he becomes convinced that he had nothing to do with it and all is of God. **Jesus Christ came into this world; he lived; he went to the Cross; he rose again.**…We did not make the story; we only received the story. Love woke within our hearts; the conviction of sin came, and with it came the experience of forgiveness and of salvation. We did not achieve that; all is of God. **That is what Paul is thinking of here.** (emphasis added)[118]

THE TRAIL OF TEARS

Kelly Commentary on Books of the Bible:

Before the cross there hung out the **gravest question** that ever was raised, [who would deliver us from the groaning of lostness] and it needed settlement in this world; but **in Christ sin is forever abolished** for the believer; and this not only in respect of what He has done, but in what He is. **Till the cross**, a converted soul might well be found **groaning in misery** at each fresh discovery of evil in himself. But now to faith all this is gone not lightly, but truly in the sight of God; so **that he may live on a** [crucified] **Saviour** that is risen from the dead as his new life.[119] (emphasis added)

The Whole Creation Groans for Golgotha

As we begin a deeper dive into our voyage, take a look at the letter symbols provided by Romans 8:22, as disclosed in the *Delitzsch Hebrew New Testament:* "For we know that the whole creation has been groaning together in the pains of childbirth until now."[120]

This was the event for which the world had waited (Isaiah 9:6–7). Here is the dramatic picture of Golgotha and its three crosses in that verse. Once again, we are looking at the three *tavs* of the Paleo-Hebrew!

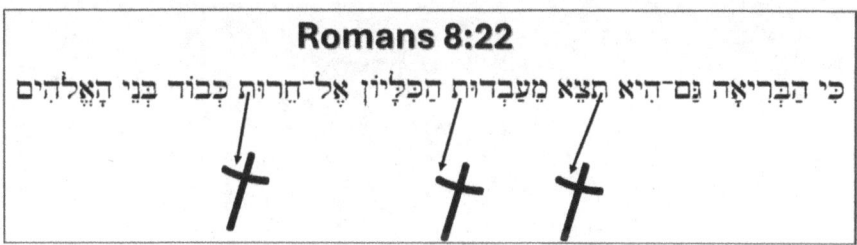

And don't forget Yeshua's own heart-wrenching proclamation that we observed in the last section:

> No one takes [my life] from me, but I lay it down of my own accord. I have authority to lay it down, and I have authority to take it up again. (John 10:18)

GOLGOTHA'S GROANING

Even there, in that gripping declaration of what Yeshua would eventually do on Golgotha, we again find the three crosses. They paint the doleful picture of that horrible, but ultimately glorious, day. This is the same type of imagery we find in the first seven words of Genesis.

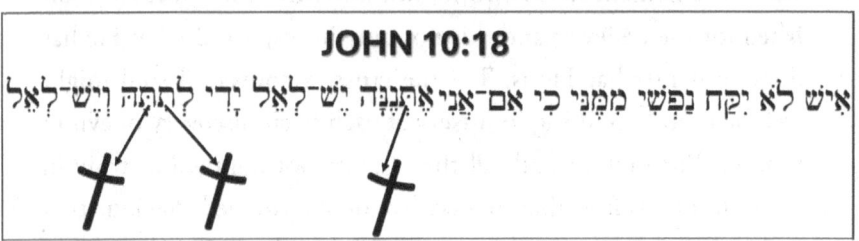

From this point forward, we will continue connecting the Old Testament to the New Testament through the supernaturally coded likenesses of Golgotha's Hill. We'll also explore several other noteworthy mysteries directly connected to those images.

27

THE GARDEN LINK

Could it be that the images we're discovering are only coincidences?

The first place in which the Word of God points directly to Golgotha *in the surface text* is found in the third chapter of Genesis, which provides the account of what took place in the Garden of Eden. It was there that Yahweh proclaimed the first prophecy of humanity's redemption, made necessary because of Eden's shame.[121]

> [The Lord God said to Satan,] And I will put enmity between **you and the woman,** and between your offspring and hers; **he will crush your head,** and you will strike his heel. (Genesis 3:15, NIV; emphasis added)

In that passage, Yahweh speaks of a male child who will come from the womb of an unknown, future woman. That child would eventually destroy Satan's kingdom and finalize his eternal doom. We now know that the crushing of Satan's head would occur at Golgotha!

Genesis 3:15 is often considered among theologians to be "the prophecy of prophecies." It is the key foretelling upon which the entire Word of God is founded. And it's the central theme of our investigation of the ultimate *scarlet cord of redemption*.[122]

And guess what letter formation is found right in the middle of that very first proclamation, spoken from our Creator's own mouth in the Garden of Eden?

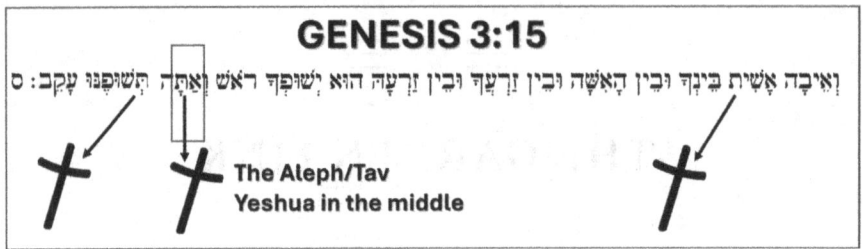

At this point in our journey, a reasonable person might indeed *expect* to find the image of Golgotha in Genesis 3:15. This is especially true if the phenomenon we're investigating truly does hold a legitimate connection to a *supernaturally encoded* message. And, sure enough, the depiction is there! In this example, the cross *tav* representing the middle one is found in the *aleph-tav*, just like the image in Genesis 1:1.[123]

The following are four additional samples to consider. These passages, taken together, tell a huge part of the New Testament Golgotha saga. And they're also in line with the ultimate fulfillment of the prophecy of Genesis 3:15.

> But when the fullness of time had come, God sent forth his Son, born of woman, born under the law, to redeem those who were under the law, so that we might receive adoption as sons. (Galatians 4:4–5)

> The true light, which gives light to everyone, was coming into the world. He was in the world, and the world was made through Him, yet the world did not know Him. He came to His own, and His own people did not receive Him. But to all who did receive Him, who believed in His name, He gave the right to become children of God, who were born, not of blood nor of the will of the flesh nor of the will of man, but of God. And the Word became flesh and dwelt among us, and we have seen his glory, glory as of the only Son from the Father, full of grace and truth. (John 1:9–14)

> He who did not spare his own Son but gave Him up for us all, how will He not also with Him graciously give us all things? (Romans 8:32)

THE GARDEN LINK

When Jesus saw His mother and the disciple whom He loved standing nearby, [at Golgotha's cross] He said to His mother, "Woman, behold, your son!" (John 19:26)

Now, for the revelation that's common to all four of those passages.

28

THE NEW TESTAMENT ICON

It is surprising to see how many of those representations actually do have an aleph-tav *located in the middle.*

Almost impossibly so, the images of the three *tav* crosses of Golgotha are found in each of the four New Testament declarations printed in the closing paragraphs of the previous chapter. And they all line up with the Genesis 1:1 image, as well as with Genesis 3:15.

Following are the exact words in which those three *tavs* are situated in each of those passages:

1. "But when the fullness of time had come, God sent forth His Son, born of woman" (Galatians 4:4).

2. "And the Word became flesh and dwelt among us, and we have seen his glory, glory as of the only Son from the Father, full of grace and truth" (John 1:14).

THE NEW TESTAMENT ICON

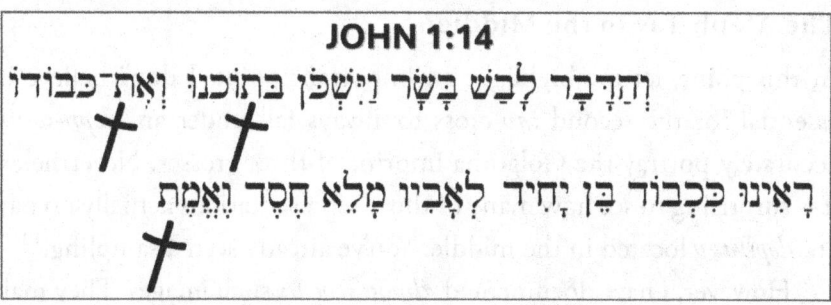

3. "He who did not spare His own Son but gave Him up for us all, how will He not also with Him graciously give us all things?" (Romans 8:32).

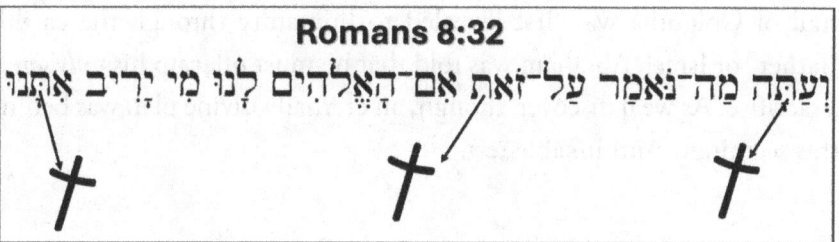

4. "When Jesus saw His mother and the disciple whom He loved standing nearby, He said to his mother, 'Woman, behold, your son!'" (John 19:26).

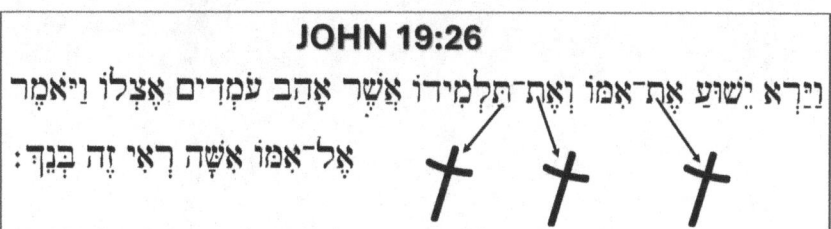

All four of those New Testament passages, when written in Hebrew, display the three *tavs*. Additionally, in each one, the middle cross is also right under an *aleph-tav*.

GOLGOTHA'S GROANING

The Aleph-Tav in the Middle?

At this point, let me highlight an important point: I don't believe it's essential for the second *tav* cross to always fall under an *aleph-tav* to accurately portray the Golgotha imprint of three crosses. Nevertheless, it is surprising to see how many of those representations actually do have an *aleph-tav* located in the middle. You've already seen a sampling.[124]

However, I have documented *almost seventy* such images. They make up more than half of all the images referenced in this book! The passages including that specific image are indexed for your convenience at this endnote.[125]

As you begin the next chapter, you'll discover where the grief-stained trail of Golgotha was first revealed to humanity through the earthly "father" of Israel. Abraham was told that he must offer up his *only son* as a sacrifice. As we'll discover, though, an eternally divine plan was behind this seemingly unthinkable test.

29

ABRAHAM'S GROANING

[God said to Abraham,] "Take your son, your only son Isaac, whom you love, and go to the land of Moriah, and offer him there as a burnt offering on one of the mountains of which I shall tell you." (Genesis 22:2)

Most who have read the book of Genesis are at least familiar with the account of the testing/tempting of Abraham. In that episode of the patriarch's life, Yahweh instructed him to sacrifice his son Isaac as a burnt offering. But there was one huge problem: Isaac was the son who had been promised to Abraham by Yahweh Himself. He was the one Yahweh declared to be destined to become the father of many nations. So, how could God tell Abraham to sacrifice that son of promise?

This biblical account can be disturbing as we grapple with the paradox of the situation—especially concerning the word "test"—or "tempt," as the KJV translates it. But the original Hebrew words hold much deeper nuances than first meet the eye.

The Journey

The Hebrew term often translated as "tempted," or "tested," is *nasah* (pronounced naw-saw).[126] *Nasah* means something along the lines of: "to be proven faithful by being put to a difficult trial." In fact, Hebrew lexicons use all of those elements to properly describe what's happening in Abraham's situation with God.

GOLGOTHA'S GROANING

A Walkabout

An easier way of thinking about *nasah* in the English-speaking mindset would be to consider it as something like an Australian aboriginal "walkabout"—a grueling spiritual and physical journey meant to challenge and teach the young generation of that ancient culture the most important lessons of life among their people.[127]

It is true that the word "tempt" can be a legitimate translation of the Hebrew word *nasah,* but only in the sense that one might find *themselves* tempted within the recesses of their own decision-making processes. The most obvious temptation would be to turn around and disobey the instruction of their own accord.

But God Himself does not "tempt" anyone, nor can He be "tempted." Scripture is clear on those points. Rather, we might call it a "test" of Abraham's *faith,* one in which he would have to struggle with his own fleshly temptation to turn back, thus disobeying the Lord.

> Let no one say when he is tempted, "I am being tempted by God," for God cannot be tempted with evil, and He Himself tempts no one. (James 1:13)

By Faith...

As we dig deeper into Genesis 22, we discover that this test of faithfulness in Abraham's life was exactly what God was accomplishing. It eventually becomes obvious that Yahweh had already laid out a plan for what He was going to teach Abraham. Additionally, the Lord preordained a way for Abraham to successfully pass the test, yet preserve his son's life in the process.

Abraham's success was that he ultimately trusted God, even though he most likely didn't understand the sum total of the test, at least in the beginning. The New Testament says Abraham trusted that Yahweh was somehow going to bring his son back to life, even if he did offer him as a sacrifice unto death. Talk about a man of faith (Hebrews 11:17–19)!

ABRAHAM'S GROANING

Yet, in that Hebraic version of a "walkabout" was an eternal lesson to be gleaned, and that experience would be remembered and celebrated among God's people until the end of earthly time.

The Lesson of Golgotha's Groanings

Unlike Abraham, Yahweh would actually carry through with the completed sacrifice of *His Only Son*. Even in the grief-stricken atmosphere of Heaven's groaning, Yeshua would indeed endure Golgotha's unspeakable sacrificial suffering. This was Abraham's lesson![128]

In fact, the God of Creation would use Abraham's incomparable test of faith to foreshadow the arrival of the ultimate sacrificial gift of Heaven. God *would* offer up His own Son on Golgotha's cross so we might be restored to Him. Think back to what we've already discovered from our study of *bereshith*, the first word in the Hebrew Bible text, and the first three *tav* crosses found in Genesis 1:1. Golgotha was planned from the beginning!

When the actual crucifixion at Golgotha finally occurred, and long afterwards, people who had *eyes to see* looked back at Abraham's days of groaning and saw a beautiful metaphor of Golgotha. And now, the book you're reading is being used to disclose the supernaturally *coded imagery* within Abraham's test of faith!

In the meantime, several thousand years of human history had to pass before that divine sacrifice would take place just outside the gates of Jerusalem. God would first raise up the nation of Israel, and through that nation would flow the written Word of God—*for all people*. That Word would also hold the prophecies of the "Coming One," the Messiah who would bring to fallen humanity the New Covenant opportunity of eternal salvation.

So there was much more to this test than Abraham could have known at the time. However, we now know the rest of Abraham's travail and of his own personal days of groaning. Abraham *did* pass the test, and we are the benefactors of his great faith. The Apostle Paul emphasized this in his letter to the Romans:

GOLGOTHA'S GROANING

That is **why it depends on faith**, in order that the promise may rest on grace and be guaranteed to all his offspring—not only to the adherent of the law but **also to the one who shares the faith of Abraham, who is the father of us all**, as it is written, "I have made you the **father of many nations**"—in the presence of the God in whom he believed, who gives life to the dead and calls into existence the **things that do not exist**. (Romans 4:16–17, emphasis added)

Now, let's have a look at the extraordinary imagery within the Paleo-Hebrew encoding of Golgotha. These iconic representations are, of course, found in Abraham's journey, as recorded in Genesis 22. But they're also found in the New Testament, and in passages linked to that corresponding Genesis account.

Think of it! How seemingly impossible would it be for *that* phenomenon to actually exist within the Golgotha pages of the New Testament?

30

ABRAHAM'S LONGEST WALK

By myself I have sworn, declares the Lord, because you have done this and have not withheld your son, your only son, I will surely bless you. (Genesis 22:16–17)

Consider the key elements of Genesis 22. Notice how closely they follow the features of the actual Golgotha event, almost two thousand years into the future beyond Abraham's lifetime.

1. Abraham was instructed to go to the land of Mt. Moriah and offer his son as a burnt offering. Eventually Jesus would be crucified at the same locale, fulfilling all the requirements of the priestly sacrifices, including those of the burnt offering.[129]
2. Isaac's journey was *three days*. During the entire trip, Isaac was as good as dead as far as Abraham knew. Yet, on the *third day*, his son would be given back to him—alive! In that way, he was "resurrected from the dead."
3. The wood for the burnt offering was "laid upon Isaac's own back," and it was Abraham who held the "knife and fire," the future priestly instruments used in offering the lamb sacrifices on the altar of the tabernacle in the wilderness and the Temple in Jerusalem.
4. At the end of the test, the Angel of the Lord provided a ram (an adult male lamb) caught by his horns in a thicket of thorns. This is a beautiful picture of Yeshua, the ultimate ram, who wore a crown of thorns as He hung upon Golgotha's cross.

GOLGOTHA'S GROANING

Now, with all those links to Golgotha in mind, let's look at something else.

Golgotha Calling

Following is the second verse of Genesis 22.

> God said, "Take your son, your only son Isaac, whom you love, and go to the land of Moriah, and offer him there as a burnt offering on one of the mountains of which I shall tell you." (Genesis 22:2)

Notice especially those words, "Your son, *your only son* Isaac, whom you love." Now, have a look at the *tav* representation found in those precise words within the original Hebrew script. It's the same as what we find in Genesis 1:1—three crosses, with Yeshua in the middle, the *aleph-tav*!

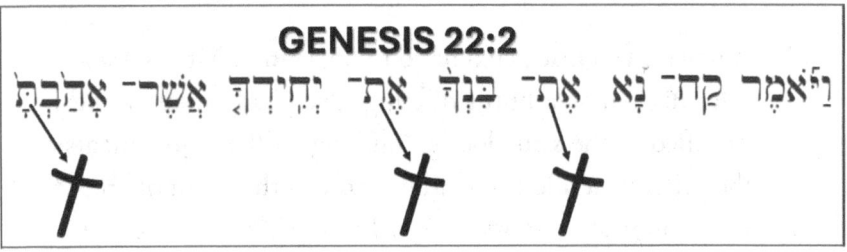

We find this same pattern in the following words of verses 4 and 5, which, when taken together, express a complete thought concerning the Golgotha foreshadowing:

> On the third day Abraham lifted up his eyes and saw the place from afar. Then Abraham said to his young men, "Stay here with the donkey; I and the boy will go over there and worship and come again to you." (Genesis 22:4–5)

Now look at what we find in those combined words.

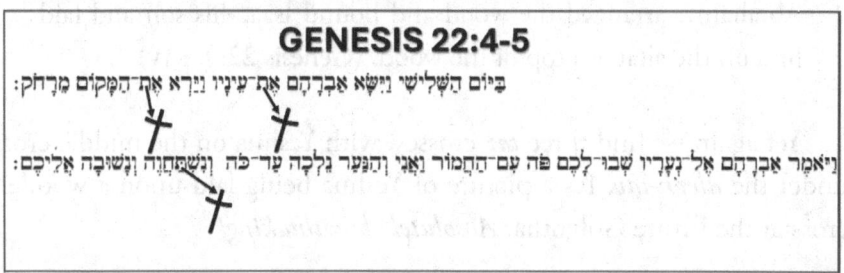

There it is again! This is the premiere passage of Scripture that paints an emotional understanding of God's divine "walkabout lesson" for Abraham. It also serves as an eternal metaphor of the greatest gift that could ever be given to humanity.

The Golgotha *tavs* are there. And, once again, the *aleph-tav* is in the middle of the three crosses. Furthermore, they are indeed nestled in the passages in which we might expect to find this supernaturally encoded wonder.

But still another image emanates from this passage in Genesis 22. The words are found in the sixth verse:

And Abraham took the wood of the burnt offering and laid it on
Isaac his son. And he took in his hand the fire. (Genesis 22:6)

In those precise, Golgotha-linked words, once again, we discover the pattern as is created in the Paleo-Hebrew letters of Genesis 1:1: three crosses, with the middle one being attached to the *aleph-tav*.

As we continue with the account of Abraham's test, we encounter the following ominous words in the ninth verse:

GOLGOTHA'S GROANING

Abraham...arranged the wood and bound Isaac his son and laid him on the altar, on top of the wood. (Genesis 22:9, NIV)

Yet again we find three *tav* crosses, with Yeshua on the middle cross under the *aleph-tav*. It's a picture of Yeshua being laid upon a wooden cross at the future Golgotha. *Absolutely breathtaking!*

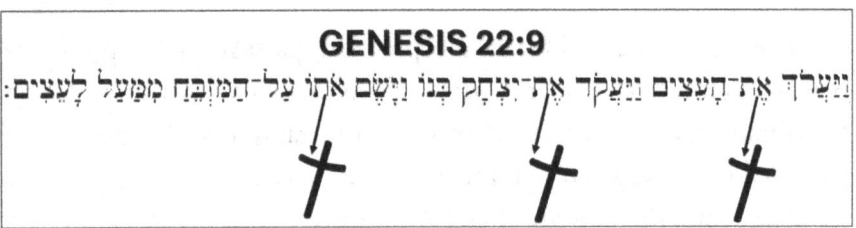

In the next chapter, we'll begin looking at a number of New Testament validations of the Golgotha passages we've just examined in Genesis 22.

31

ABRAHAM LONGED TO SEE MY DAY

Does Yeshua's statement mean Abraham knew something of the coming groanings of Golgotha?

Let's begin by looking at a passage in the New Testament book of Hebrews that answers the question of how Abraham could even consider the possibility of sacrificing his only son.

The response to that query is in the surface text of these three verses. However, especially note the emphasized words; they are the most important.

> **By faith Abraham, when he was tested,** offered up Isaac, and he who had received the promises offered up his only begotten son, of whom it was said, "In Isaac your seed shall be called," **considered that God was able to raise him up, even from the dead, from which he also received him** in a figurative sense. (Hebrews 11:17–19, NKJV; emphasis added)

Those emphasized words, encompassing the phrase concerning Abraham's trust in Yahweh, indicate exactly what it was that Yahweh/Yeshua wanted us to see as confirmation of Abraham's faith walk.

They are words that once again paint a portrait. The three *tav* images, with the middle cross represented by the *aleph-tav* concealed within those words, are like a bolt of lightning that illuminates the biblical truth. Here is yet another dramatic portrayal of the iconic image we first found in Genesis 1:1. As a matter of fact, we find the three *tav* crosses within the words "to raise even the dead."

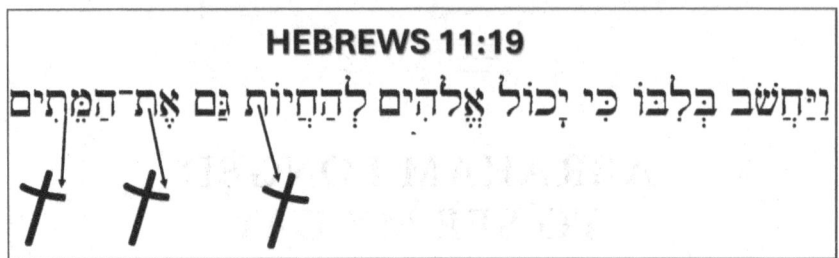

It's becoming increasingly obvious that our personal faith is meant to be strengthened, dramatically so, by seeing these uncanny images.

Rejoiced to See My Day

A verse found in the New Testament book of John confirms that Abraham was indeed given a supernatural glimpse of what would eventually come to pass at Golgotha. That assurance is spoken from the mouth of Yeshua Himself:

> Your father Abraham rejoiced to see my day; and he saw it, and was glad. (John 8:56, KJV)

Certainly the "my day" of which Yeshua was speaking would have included His sacrificial death that took place in much the same manner as Isaac's death almost came about when Abraham was commanded to offer up his own son. Several leading biblical scholars and scholarly sources agree, including the following:

Ellicott's Commentary for English Readers:

> **God foretold his advent clearly to [Abraham]**, Galatians 3:16; "Now to Abraham and his seed were the promises made. He saith not, And to seeds, as of many; but as of one, and to thy seed, which is Christ." **Abraham was permitted to have a view of the death of the Messiah** as a sacrifice for sin, represented by the command to offer Isaac. The death of the Messiah as a sacrifice…**was represented to Abraham clearly** by the command to offer his son.[130] (emphasis added)

ABRAHAM LONGED TO SEE MY DAY

John 8:56, when examined at the *spiritual DNA* level, offers yet another affirmation. In the words, "Abraham rejoiced to see my day; and he saw it, and was glad," we find the same Golgotha imagery: three *tavs*, right in the middle of the verse.

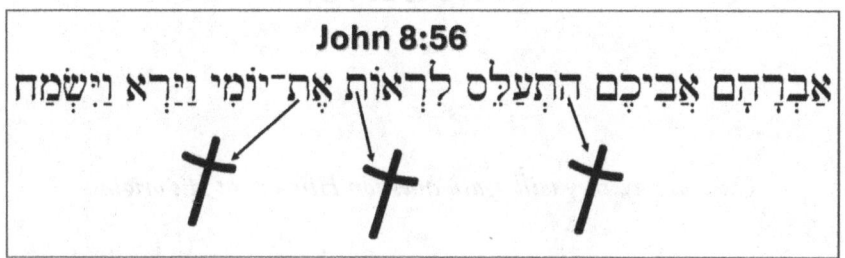

This time, the *tav* cross that represents the one in the middle (Yeshua) is at the end of the *aleph-tav* letters that are also sandwiching the Hebrew letter *waw* (*vav* in modern Hebrew[131]). And within that specific Hebrew letter arrangement is yet another staggering revelation.

The ancient Hebrew ideogram for the *waw* is the peg, nail, or hook. It can also mean *a spear*. So, in those three letters, we are looking at the *aleph*, the Eternal God—embedded with nails and pierced with a spear, *waw*—who is making the covenant, *tav*, with humanity through the cross, *tav*, of Golgotha![132]

Don't forget, this depiction emerges from the Golgotha statement given by Yeshua Himself about Abraham "seeing His day."[133]

Within this *aleph/waw/tav* combination we have yet another seemingly impossible picture/message made with the Paleo-Hebrew letters.

However, the two verses *after* John 8:56 (verses 57–58) also have embedded revelations. It's in those directly interlinked verses that Yeshua answers His detractors with yet another colossal response.

32

ORIGINS

On that day, they will again question Him about His origins.

In the Gospel of John, chapters 7 and 8, we find Yeshua in Jerusalem again. He's at the Temple Mount in early to mid-October to attend the Feast of Tabernacles with His disciples. That is the last of the Seven Feasts of the Lord that occur each Jewish liturgical year (Leviticus 23).

About six months later, at the *first feast* of the liturgical new year, the Feast of Passover, Yeshua will be groaning upon Golgotha's cross.[134]

The Feast of Tabernacles

While at the Feast of Tabernacles, Yeshua once again speaks to the gathering crowds piling into the Temple teaching area of Solomon's Colonnade. The elders, rabbis, and priests harass Him unmercifully, as they have during almost the entire three years of His ministry. They hurl false accusations at Him and continually pelt Him with verbal "stones" of slanderous innuendos. To no avail, they persistently attempt to turn the masses against Him. On that day, they again question Yeshua about His origins, just as they've done on several occasions prior to this event.

Following is Yeshua's seemingly audacious declaration to the Jewish religious elite. Again, this exchange takes place about five months before Golgotha's reality will burst to life.

> The Jews therefore said unto him, thou art not yet fifty years old, and hast thou seen Abraham? Jesus said unto them, Verily, verily, I say unto you, before Abraham was born, I am. (John 8:57–58, KJV)

ORIGINS

There it is again, right where we might expect it to be. In those two verses, there are only three *tavs*. In them can be seen the three *tav* crosses of Golgotha with Yeshua (*aleph-tav*) in the middle.

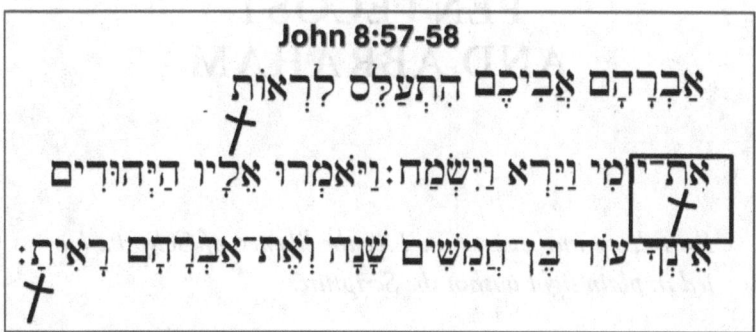

The Church Is Born

Months later, only a few days after the birth of the Church, a powerful sermon will be delivered within earshot of the public and religious elite.

But this time, it is the Apostle Peter who will preach to the gathering throngs in the Temple area. He will pick up where Yeshua left off, and he will once again invoke the prophecy of the Genesis 22 saga.

In so doing, Peter will be certain to include the name of Abraham.

33

PENTECOST AND ABRAHAM

I'm still stunned every time I see the likeness of Golgotha buried in plain sight within the Scripture.

In the third chapter of the book of Acts, we run into the words of Peter's fiery preaching at the Temple a few days after the birth of the Church, during the Feast of Pentecost, fifty days after Yeshua's resurrection. A huge crowd has gathered at the Temple teaching area when Peter proclaims the following:

> The God of Abraham, the God of Isaac, and the God of Jacob, the God of our fathers, glorified his servant **Jesus, whom you delivered over and denied** in the presence of Pilate, when he had decided to release him. (Acts 3:13, emphasis added)

In the **boldfaced** words describing exactly how Yeshua was delivered up to Golgotha's groanings, we find the same picture: the three crosses in the form of Golgotha's dark effigy.

PENTECOST AND ABRAHAM

Continuing into the heart of Peter's sermon in Acts 3, we see yet another direct reference to the Genesis 22 account of Abraham and Isaac, and God's covenant with Abraham:

> You are the sons of the prophets and **of the covenant** that God made with your fathers, saying to Abraham, "And in your offspring shall all the families of the earth be blessed." (Acts 3:25, emphasis added)

Notice the word "covenant" in this portion of Peter's sermon. This is important, because we've already seen the message of the "Covenant House of God" in the first word of Genesis 1:1, *bereshith*. And we know the *tav* represents the concept of "the covenant" in the ancient Hebrew alphabet ideograms.

Peter quotes Yahweh's pledge to Abraham right out of Genesis 22:18: "And in your offspring shall all the nations of the earth be blessed, because you have obeyed my voice."

Following are those exact Hebrew words, as recorded in Acts 3:25:

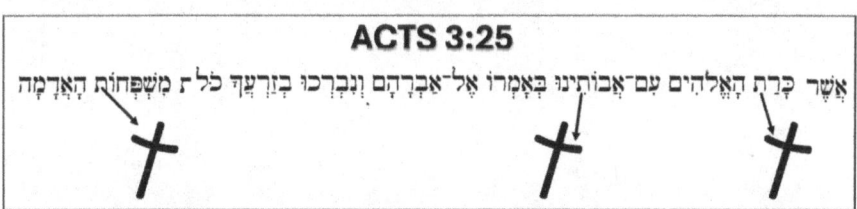

There they are, once more. The ages-old images of the three *tav* crosses of Golgotha are plainly depicted. It testifies of the *blessing* to the world that God promised would come from Abraham's seed: *the Lamb slain from the foundation of the world.*

I'm still stunned every time I see the likenesses of Golgotha that were supernaturally buried within the Scriptures well over two thousand years ago.

Again, what you choose to do with the knowledge of these images is up to you. The biggest obstacle to those who wish to simply dismiss the matter is that the uncanny *tav* portrait is practically impossible to

GOLGOTHA'S GROANING

forget. Once you see it, especially when it's presented in this manner, it's almost impossible to "unsee"!

As Messianic Rabbi Zev Porat said early in this book, the obviously preordained places in which we repeatedly see these iconic figures cannot be chalked up to mere coincidence.

We are now far beyond the possibility of happenstance. Nor is this phenomenon some sort of cosmic joke. We are looking at a supernaturally encoded message, apparently placed there for our generation!

Now, let's go back to the Old Testament and examine yet another seemingly impossible prophecy of Golgotha's groaning. This sensational declaration, written a full one thousand years before Yeshua goes to His cross of suffering, was supernaturally penned by ancient Israel's King David.

≡ 34 ≡

THE COMPOUNDING OF PSALM 22

> *The heart of this psalm is all about Golgotha—an event that wouldn't happen for another one thousand years into David's future.*

The paintings, drawings, and various movie and video interpretations of Golgotha almost always display *three* crosses. That's because the imagery, in one form or another, has been exhibited all over the planet since its significance was first punctuated by the actual Golgotha and resurrection events.

For two thousand years and counting, that likeness has been firmly implanted in the minds of a mammoth portion of the world's population, regardless of whether or not people believe Yeshua is the long-awaited Messiah. It is simply one of the most recognizable illustrations on the planet to this day—to Satan's dismay.

However, until now, almost no one knew that this prototypical imprint was also emblazoned in the Golgotha passages found throughout the Old Testament. Nor could they have imagined that the imagery could be found in the majority of the *Delitzsch Hebrew New Testament* Scriptures that tie directly to the crucifixion of Yeshua. What we are now seeing is no small thing!

- "The LORD gives wisdom to the wise and knowledge to the discerning. He reveals deep and hidden things" (Daniel 2:21–22, BSB).

- "But we impart a secret and hidden wisdom of God, which God decreed before the ages for our glory" (1 Corinthians 2:7).

Introduction to Psalm 22

Psalm 22, which features a compound prophecy, may be the most astonishing Golgotha passage in the Psalms, and perhaps in the entire Old Testament.

A *compound prophecy* begins by addressing the prophet's own time period and/or personal experiences, but morphs into a prophecy about Yeshua, Satan, or the ultimate *time of the end*.[135]

However, the compound prophecy in Psalm 22 is practically impossible to miss. It turns out that the heart of this passage is obviously about Golgotha, an event that wouldn't happen for another thousand years into David's future. And in this Psalm, several of the now most recognizable New Testament elements of what took place on Golgotha are *described* in exact detail.

So the question arises yet again: Are the hidden images of that historically recognized event also present within the text of Psalm 22? After observing what we've thus far uncovered, it only seems logical that they would be.

35

DAVID'S AGONY

My God, my God...why are you so far...from the words of my groaning? (Psalm 22:1)

Couched in the middle of Psalm 22 are several specific events that came to pass at Golgotha, and they're spoken of in the plain surface text.

The events dolefully express the echoing depths of Golgotha's groanings that wouldn't happen until a millennium after they were first written about by David. The prophecies also include words that would be uttered from the mouth of the crucified Yeshua Himself! These events described by David would eventually converge into that one iconic image imprinted on a large portion of the collective human psyche.

What is particularly noticeable is that those Golgotha words of Psalm 22 are written in the first person, as though David himself is actually feeling the agony of what is happening as he's writing. The problem is, he did not personally experience certain elements of that suffering—not in the way he describes it in that text.

But Yeshua did experience them—every one of them, to the letter. Following are some of the compound-prophecy verses of Psalm 22:

- "My God, my God, why have you forsaken me? Why are you so far from saving me, from the words of my groaning?" (verse 1).
- "But I am a worm and not a man, scorned by mankind and despised by the people. All who see me mock me; they make mouths at me; they wag their heads; 'He trusts in the Lord; let him deliver him; let him rescue him, for he delights in him!'" (verses 6–8).

GOLGOTHA'S GROANING

- "I am poured out like water, and all my bones are out of joint; my heart is like wax; it is melted within my breast; my strength is dried up like a potsherd, and my tongue sticks to my jaws; you lay me in the dust of death. For dogs encompass me; a company of evildoers encircles me; they have pierced my hands and feet—I can count all my bones—they stare and gloat over me; they divide my garments among them, and for my clothing they cast lots" (verses 14–18).

You'll most likely recognize that the first verse of Psalm 22 was actually quoted by Yeshua as He was taking His dying breaths upon Golgotha's cross. These were some of the last words He would speak on that horrific day of agony. Have a look at Psalm 22:1 again: "My God, my God, why have you forsaken me? Why are you so far from saving me, from the words of my groaning?" (Psalm 22:1).

Nothing Else Like It

Does the following illustration shock you? Probably not at this point in our study. But still, I am gobsmacked every time I see the illustration created in the Paleo-Hebrew script for those precise words.

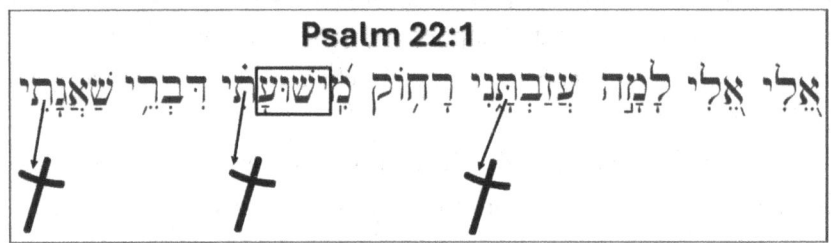

The Psalm 22 depiction of Golgotha's groaning is significantly different from the ones we've seen previously, although at first glance the arrangement of the three *tavs* might not seem unique. But notice the four Hebrew letters in the black box. Those letters are *yud, shin, waw, and ayin*—the letters that spell the *Hebrew name* of Yeshua/Jesus!

DAVID'S AGONY

Not only does Psalm 22:1 display the three *tavs* of Golgotha, but the middle *tav* in the image is attached to the name of Yeshua Himself—tucked away inside a single Hebrew word.

It has been there for more than three thousand years.

≡ 36 ≡

THE RABBI'S DISCOVERY

It was secretly tucked away within a Hebrew expression!

My global ministry partner, Messianic Rabbi Zev Porat, made that discovery while we were on a phone call. I had called him from my office in Florida, and he was at his Tel Aviv office in Israel.

During the conversation in which we had been discussing Psalm 22, Zev blurted out, "Carl! Look at Psalm 22 again...that first verse! Yeshua's name is there, *hidden* inside another word!

The Hebrew word he was talking about is pronounced "mee-shoe-ah-TEE," which expresses the English words "from helping me" or "from saving me." It is similar to the Hebrew *bereshith,* the first word of Genesis 1:1, which expresses twelve other distinct Hebrew words within it.

So, unless a person can read Hebrew and is paying close attention, many readers—even Hebrew-speaking people—will miss the name of Yeshua entirely! *But it's there.*

Think of that! This is a particularly striking revelation. The one and only Old Testament verse quoted by Yeshua while on the cross of Golgotha was this one! He groaned it out in the depths of His agony. And, of all things, the words he quoted *contain His name* furtively tucked away within a Hebrew expression.

Words Within a Word

This same phenomenon occurs in the English language. Sometimes we read a word, time and time again, without even noticing that it contains several other English words. For example, "decadence" includes the words "decade," "den," and "cadence," as well as the often-used prefix "deca." You might have looked at that word many times and never noticed the other words within it. This is the same type of thing that occurs in Psalm 22:1.

However, even as Yeshua quoted that line of Scripture while on the cross, everything spoken of in David's thousand-year-earlier Golgotha vision was taking place at that very moment, right under Yeshua's feet. In speaking the first verse of Psalm 22, Yeshua was actually directing those who had the spiritual "ears to hear and eyes to see" to consider the prophecy of the 22nd Psalm.

More than likely, this was one reason the Roman centurion in charge of the crucifixion exclaimed the unfolding truth:

> The centurion, seeing what had happened, praised God and said, "Surely this was a righteous man." (Luke 23:47, NIV)[136]

Would it surprise you to discover that the words spoken by the centurion have a familiar symbol within them, when written in Hebrew? Have a look:

LUKE 23:47

וַיַּרְא שַׂר־הַמֵּאָה אֵת אֲשֶׁר נִהְיָתָה וַיִּתֵּן כָּבוֹד לֵאלֹהִים וַיֹּאמַר אָכֵן הָאִישׁ הַזֶּה צַדִּיק הָיָה

☦ ☦ ☦

There they are—the three *tav* crosses of Golgotha! It seems this long-hidden messaging is as legitimate as it gets. However, we still haven't even begun to completely unravel where we're ultimately headed.

37

IN THE DUST OF DEATH

How can this be, apart from the supernatural inspiration of the Spirit of Yahweh?

Let's continue by examining several more noteworthy discoveries. They are also found in Psalm 22, as well as in the New Testament passages that echo them.

Verses 6–8 of Psalm 22 express the mournful groaning of a despised soul who is suffering in the unimaginable depths of despair. While David surely may have experienced similar emotions in his lifetime, and even heard comparable words spoken about him from the lips of his enemies, there is no way we can deny that these sentiments, almost in the same words recorded by David, were also hurled at Yeshua while on the cross (Matthew 27:43–44).[137]

> But I am a worm and not a man, scorned by mankind and despised by the people. All who see me mock me; they make mouths at me; they wag their heads; "He trusts in the Lord; let him deliver him; let him rescue him, for he delights in him!" (Psalm 22:6–8)

When we examine this passage, we discover that in those three undeniably connected Golgotha verses, there are only three *tavs*. And they form a picture of the three crosses. All three *tavs* are found in verse 6, the one that describes the emotional pain of that horrible day.

> But I am a worm and not a man, scorned by mankind and despised by the people. (Psalm 22:6)

IN THE DUST OF DEATH

Following is the corresponding Paleo imagery of that verse:

However, that's not all we find in Psalm 22. There are additional words David uttered in verse 15. They are connected to an announcement that Yeshua would eventually cry out during His six-hour ordeal: the agonizing words, "I thirst!"

Following is the Psalm 22 prediction of that excruciating dehydration Yeshua would be forced to endure:

> My mouth is dried up like a potsherd, and my tongue sticks to the roof of my mouth; you lay me in the dust of death. (Psalm 22:15, NIV)

Here is what that verse from Psalm 22 illustrates for us in the Paleo-Hebrew—the same, unmistakable image of Golgotha's outrage:

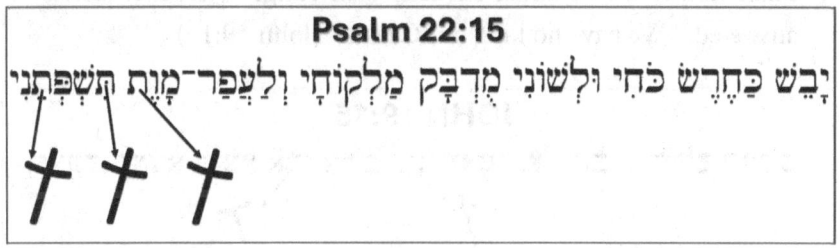

How can these dramatic images be there, apart from the supernatural inspiration of the Holy Spirit of Yahweh?

By now, the answer is obvious: They can't be.

☰ 38 ☰

TAKE HIM AWAY!

And He went out, bearing His own cross, to the place called The Place of a Skull, which in Aramaic is called Golgotha. (John 19:17)

The four Gospels, as rendered in the Hebrew language, spill over with the same iconic figure of the three *tav* crosses, predominately found in the places we might expect to find a corresponding, supernaturally placed code. Moving forward, you will see the *exact wording* in which Golgotha's three crosses are revealed, straight from the Hebrew translation of the New Testament.

The first example is John 19:15, and the three *tav* crosses are there, with the *aleph-tav* as the middle one.

> They cried out, "Away with him, away with him, crucify him!" Pilate said to them, "Shall I crucify your King?" The chief priests answered, "We have no king but Caesar." (John 19:15)

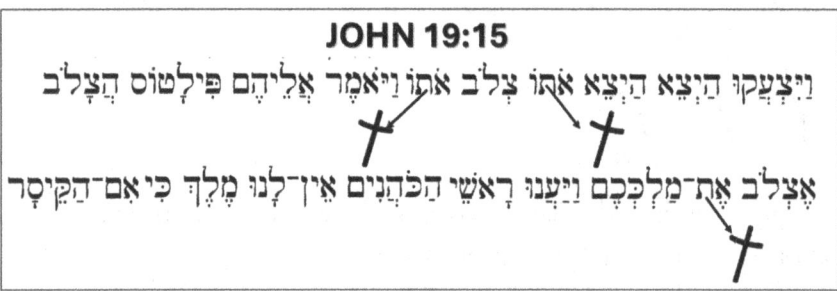

Here's the next verse:

TAKE HIM AWAY!

So [Pilate] delivered [Yeshua] over to them to be crucified. (John 19:16)

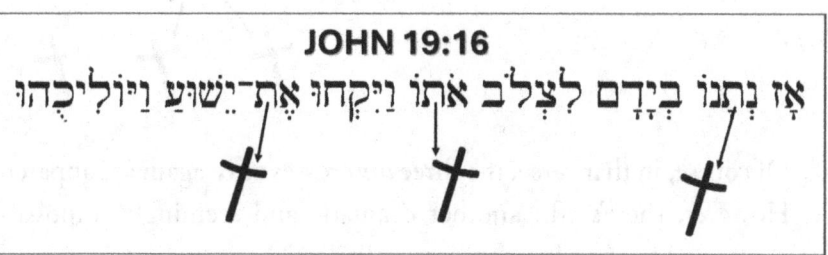

There it is again. The Golgotha image—three *tavs*. And the middle one is the *aleph-tav*.

Then, verse 17 tells us:

He went out, bearing His own cross, to the place called The Place of a Skull, which in Aramaic is called Golgotha. (John 19:17)

Using the exact wording from verse 17 that reads, "to the place called the Place of a Skull, which in Aramaic is called Golgotha," we find the following revelation. The three *tavs* are there.

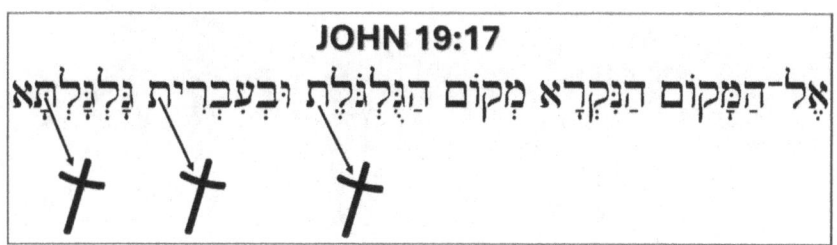

Now we come to verse 19, where we find a particularly infamous reminder of that hideous day. Pilate ordered a sign to be constructed and then hung over Yeshua's head as a jeering derision.[138]

Pilate also wrote an inscription and put it on the cross. It read, "Jesus of Nazareth, the King of the Jews." (John 19:19)

> **JOHN 19:19**
>
> וַיִּכְתֹּב פִּילָטוֹס כְּתֹבֶת כְּתֹבֶת עַל־לוּחַ הַנָּצְרִי וַיְשִׂימֵהוּ עַל־הַצְּלָב יֵשׁוּעַ מֶלֶךְ הַיְּהוּדִים

Of course, in that verse, the three *tav* crosses once again are apparent. However, there's still another dramatic and seemingly impossible detail we need to examine concerning Psalm 22.

≡ 39 ≡

CASTING LOTS

What are the chances that there would be a clear Golgotha depiction in the precise words that speak of that specific Psalm 22 prophecy?

One of the most noteworthy features of Psalm 22 is the fact that David, within the revelation of his prophetic vision, actually saw the soldiers casting lots for Messiah's clothing.

All four Gospels record the account of the soldiers gambling for Yeshua's clothing at the foot of His cross. Take note of the emphasized words in the following:

> **Then they crucified Him, and divided His garments, casting lots**, that it might be fulfilled which was spoken by the prophet: "They divided My garments among them, And for My clothing they cast lots. **Sitting down, they kept watch over Him there.**" (Matthew 27:35–36, NKJV; emphasis added)

What are the chances there would be a clear Golgotha depiction in the *exact words* that speak of the Psalm 22 prophecy? Apparently, the chances are 100 percent!

In those two verses are the three *tav* crosses with the *aleph-tav* in the middle, found in the emphasized words, "Then they crucified Him, and divided His garments, casting lots.… Sitting down, they kept watch over Him there."

GOLGOTHA'S GROANING

The words that are not emphasized in that verse simply indicate, in a parenthetical declaration, that the lot-casting was indeed prophesied in Psalm 22.

Golgotha's image is glaring at us, straight from the text of Matthew 27, as it perfectly mirrors the fulfillment of David's thousand-year-old prophecy.

The iconic Golgotha three-*tav* image is also found in John's account of that day:

> So they said to one another, "Let us not tear it, but cast lots for it to see whose it shall be." This was to fulfill the Scripture which says, "They divided my garments among them, and for my clothing they cast lots." (John 19:24)

There's More!

The same pattern of precisely three *tavs* displaying the numinous imagery of Golgotha is also found in the following New Testament passages. Each has an endnote reference so you can examine the three *tavs* for yourself.

- "And they offered him wine mixed with myrrh, but he did not take it" (Mark 15:23).[139]
- "And they crucified him and divided his garments among them, casting lots for them, to decide what each should take. And it was the third hour when they crucified him" (Mark 15:24–25).[140]
- "And the inscription of the charge against him read, 'The King of the Jews'" (Mark 15:26).[141]
- "Then two robbers were crucified with him, one on the right and one on the left. And those who passed by derided him, wagging their heads" (Matthew 27:38–39).[142]

The Foremost Fulfillment

Still another important passage in the *Delitzsch Hebrew New Testament* connects directly to Psalm 22. It is a passage from Luke 23, and it encompasses a complete thought expressed in four verses. Together, they speak of casting lots for Yeshua's clothing, as well as the exact words of mocking that Yeshua endured from the religious leaders and soldiers. As we've already seen, both the gambling for Yeshua's clothing and the sadistic scoffers are foreshadowed in Psalm 22.[143]

Here is what Luke says about that day:

> And Jesus said, "Father, forgive them, for they know not what they do." And they cast lots to divide his garments. And the people stood by, watching, but the rulers scoffed at him, saying, "He saved others; let him save himself, if he is the Christ of God, his Chosen One!" The soldiers also mocked him, coming up and offering him sour wine and saying, "If you are the King of the Jews, save yourself!" (Luke 23:34–37, emphasis added)

In the midst of the entire four verses are only three *tav* crosses. That quartet of verses describes what David saw as recorded in the 22nd Psalm.

See the endnote for a link where you can identify the three *tavs* for yourself.[144]

40

ISAIAH AND THE ARM OF THE LORD

Isaiah 52:10 represents the exact ideographic message of Yeshua's name. Coincidence, or a supernaturally encoded verse?

Most students of the Word of God know Isaiah 52 and 53 are two of the most remarkable prophetic Old Testament chapters in the Scriptures. The chapters address, in the greatest detail, the coming of Messiah and His travail on Golgotha's cross.

Isaiah 53 even features prophecies about Yeshua being crucified along with criminals and being "with a rich man in his death." In addition, the passage includes an emphasis on the resurrection event itself. We'll examine those elements in more detail in the next chapter.

Forbidden Words

The prophetic words of Isaiah 53 are so unexpectedly in line with what would ultimately take place at Golgotha that the Orthodox Jewish synagogue liturgical readings purposely skip over them, including a section of chapter 52. Because of the Golgotha features of those prophecies, this section is often referred to as the "forbidden chapter."[145]

In light of that fact, a large number of Orthodox Jewish people have no idea these passages exist. Let's discover why.

The Whole World Will See It

Most of this next revelation is first seen within the surface text alone.

Isaiah 52 is the setup for the truths found in Isaiah 53. Therefore, the Scripture we will concentrate on for now is Isaiah 52:10:

ISAIAH AND THE ARM OF THE LORD

The LORD has bared his holy arm before the eyes of all the nations, and all the ends of the earth shall see the salvation of our God. (Isaiah 52:10)

For most believers, this verse is fairly straightforward. But the more we peel back the layers that go deeper than the English surface text, the more exceptional the message becomes.

Salvation

The English word "salvation" in Isaiah 52:10 is actually the Hebrew word *yeshua*.[146] Of course, we also know this is the Name above all names—*Yeshua/Jesus*!

Knowing that piece of information, think of what Isaiah 52:10 is actually saying as we read it in English, but with the Hebrew understanding of the word "salvation." It would read like this: "The LORD has bared his holy arm before the eyes of all the nations, and all the ends of the earth shall see the *Yeshua/Jesus* of our God."

And that's just the *surface text* revelation.

The Name

But there are still additional supernatural connections to explore.

You'll remember from a previous chapter that the name *Yeshua* is found inside a word in the first verse of Psalm 22, what Yeshua quoted on the cross: "My God, my God why have you forsaken me?"

However, what I did not disclose in that earlier chapter is the ideographic *meaning* of *Yeshua*. That meaning is based on the Hebrew letters that make it up. In this way, the name itself delivers a distinctive message. Reading the letters of *Yeshua* from right to left, as it would be read in Hebrew, they are *yud, shin, waw,* and *ayin*.

Here are the anciently established ideograms of each of those letters.

The *yud/yod*.[147] This letter represents the hand, or the outstretched arm(s). The *yud* is also in the name *YHWH*.[148]

The *shin*. This letter represents the Name

133

GOLGOTHA'S GROANING

of God/*El Shaddai*. As demonstrated in an earlier chapter, it is for this reason that the *shin* is emblazoned upon almost every Hebrew *mezuzah* around the world.

The *vav/waw*.[149] The *waw* represents a hook, peg, nail, spear, or spike. It carries the connotation of fastening one thing to another. It, too, is in the name *YHWH*.[150]

The *ayin*. The *ayin* is the sixteenth letter of the Hebrew alphabet. According to Chabad.org, its meaning is: 1. Eyes 2. Salvation. 3. To see salvation.[151]

So then, here is the beautiful ideographic message of Yeshua's name: "Through the outstretched arms of God Almighty, and the nails and the spear, the whole world will see my salvation in Yeshua!"

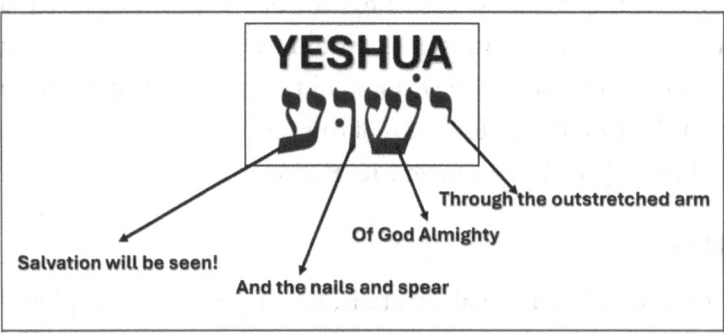

Think of that: The message in the letters of Yeshua's name also make up the entire surface-text message of Isaiah 52:10! Coincidence, or a supernaturally encoded verse?

And don't forget, that same message is represented in the first word of Genesis 1:1 (*bereshith*). Additionally, it is found in the three crosses/*tavs* within the seven words of Genesis 1:1…the first *tav* picture of Golgotha.

Once again, we see the previously unimaginable link between Genesis 1:1 and important portions of every other Golgotha reference throughout the Old Testament…and even in the Hebrew New Testament!

ISAIAH AND THE ARM OF THE LORD

The Sensational Finale to Isaiah 52:10

Guess what else we find in Isaiah 52:10? Surely you know by now: the three crosses of Golgotha's Hill shining like the noonday sun.

> The LORD has bared his holy arm before the eyes of all the nations, and all the ends of the earth shall see the salvation of our God. (Isaiah 52:10)

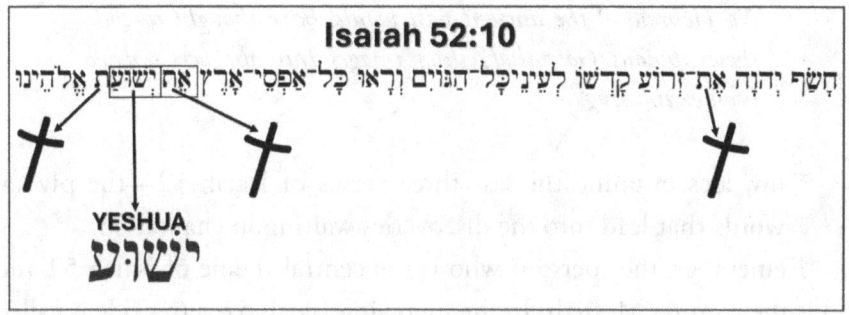

Not only are the three *tav* crosses there, but the middle one is under the *aleph-tav*. And that *aleph-tav* ("the first and the last, the beginning and the end") is right next to Yeshua's name (*yud, shin, wav, ayin*).

The Golgotha depiction of Isaiah 52:10 is truly miraculous to behold!

41

THE INTERLUDE

No Hebrew of the ancient past would have thought to code these obvious Golgotha/Yeshua images into the verses we've been examining.

Now, let's examine the last three verses of Isaiah 52—the pivotal words that lead into the discoveries waiting in chapter 53.

Remember, the "person" who is the central theme of Isaiah 52 and 53 is the coming Messiah. In the following Isaiah 52 verses, He is called "My Servant." Of course, we now know this "servant" is none other than *Yeshua HaMashiach*, the central figure of the Word of God.

> Behold, My Servant will prosper, He will be high and lifted up and greatly exalted. Just as many were appalled at you, My people, So His appearance was marred beyond that of a man, And His form beyond the sons of mankind. So He will sprinkle many nations, Kings will shut their mouths on account of Him; For what they had not been told, they will see, And what they had not heard, they will understand. (Isaiah 52:13–15, NASB)

This vital information about the "servant" seamlessly slides the reader right into chapter 53. But this three-verse passage, taken as a whole, and expressing the complete thought of that transition, contains (you guessed it!) precisely three *tav* crosses as well.[152]

Those verses display yet another mind-boggling depiction of Golgotha, which is exactly what chapters 52 and 53 are all about. The picture is right where it *ought* to be.

THE INTERLUDE

Unarguably Supernatural

Think of it: No Hebrew person of the ancient past would have thought to code these obvious Golgotha/Yeshua images into the verses we've been examining—much less beginning with Genesis 1:1. In fact, other than "seeing" Golgotha through supernatural revelation, they wouldn't even know what their prophetic utterances meant. Yet there they are.

Not only that, but when we consider that the New Testament was first written in Greek and then, much later, was translated to Hebrew, we have evidence of an even deeper supernatural overlay.

After all, apparently the Holy Spirit of God had to first inspire the men who wrote the New Testament documents. That had to have been done in such a way that when the Hebrew translation was eventually produced from the original Greek words, the *tav* crosses would still be present in that Hebrew translation—and *in just the right passages*! Unbelievable, but true.

In a world that would somehow be utterly devoid of any possibility of supernatural involvement, what we've been observing, page after page, would be nothing less than absolute impossibility—especially in the numbers in which we're finding them, and in the exact places that match the overall messages the figures of Golgotha convey.

With this understanding of the reality of the supernatural *Golgotha codes*, let's take a much closer look at Isaiah 53—that, regrettably, "forbidden chapter."

42

ISAIAH'S GROANING

Once again we're being dramatically reminded that Golgotha was planned from the beginning.

The surface text of Isaiah 53 opens with a vivid description of the coming Messiah. Verses 2–4 form a cohesive declaration about the Coming One. Also, the overarching message of the passage centers on the misery-laden groanings of Golgotha's necessity. The emphasized words in the following portray that precise language:

> For he grew up before him like a young plant, and like a root out of dry ground; he had **no form or majesty** that we should look at him, and **no beauty** that we should desire him. He was **despised** and **rejected** by men, a man of **sorrows** and acquainted with **grief**; and as one from whom men **hide their faces** he was **despised**, and we **esteemed him not**.
>
> Surely he has borne **our griefs** and carried **our sorrows**; yet we **esteemed him stricken**, **smitten** by God, and **afflicted**. (Isaiah 53:2–4, emphasis added)

So, if the three-*tav* phenomenon truly is supernaturally orchestrated by the Holy Spirit of God, how could it be that these three verses, as a complete declaration, might *not* possess a Paleo-Hebrew imprint of Golgotha? Don't worry; that won't be a problem, because they do. View them at this endnote.[153]

ISAIAH'S GROANING

Groaning Magnified

Not surprisingly, the same phenomenon is repeated in verses 5–6, where another complete thought is expressed. Once again, the emphasized words in the two verses that follow illustrate the agonizing consequences of Golgotha. And in that entire expression are three *tav* crosses:

> But he **was pierced** for our transgressions; he was **crushed** for our iniquities; upon him was the **chastisement** that brought us peace, and with **his wounds** we are healed. All we like sheep have gone astray; we have turned—everyone—to his own way. (Isaiah 53:5–6, emphasis added)

The vividly expressed human misery is the message being conveyed in the surface text, as well as in the three-*tav* verification of the three crosses.[154]

Once more, we're being dramatically reminded that Golgotha was planned from the beginning, even before Adam took in his first gasp of earth's newly created air. The three *tav* crosses are there within the completed thought of those two verses, right up through the words "everyone to his own way."

Planned from the Beginning

In the six remaining Hebrew words of that two-verse section, we discover the following complete statement: "And the Lord has laid upon Him the iniquity of us all."

In that one sentence, we find only one *tav* cross. But here's the clincher. Right in the middle of those words, the "Him" being spoken of is represented by the *aleph-tav*.

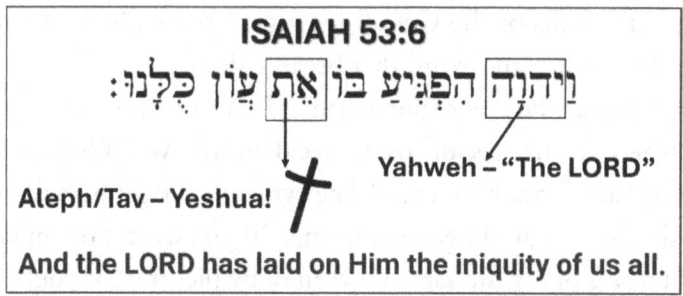

GOLGOTHA'S GROANING

Yet again, even within the last words of the passage, we find confirmation that the *aleph-tav*—Yahweh/*Yeshua*—is the One who will go to Golgotha...*the Lamb slain from the beginning*. What majesty!

Do You Want to Know Who I Am?

Furthermore, the Hebrew word for LORD is *Yahweh,* which, as we've noted, is spelled with the letters *yud, heh, waw, heh*. The ideographic meaning of those letters is also anciently verified. They translate to: "Behold the hands/arms, behold the nails/spear!"[155]

Yahweh—"LORD"—is found almost seven thousand times in the Old Testament. Therefore, even the most frequently used name for God speaks the message of Golgotha in *ideographic interpretation*, a practice that is thousands of years old![156]

A Vivid Lesson

Repeatedly, the Golgotha images, as well as precise ideographic messages, command us to see the truth. They do so in the surface text of Isaiah as well as in the accompanying *tav* images in that text. The message is encoded in the name of Yeshua, and it's in the name of Yahweh as well. All of that exists so that we simply cannot miss the communication of the central focus of the Gospel message: "Yeshua is the Lamb slain from the beginning, the Word that became flesh."

Golgotha was the preordained plan of Heaven's throne. It was not the world's plan or some type of cosmic accident, nor was it Satan's plan. In fact, it was Satan's death sentence! The evidence is right before our eyes.

It's almost as if our Creator is saying, "If you can't quite understand the plain *words* of my message, I'll even draw pictures for you!"

43

DEATH AND RESURRECTION

Isaiah 53:9 speaks of Yeshua being crucified with criminals.

Following the incredible message we've just seen in the fifth and sixth verses of Isaiah 53, we now focus on verses 7 and 8. These verses express yet another complete thought of Isaiah's prophecy. They also speak of Yeshua's *groaning* agony, especially the certain outcome of the ordeal: His sacrificial death. Again, these two verses embody exactly three *tav* crosses.[157]

> He was **oppressed**, and he was **afflicted**, yet he opened not his mouth; like a lamb that is **led to the slaughter**, and like a sheep that before its shearers is **silent**, so he **opened not his mouth**.
>
> By **oppression** and **judgment** he was **taken away**; and as for his generation, who considered that he was **cut off** out of the **land of the living, stricken** for the transgression of my people? (Isaiah 53:7–8, emphasis added)

Yeshua Wasn't Alone at Golgotha

Next, we confront another surprising fact: Isaiah 53:9 speaks of Yeshua being crucified with criminals, as well as introduces the idea that Yeshua would be buried in a rich man's tomb after the crucifixion.[158]

> They intended to bury Him with criminals, but He ended up in a rich man's tomb, because He had committed no violent deeds, nor had He spoken deceitfully. (Isaiah 53:9, NET)

Within the specific words of verse 9, "His grave was with the wicked and with a rich man in His death," we discover to no surprise that the pictures are there again...the three Paleo *tavs* of Golgotha, with the *aleph-tav* in the middle.

The Revenant

Now we come to verses 10 and 11 of Isaiah 53, which not only express a completed thought that points to Golgotha, but also speak of *the resurrection* of the prophesied Coming One.

Here are the words in the surface text.

> Yet it was **the Lord's will** to **crush him** and **cause him to suffer**, and though the Lord **makes his life an offering for sin**, he will **see his offspring** and **prolong his days**, and the will of the Lord will prosper in his hand.
>
> **After he has suffered**, he **will see the light of life** and be satisfied; by his knowledge my righteous servant will justify many, and he will **bear their iniquities**. (Isaiah 53:10–11, NIV; emphasis added)

The *Pulpit Commentary* sums up what a number of scholars say about this passage:

> As Delitzsch says, "His continued taking of our trespasses upon himself is merely the constant presence and presentation of his atonement, which has been offered once for all. **The dead yet**

DEATH AND RESURRECTION

living One, because of his one self-sacrifice, is **an eternal Priest**, who **now lives** to distribute the blessings which he has acquired" ("Commentary on Isaiah," vol. 2:p. 338).[159] (emphasis added, parentheses in original)

And of course, within Isaiah 53:10–11, there are only three Paleo *tav* crosses, forming the image of Golgotha.[160] By now, we shouldn't be surprised in the least.

Now let's investigate to see if there are any corresponding Isaiah 53 Golgotha pictures within the Hebrew New Testament Scriptures.

… 44 …

ISAIAH'S CRIMINALS

There are only two kinds of people that Heaven's throne sees when the Lord of Glory looks at humanity.

One of the most arresting features of Isaiah 53, on our historical side of the fulfillment of Golgotha, is a detailed prophecy of the look and feel of what were *then* the "coming" events that would take place on Golgotha.

That ancient foretelling indicated Yeshua would be crucified along with criminals. Certainly, this was a prophetic oddity I had to investigate within the Golgotha passages found in the *Delitzsch Hebrew New Testament*.

First, let's have a look at two prominent New Testament passages that speak of the crucified thieves on that day at Golgotha:

- "They crucified two criminals with Him, one on His right and one on His left. **So the Scripture was fulfilled** that says: And He was counted among outlaws" (Mark 15:27–28, HCSB; emphasis added).
- "And when they came to the place that is called The Skull, there they crucified him, and the criminals, one on his right and one on his left" (Luke 23:33).

Notice the passage in Mark 15 references the "fulfillment of Scripture." All the reputable scholars agree that Mark is referring to Isaiah 53. How could it *not* be? Now look at the imagery from both Mark 15 and Luke 23.

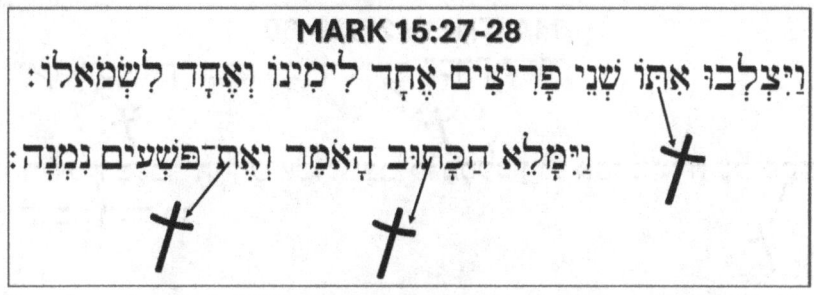

Not only does the surface text of Isaiah 53 predict this specific aspect of Yeshua's crucifixion on Golgotha's Hill, but the New Testament surface text also confirms it. And the Paleo-Hebrew *tav* depictions found in both the Old Testament and the Hebrew New Testament confirm it as well!

Buried with the Rich

The same phenomenon concerning the burial of Yeshua in a rich man's tomb is also present. We know that Joseph of Arimathea was the rich man through whom this prophecy was finally fulfilled. The following is Matthew's New Testament account:

> And Joseph took the body and wrapped it in a clean linen shroud and laid it in his own new tomb, which he had cut in the rock. And he rolled a great stone to the entrance of the tomb and went away. (Matthew 27:59–60)

We see exactly what Isaiah prophesied in the Paleo-Hebrew depiction of Golgotha—exactly three *tav* crosses running right through Matthew 27:59–60.

GOLGOTHA'S GROANING

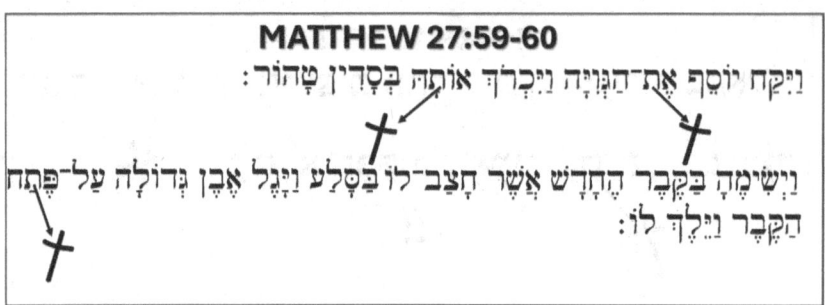

As I explained at the outset of this book, what we're finding throughout Scripture, beginning in Genesis 1:1, is something akin to looking at the *spiritual DNA* of the Word of God!

The more we examine this phenomenon, the more we see that it is certainly an intentionally and supernaturally placed *code*. As Messianic Rabbi Zev Porat said, "This could be nothing else!"

And that code, similar to DNA, is formulated by a distinctive arrangement of certain Hebrew letters to produce an image that conveys a message.

What we're looking at, once again, is the central theme of Scripture: *Golgotha*.

Two Kinds of People

Also consider this important *human image* of Golgotha. Think of the imagery created by the thieves on either side of Yeshua on that ominous day. The people attending the event were actually seeing yet another divine message displayed right in front of them, in the flesh.

The message was that there are only *two kinds of people* Heaven's throne sees when the LORD of Glory looks upon all of humanity: 1) the ones who deny and mock Yeshua as one of the thieves did; and 2) multitudes of people who repent in humility and believe what Yeshua has done for them at Golgotha, which is what the other thief did.

And, most importantly, Our Father in Heaven sees Yeshua situated right in the middle of this pitiful human condition, suspended between Heaven and Earth! He is humanity's *Chief Mediator* before the throne of God—ready to be the Savior for all who call upon Him.

ISAIAH'S CRIMINALS

Not only do we find verification of this truth in 1 Timothy 2:5–6, but we also discover the *tav* picture within that confirmation. It's found in the complete thought of the first sentence of those two verses:

> For there is one God, and there is **one mediator** between God and men, the man Christ Jesus, who gave himself as a ransom for all. (1Timothy 2:5–6, emphasis added)

Of course, the Golgotha *tav* image is there. Because, as our divine mediator, Yeshua "gave Himself" on that hill!

And the *aleph-tav* in the middle of that imagery...is *Yeshua HaMashiach*.

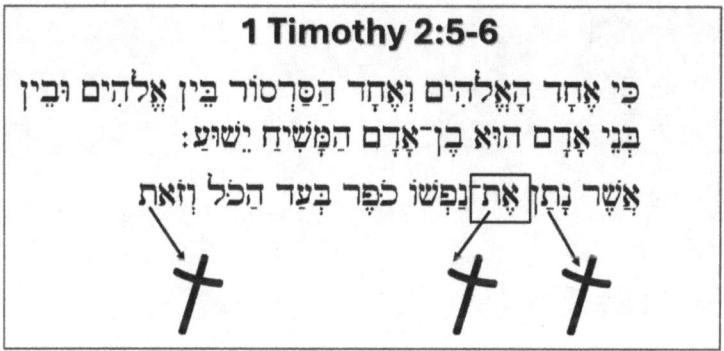

Part Six

A LAMB AND A HIGH PRIEST

The blood shall be a sign for you, on the houses where you are. And when I see the blood, I will pass over you, and no plague will befall you to destroy you, when I strike the land of Egypt. (Exodus 12:13)

≡ 45 ≡

THE LAMB

Renowned scholars agree that Yeshua was indeed "David's Lamb" of Psalm 22.

In part five we examined the prophecy about Abraham's sacrifice of Isaac. We also analyzed David's vision of the crucified Savior and Isaiah's revelation of the gruesomeness of the Suffering Servant's travail, as well as His resurrection.

Within two of those three Golgotha prophecies, Genesis 22 and Isaiah 53, the crucifixion of Yeshua was directly compared to that of a *sacrificial lamb*. And even in the third one, David's Psalm 22, there is an inarguable reference to the Lamb of Golgotha. I use the word "inarguable" because that fact is confirmed by Yeshua's own words, as recorded in the New Testament.

First, let's have another look at the first two "lamb" statements of Genesis 22 and Isaiah 53. Especially note the emphasized words.

- "And Isaac said to his father Abraham, 'My father!' And he said, 'Here I am, my son.' He said, 'Behold, the fire and the wood, but **where is the lamb** for a burnt offering?' Abraham said, '**God will provide for himself the lamb** for a burnt offering, my son.' So they went both of them together" (Genesis 22:7–8, emphasis added).
- "He was oppressed, yet when he was afflicted he opened not his mouth; **as a lamb that is led to the slaughter**, and **as a sheep** that before its shearers is dumb, so **he opened not his mouth**" (Isaiah 53:7, ASV; emphasis added)

GOLGOTHA'S GROANING

The "Third Lamb"

Now explore the almost "coded" indication of the ultimate sacrifice of the Lamb of God that's found in Psalm 22. It's not nearly as obvious as it is in Genesis 22 and Isaiah 53, but it's there.

The statement is made in Psalm 22:1–25. After the Golgotha sacrifice is offered (described in detail through the first two dozen verses of Psalm 22), there arises a deep New Testament Golgotha connection. Here's that verse from David's prophecy:

> The afflicted shall eat and be satisfied; those who seek Him shall praise the LORD! May your hearts live forever! (Psalm 22:26)

Renowned scholars agree Yeshua was indeed "David's Lamb" of Psalm 22. And David's prophecy proclaims that those who "eat of that Lamb" will be "satisfied" and will "live forever." The reference to the "heart" living forever is a Hebrew expression that signifies *the person* experiencing eternal life.[161]

Besides the following commentary that confirms these truths, see the endnote for two others like it.[162]

MacLaren's Expositions on the Scripture (Psalm 22:26):

> **Jesus Christ laid His hand on this wonderful psalm** of desolation, despair, and deliverance **when on the Cross**...None to whom that voice that rang through the darkness on Calvary [Golgotha] is the voice of the Son of God, can hesitate as to **who it is whose very griefs and sorrows are thus the spiritual food that gives life** to the whole world.[163] (Emphasis added)

Eat My Flesh, Drink My Blood

Now look at what Yeshua Himself says in John 6, beginning with verse 52. Also notice the emphasized similarities between what He declares and what Psalm 22 plainly asserts.

THE LAMB

The Jews then disputed among themselves, saying, **"How can this man give us his flesh to eat?"** So Jesus said to them, "Truly, truly, I say to you, **unless you eat the flesh** of the Son of Man and drink his blood, **you have no life** in you. Whoever feeds on my flesh and drinks my blood has eternal life, and **I will raise him up** on the last day. **For my flesh is true food, and my blood is true drink.** Whoever feeds on my flesh and drinks my blood abides in me, and I in him. As the living Father sent me, and I live because of the Father, so **whoever feeds on me**, he also will live because of me. This is the bread that came down from heaven, not like the bread the fathers ate, and died. Whoever feeds on this bread **will live forever."** (John 6:52–58, emphasis added)

There should be no doubt that Psalm 22:26 is in fact a reference to the Lamb of God, Yeshua, of whom we must "eat" in order to receive the promise of eternal life.

Golgotha Emerges

By now, the next disclosure should come as little surprise. The Golgotha picture of three *tavs* arises from the Hebrew translation of Yeshua's exact words recorded in John 6:56, "Whoever feeds on my flesh and drinks my blood abides in me, and I in him."

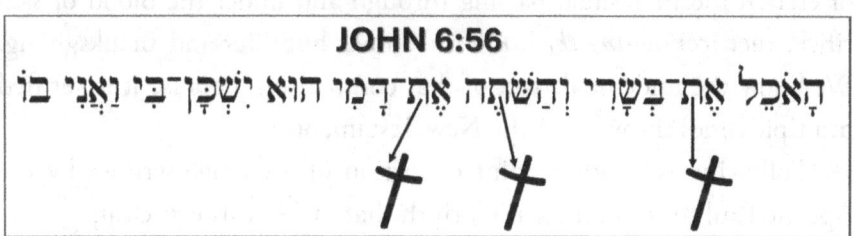

It seems there is simply no escaping the supernatural Golgotha spectacle we keep running into. It's there. *It's there often*—and it's right where we might expect it![164]

Now let's examine the *first* Old Testament instance of "eating a lamb" that states the necessity of that ritual, especially in regard to our "salvation."

46

WHEN I SEE THE BLOOD

Without even knowing it, Abraham's descendants, the Hebrew people, were "painting" the picture of a blood-stained cross every time they did this.

At this point in our journey, we might ask where in the Word of God do we first see a clear connection of "eating of a sacrificial lamb" that's also tied directly to the foreshadowing of Golgotha?

The Passover narrative in Exodus 12 is where we first come upon the stark details involving Yeshua's eventual sacrificial offering on Golgotha. Practically every element of the Passover event was a foreshadowing of Golgotha. It also foretells of the entire *born-again* journey making its way through the wilderness of a fallen world, on the way to the ultimate Promised Land of eternal reward.

The journey began for those who were willing to enter the door of eternal life in Yeshua, passing through and under the blood of sacrifice, then *consuming the lamb* in somber humility and thanksgiving. We know the undeniable fact of that comparison, because it is verified multiple times throughout the New Testament.

Following is a rather pointed portion of a passage written by the Apostle Paul to the church at Corinth that makes this fact clear.

> For I do not want you to be unaware, brothers, that **our fathers were all under the cloud, and all passed through the sea, and all were baptized into Moses in the cloud and in the sea, and all ate the same spiritual food, and all drank the same spiritual drink.**

WHEN I SEE THE BLOOD

> For they drank from the spiritual Rock that followed them, and the Rock was Christ.... Now these things took place as examples for us, that we might not desire evil as they did.... Now these things happened to them as an example, but they were written down for our instruction, on whom the end of the ages has come. (excerpted from 1 Corinthians 10:1–11, emphasis added)

As you've probably already surmised, the image found in the emphasized words of 1 Corinthians 10:1–4 is that of the three *tav* crosses of Golgotha! Remember, these words were first written in Greek, and then, almost two thousand years later, they were translated into Hebrew. Yet when that translation was completed, the three *tav* crosses are somehow there, right where they should be. *Incredible!*

1 CORINTHIANS 10: 1-4

הֶעָנָן וְכֻלָּם עָבְרוּ בְּתוֹךְ הַיָּם וְכֻלָּם נִטְבְּלוּ לְמֹשֶׁה בֶּעָנָן וּבַיָּם וְכֻלָּם אָכְלוּ מַאֲכָל אֶחָד רוּחָנִי

וְכֻלָּם שָׁתוּ מַשְׁקֶה אֶחָד רוּחָנִי כִּי שָׁתוּ מִן־הַצּוּר הָרוּחָנִי הַהֹלֵךְ עִמָּהֶם וְהַצּוּר הַהוּא הַמָּשִׁיחַ

Even Yeshua Himself drives home the fact that He alone is the "spiritual food" of Psalm 22 when He eats the last Passover meal with His disciples. He declared the Passover ritual had *always* been about Him, and it was the foreshadowing of the reason He was going to the cross. He also told the disciples it was around that specific meal that the *groaning of Golgotha* would finally come to a head.

So, then, the obvious path of exploration would be to determine the potential for the hidden icons of Golgotha to appear in the Passover narrative of Exodus 12. If that imagery does indeed exist, that would be something indeed.

GOLGOTHA'S GROANING

The Tenth Day of Nisan

According to Exodus 12, the Passover ordinances begin with choosing the lamb on the tenth day of Nisan. It also declares Nisan as the first month of the Hebrew calendar from that day forward.

The tenth of Nisan would also prophetically correspond to the day Yeshua entered Jerusalem on the back of a donkey to the shouts of "Hallelujah to the Son of David," a distinctly Old Testament Messianic term. On that day, unbeknownst to them, the people were *choosing* their Passover lamb![165]

Now look at the scriptural command for choosing the lamb on the tenth day of the first month, and its corresponding *tav* arrangement.

> Tell all the congregation of Israel **that on the tenth day of this month every man shall take a lamb according to their fathers' houses, a lamb for a household.** (Exodus 12:3, emphasis added)

Note the emphasized words of that verse, then look at the picture they produce. Again, the image of Golgotha is there!

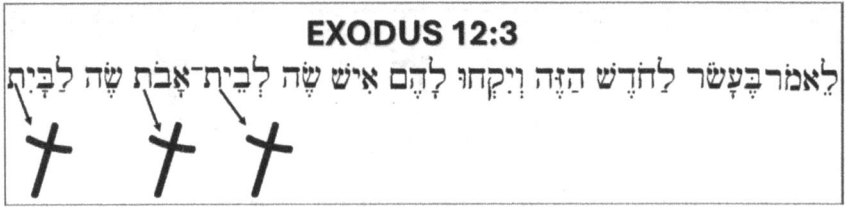

In the New Testament, the event that lights the fuse for choosing Yeshua as the people's collective "lamb" is His riding into Jerusalem on the back of a donkey through the Eastern Gate. This was prophesied by Zechariah four hundred years before it happened. But when it finally unfolded in Yeshua, it took place on the tenth of Nisan.[166]

> Rejoice greatly, O daughter of Zion! **Shout aloud, O daughter of Jerusalem! Behold, your king is coming to you; righteous and having salvation is he, humble and mounted on a donkey, on a colt, the foal of a donkey.** (Zechariah 9:9, emphasis added)

WHEN I SEE THE BLOOD

Take note of the emphasized words of Zechariah 9:9. In that lengthy declaration are found only three *tavs*, presenting yet again the picture of Golgotha—three crosses on a hill. The middle cross is under the *aleph-tav*.

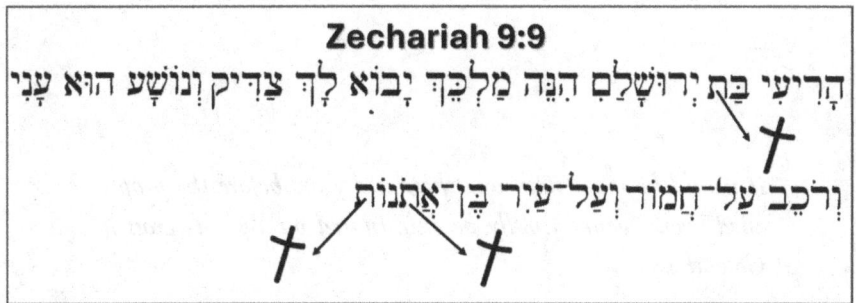

Matthew 21:5 quotes Zechariah 9:9 almost verbatim. And, of course, the same image of Golgotha is implanted there, within the Hebrew rendition of the New Testament.

> Say to the daughter of Zion, 'Behold, your king is coming to you, humble, and mounted on a donkey, on a colt, the foal of a beast of burden.'" (Matthew 21:5)

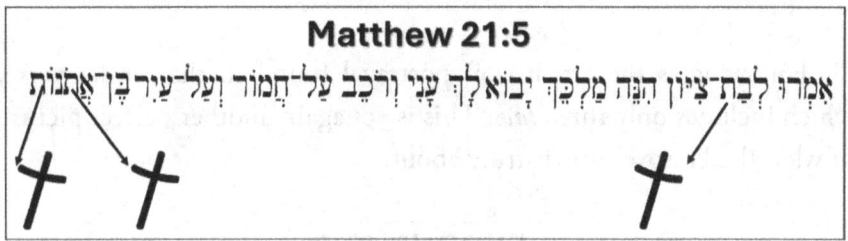

Notice again the frequent occurrence of the middle cross, found in connection with the *aleph-tav*, continues to make its appearance.

In the next chapter we'll look at the treasures waiting for us in the Exodus 12 account of Passover, found in the Hebrew New Testament.

⊰ 47 ⊱

THE LAMB OF SACRIFICE

It would be more than one thousand years before the prophesied event would finally be culminated on Yeshua's cross at Golgotha.

The slaughtering of the lamb was prescribed by the Passover ritual to be done on the fourteenth day of Nissan. This was the *very day* Yeshua was crucified, more than fifteen hundred years after that first Passover event.[167]

> …and you shall keep [the lamb] until the fourteenth day of this month, when the whole assembly of the congregation of Israel shall kill their lambs at twilight. (Exodus 12:6)

Following is the crucifixion portrayal found in that entire verse, which includes only three *tavs*. This is yet again another perfect picture of what the Passover was/is truly about.

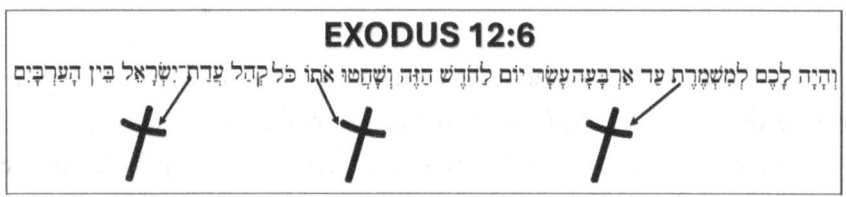

After the lamb had been slaughtered, the people were instructed to put splashes of the sacrificial blood on doorposts and along the top door frame, or the lintel. That configuration of blood ensured that the doorway was symbolically "under the blood-stained cross" of the Lamb, who

THE LAMB OF SACRIFICE

was to fulfill our ultimate salvation. The highlighted words of that verse include three *tavs*.

> **Then they shall take some of the blood and put it on the two doorposts and the lintel** of the houses in which they eat it. (Exodus 12:7, emphasis added)

Following is the imagery created by that instruction:

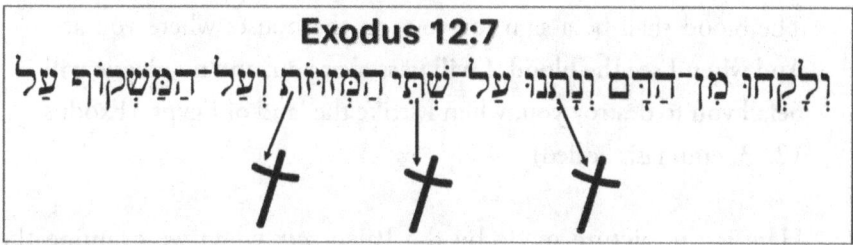

Without even knowing it, Abraham's descendants, the Hebrews, were "painting" the picture of a blood-stained cross every time they applied the blood of the lamb to their doorposts and lentils. It would be more than a thousand years before the prophesied event would finally take place on the middle cross at Golgotha.[168]

[169]

Remember, when Passover was first instituted at the initial Exodus event, the form of execution now known as *crucifixion* had not yet been used. In fact, crucifixion wouldn't have been even in its earliest stages of development for many hundreds of years into the future.[170]

GOLGOTHA'S GROANING

Covenant of Salvation

In Exodus 12:13, God promised His people that when they had faithfully completed everything He had prescribed concerning the sacrifice of the Passover Lamb, He would then *pass over* them and withhold His wrath.

As you might have guessed, that beautiful promise has an astounding reference attached to it—made up of three *tav* crosses.

> The blood shall be a sign for you, on the houses where you are. **And when I see the blood, I will pass over you, and no plague will befall you** to destroy you, when I strike the land of Egypt. (Exodus 12:13, emphasis added)

Here is the picture made by the Paleo *tavs* when we examine the words in bold. The picture of Golgotha is right in the middle of those words. The middle cross is under the *aleph-tav*.

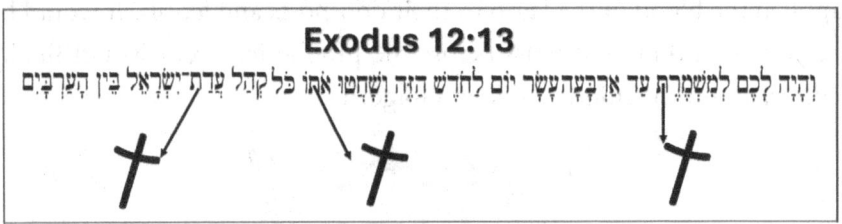

From Beginning to End

In an earlier chapter, I said these Golgotha letter images we've seen in the Old Testament range from Genesis 1:1 to Malachi, the last book of the Old Testament.

Next, I'll show you the truth of that declaration.

… 48 …

THE MESSENGER OF THE COVENANT

They came to test Him, embarrass Him, challenge Him, harass Him, and to try and turn the crowds against Him.

There are only four chapters in the book of Malachi. Yet, that relatively short book is rich with declarations of Messianic expectations.[171]

Most of the last statements of Malachi point directly to the "Coming One" and, subsequently, to Golgotha's blood covenant. They were written almost four hundred years before Yeshua went to the cross of our salvation.

The words we'll explore now are found in Malachi 3:1, in which Yahweh is speaking through the prophet Malachi. He is speaking of Himself as the One whom they are desperately seeking—*the Messiah*, the ultimate *bringer of the final Covenant*. God Himself will be the One who opens the way for salvation!

In that manner of speaking, Yahweh is proclaiming the absolute deity of the Messiah. Of course, we're now blessed to know *exactly* whom this verse is speaking of, and who the Man in the Middle of the Golgotha image actually is.

> "I will send my messenger, who will prepare the way before me. Then suddenly the Lord you are seeking will come to his temple; the messenger of the covenant, whom you desire, will come," says the LORD Almighty. (Malachi 3:1, NIV)

Take a look at a couple of scholarly commentary entries regarding Malachi 3:1.

GOLGOTHA'S GROANING

The Pulpit Commentary:

He is **identified with the Lord**… The **Divinity of Messiah** is thus **unequivocally asserted**. In him are fulfilled all the promises made under the old covenant, and he is called (Hebrews 9:15) "the Mediator of the new covenant." Some render, "and the Messenger."[172] (Emphasis added)

Barnes' Notes on the Bible:

He who speaks, is He who should come, God the Son. For it was before Him Who came and dwelt among us, that the way was to be prepared. He speaks here in **His divine nature**, as the Lord Who should send, and **Who should Himself come in our flesh**. In the Gospel, when **He was come in the flesh**, He speaks not of His own Person but of the Father.[173] (emphasis added)

The divine declaration of Malachi 3:1 appears in the following: "I will send my messenger, who will prepare the way before me. Then suddenly the Lord you are seeking will come to his temple; the messenger of the covenant." In those words, we find the following iconic image of Golgotha.

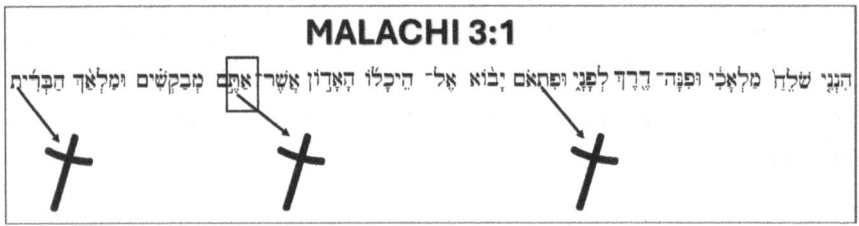

Of course, it is the three cross *tavs*, with the *aleph-tav* representing the One in the middle. This is none other than *Yahweh/Yeshua*.

And don't forget the Paleo-Hebrew *tav* also carries the ideographic meaning of "the covenant," in the shape of a crucifixion cross. Therefore, the *tav* represents the covenant in general, but specifically the "covenant" Yahweh is referring to in Malachi 3:1.

THE MESSENGER OF THE COVENANT

From Genesis 1 to Malachi 3, the persistent biblical icon of Golgotha's groaning is there.[174]

No One Can Stand Against Him

The prophecy of Malachi 3 was fulfilled to the letter when Yeshua appeared in the Temple during the last week of His life. It was there where He taught the attending throngs of people. So, it truly was the Creator Himself standing in Solomon's Colonnade teaching the people, in human flesh, in the person of Yeshua! Most had no idea whose face they were actually beholding.

In the very next verse, Malachi 3:2, we read a prophecy of Yeshua's main mission as He taught the Kingdom truths while in those Temple courts.

> But who can endure the day of his coming, and **who can stand when he appears?** For he is like a refiner's fire and like fullers' soap. (Malachi 3:2, emphasis added)

The New Testament records that every time Yeshua was at the Temple, the Pharisees, Sadducees, Sanhedrin Council, and even the Herodians were there. They came to test Him, embarrass Him, challenge Him, harass Him, and try to turn the crowds against Him. But the opposite happened. Each of those groups was consistently rebuked by the Word that had become flesh, *Yeshua HaMashiach*. They "could not stand" in His presence. He had truly stood before them as "a refiner's fire."

The prophecy of Malachi had been lived out right in front of them! They were challenging God in the Flesh, their Creator from the beginning, and didn't even know it. They didn't have the "eyes to see."[175]

Now let's follow the New Testament trail of Golgotha. We will begin with the last Passover of Yeshua's earthly life and ministry. It is, of course, the one we experienced through the *theater of our minds* in the opening chapters of part one.

49

PASSOVER FULFILLED

Prepare to be stunned by the perfect complexity, human impossibility, and sheer spiritual beauty of the unfolding account of the lead-up to the Golgotha event.

At this point, we might ask whether other Golgotha images are found in the New Testament passages about the Passover. The answer is a resounding "yes." But by now, why would we expect anything different?[176]

Rather than pummeling readers with page after page of the same type of illustrations we've already featured, I will simply quote the passages that apply. At the endnote of each passage, you'll find a link to follow so you can verify the *tav* placements for yourself.

Each of the passages listed (either a single verse or several consecutive verses that complete a thought) contain three *tavs*. Only one passage I've quoted has bold print in it, and those emphasized words are the Hebrew words that contain the three *tavs* within the *Delitzsch Hebrew New Testament* translation. They form the core of the message.

The Murder of Yeshua Set in Stone

> It was now two days before the Passover and the Feast of Unleavened Bread. And the chief priests and the scribes were seeking how to arrest [Yeshua] by stealth and kill him. (Mark 14:1)[177]

Entrance into Jerusalem—Nisan 10

> Say to the daughter of Zion, "Behold, **your king is coming to you,**

PASSOVER FULFILLED

humble, and mounted on a donkey." (Matthew 21:5, emphasis added)[178]

Then one of the twelve, whose name was Judas Iscariot, went to the chief priests and said, "What will you give me if I deliver him over to you?" And they paid him thirty pieces of silver. (Matthew 26:14–15)[179]

The Passover Meal

Now on the first day of Unleavened Bread the disciples came to Jesus, saying, "Where will you have us prepare for you to eat the Passover?" (Matthew 26:17)[180]

Now as they were eating, Jesus took bread, and after blessing it broke it and gave it to the disciples, and said, "Take, eat; this is my body." (Matthew 26:26)[181]

And he took a cup, and when he had given thanks he gave it to them, saying, "Drink of it, all of you." (Matthew 26:27)[182]

Peter said to him, "Even if I must die with you, I will not deny you!" And all the disciples said the same. (Matthew 26:35)[183]

And Jesus said to [Peter], "Truly, I tell you, this very night, before the rooster crows twice, you will deny me three times." (Mark 14:30)[184]

As soon as Judas took the bread, Satan entered into him. So Jesus told him, "What you are about to do, do quickly." (John 13:27, NIV)[185]

As soon as Judas had taken the bread, he went out. And it was night. (John 13:30, NIV)[186]

GOLGOTHA'S GROANING

For I tell you that this Scripture must be fulfilled in me: "And he was numbered with the transgressors." For what is written about me has its fulfillment. (Luke 22:37)[187]

The Garden of Gethsemane

When Jesus had spoken these words, he went out with his disciples across the brook Kidron, where there was a garden, which he and his disciples entered. (John 18:1)[188]

Now Judas His betrayer also knew the place, because Jesus had often met there with His disciples. (John 18:2, MSB)[189]

Then Jesus, knowing all that would happen to him, came forward and said to them, "Whom do you seek?" (John 18:4)[190]

And taking with him Peter and the two sons of Zebedee, he began to be sorrowful and troubled. (Matthew 26:37)[191]

"Father, if you are willing, remove this cup from me. Nevertheless, not my will, but yours, be done." (Luke 22:42)[192]

Then Jesus returned to the disciples and found them sleeping. "Were you not able to keep watch with Me for one hour?" He asked Peter. (Matthew 26:40, BSB)[193]

And immediately, while he was still speaking, Judas came, one of the twelve, and with him a crowd with swords and clubs, from the chief priests and the scribes and the elders. (Mark 14:43)[194]

But one of those who stood by drew his sword and struck the servant of the high priest and cut off his ear. (Mark 14:47)[195]

As important as each of those preceding passages is, remember the earth-shattering consequences of Yeshua's prayer uttered in Gethsemane, after He and His disciples had eaten the Passover meal. If He had not said these words, there would have been no offer of salvation for humanity: "Father, if you are willing, take this cup from me; yet not my will, but yours be done" (Luke 22:42, NIV).

The three *tav* crosses are also found in those words. They depict Golgotha's hill, with the *aleph-tav* in the middle, representing none other than the Lamb slain before the foundation of the world.

Once again, in the very words Yeshua spoke, we discover a Golgotha image that points all the way back to Genesis 1:1!

Next, we'll move to the arrest and trial of Yeshua, and then to the actual Golgotha event. We'll continue by examining several pertinent Gospel passages about the resurrection of Yeshua.

What is this we're seeing—over, and over, and over again?

≡ 50 ≡

GOLGOTHA'S GROANING

This persistently nagging question must once again be highlighted.

As we dive into the day of Golgotha's sacrifice, we'll examine the New Testament passages to determine if they, too, feature the Golgotha imagery in their Hebrew translation.

Following are the passages with only three *tavs*. In each of these examples, try to visualize the Golgotha image as you read…*because it is there*!

The Arrest and Trial

> Now the chief priests and the whole council were seeking testimony against Jesus to put him to death, but they found none, For many bore false witness against him, but their testimony did not agree. (Mark 14:55–56)[196]

> Then those who had seized Jesus led him to Caiaphas the high priest, where the scribes and the elders had gathered. (Matthew 26:57)[197]

> And the high priest stood up and said, "Have you no answer to make? What is it that these men testify against you?" But Jesus remained silent. And the high priest said to him, "I adjure you by the living God, tell us if you are the Christ, the Son of God." (Matthew 26:62–63)[198]

GOLGOTHA'S GROANING

And Peter remembered the saying of Jesus, "Before the rooster crows, you will deny me three times." And he went out and wept bitterly. (Matthew 26:75)[199]

When morning came, all the chief priests and the elders of the people took counsel against Jesus to put him to death. And they bound him and led him away and delivered him over to Pilate the governor. (Matthew 27:1–2)[200]

The Day of Golgotha—Nisan 14

Now Jesus stood before the governor, and the governor asked him, "Are you the King of the Jews?" Jesus said, "You have said so." (Matthew 27:11)[201]

Now at the feast the governor was accustomed to release for the crowd any one prisoner whom they wanted. And they had then a notorious prisoner called Barabbas. (Matthew 27:15–16)[202]

And some began to spit on him and to cover his face and to strike him, saying to him, "Prophesy!" And the guards received him with blows. (Mark 14:65)[203]

Then the soldiers of the governor took Jesus into the governor's headquarters, and they gathered the whole battalion before him. (Matthew 27:27)[204]

Then Pilate took Jesus and flogged him. And the soldiers twisted together a crown of thorns and put it on his head and arrayed him in a purple robe. They came up to him, saying, "Hail, King of the Jews!" and struck him with their hands. (John 19:1–3)[205]

GOLGOTHA'S GROANING

The Crucifixion

And when they came to the place that is called The Skull, there they crucified him, and the criminals, one on his right and one on his left. (Luke 23:33)[206]

And over his head they put the charge against him, which read, "This is Jesus, the King of the Jews." (Matthew 27:37)[207]

So also the chief priests, with the scribes and elders, mocked him, saying, "He saved others; he cannot save himself. He is the King of Israel; let him come down now from the cross, and we will believe in him. He trusts in God; let God deliver him now, if he desires him. For he said, 'I am the Son of God.'" (Matthew 27:41–43)[208]

When Jesus saw his mother and the disciple whom he loved standing nearby, he said to his mother, "Woman, behold, your son!" (John 19:26)[209]

Now from the sixth hour there was darkness over all the land until the ninth hour. (Matthew 27:45)[210]

And behold, the curtain of the temple was torn in two, from top to bottom. And the earth shook, and the rocks were split. (Matthew 27:51)[211]

For these things took place that the Scripture might be fulfilled: "Not one of his bones will be broken." (John 19:36) [212]

Now in the place where he was crucified there was a garden, and in the garden a new tomb in which no one had yet been laid. So because of the Jewish day of Preparation, since the tomb was close at hand, they laid Jesus there. (John 19:41–42) [213]

GOLGOTHA'S GROANING

The Resurrection

> Now when he rose early on the first day of the week, he appeared first to Mary Magdalene, from whom he had cast out seven demons. (Mark 16:9)[214]

> She went and told those who had been with him, as they mourned and wept. But when they heard that he was alive and had been seen by her, they would not believe it. (Mark 16:10–11)[215]

> After these things he appeared in another form to two of them, as they were walking into the country (Mark 16:12)[216]

> And stooping to look in, [Peter] saw the linen cloths lying there, but he did not go in. (John 20:5)[217]

> The cloth that had been around Jesus' head was rolled up, lying separate from the linen cloths. (John 20:7, BSB)[218]

> …but these are written so that you may believe that Jesus is the Christ, the Son of God, and that by believing you may have life in his name. (John 20:31)[219]

Believe it or not there are still more to see!

≡ 51 ≡

THE HIGH PRIEST OF OLD

He shall make atonement for the priests and for all the people of the assembly. (Leviticus 16:33)

I've spent more than four decades preaching the contextually connected Word of God. In so doing, I've taught numerous times on the high priest of Leviticus 16 and his role in the Yom Kippur (Day of Atonement) rituals as prescribed by Yahweh at Mt. Sinai.

The interconnectivity of that ancient Levitical chapter to the Golgotha event illustrates yet another *biblical type* of Yeshua. In Leviticus 16, not only is Yeshua the Yom Kippur sacrificial Lamb of God, as well as the *scapegoat* that bears our sin; He is also our Great High Priest who reigns forever.

Of course, all the elements of the ceremonial *rehearsal*[220] of the Yom Kippur observation were eventually fulfilled through Yeshua at Golgotha's cross—the focus of our entire exploration.

It was at Golgotha where humanity witnessed the melding together of the *Lamb of God*, the *scapegoat* of our sin, and the officiating *High Priest* of all eternity as "the man in the middle," the central figure among the three crosses of Golgotha.

You can read a couple of short but powerful summaries of that linkage within the highly acclaimed classical biblical scholarship of *Matthew Henry's Commentary on the Bible* and the *Keil and Delitzsch Biblical Commentary on the Old Testament*. Simply go to the endnote link at the close of this paragraph, where their commentary on the topic has been provided.[221]

THE HIGH PRIEST OF OLD

The Golgotha Pictures of Leviticus 16

In the meantime, let's have a look at the supernatural linkages between Leviticus 16 and the New Testament Golgotha fulfillment, as it is represented in the Hebrew translation.

I will provide Scripture passages directly from Leviticus 16. Taken as whole, these will give an overview of Yom Kippur. They will each contain only three *tavs*.

> And he shall take from the congregation of the people of Israel two male goats for a sin offering, and one ram for a burnt offering. (Leviticus 16:5)[222]

> Aaron shall offer the bull as a sin offering for himself and shall make atonement for himself and for his house. (Leviticus 16:6)[223]

> Then he shall take the two goats and set them before the LORD at the entrance of the tent of meeting. (Leviticus 16:7)[224]

> Aaron shall bring the goat whose lot falls to the LORD and sacrifice it for a sin offering, But the goat chosen by lot as the scapegoat shall be presented alive before the LORD to be used for making atonement by sending it into the wilderness as a scapegoat. (Leviticus 16:9–10, NIV)[225]

> The goat shall bear all their iniquities on itself to a remote area, and he shall let the goat go free in the wilderness. (Leviticus 16:22)[226]

> For on this day shall atonement be made for you to cleanse you. You shall be clean before the LORD from all your sins. (Leviticus 16:30)[227]

> He shall make atonement for the holy sanctuary, and he shall make atonement for the tent of meeting and for the altar, and he shall make atonement for the priests and for all the people of the assembly. (Leviticus 16:33)[228]

GOLGOTHA'S GROANING

You can see how the Old Testament dialect of Leviticus 16 speaks of the ultimate fulfillment of the high priesthood in *Yeshuah HaMashiach Adonai*. And throughout that language is the *image of all images*...the *tavs* of Golgotha. Everything the high priest of Israel did pointed toward Golgotha and Yeshua's sacrificial offering of Himself.

But does the New Testament have anything to say about Leviticus 16 and the high priest? Actually, it reveals quite a bit about that holy ritual.

In fact, an entire book in the New Testament is largely dedicated to that topic, as well as provides a direct connection to John 13 and the Passover evening before Golgotha.

≡ 52 ≡

OUR GREAT HIGH PRIEST

For it was indeed fitting that we should have such a high priest, holy, innocent, unstained, separated from sinners, and exalted above the heavens. (Hebrews 7:26)

Nine of the thirteen chapters of the book of Hebrews point all the way back to Leviticus 16 and the role of the high priest. Following are ten entries from Hebrews illustrating this fact. Each possesses the same iconic display of the three *tavs*. All contain only three *tavs* each.

Hebrews and the High Priest

For we do not have a high priest who is unable to sympathize with our weaknesses, but one who in every respect has been tempted as we are, yet without sin. Let us then with confidence draw near to the throne of grace, that we may receive mercy and find grace to help in time of need. (Hebrews 4:15–16)[229]

We have this as a sure and steadfast anchor of the soul, a hope that enters into the inner place behind the curtain, where Jesus has gone as a forerunner on our behalf, having become a high priest forever after the order of Melchizedek. (Hebrews 6:19–20)[230]

Consequently, he is able to save to the uttermost those who draw near to God through him, since he always lives to make intercession for them. For it was indeed fitting that we should have such a high priest, holy, innocent, unstained, separated from sinners, and exalted above the heavens. (Hebrews 7:25–26) [231]

For the law appoints men in their weakness as high priests, but the word of the oath, which came later than the law, appoints a Son who has been made perfect forever. (Hebrews 7:28) [232]

These preparations having thus been made, the priests go regularly into the first section, performing their ritual duties. (Hebrews 9:6) [233]

But into the second only the high priest goes, and he but once a year, and not without taking blood, which he offers for himself and for the unintentional sins of the people. By this the Holy Spirit indicates that the way into the holy places is not yet opened as long as the first section is still standing. (Hebrews 9:7–8) [234]

How much more will the blood of Christ, who through the eternal Spirit offered himself without blemish to God, purify our conscience from dead works to serve the living God. (Hebrews 9:14) [235]

So Christ, having been offered once to bear the sins of many, will appear a second time, not to deal with sin but to save those who are eagerly waiting for him. (Hebrews 9:28) [236]

But in these sacrifices there is a reminder of sins every year. For it is impossible for the blood of bulls and goats to take away sins. Consequently, when Christ came into the world, he said, "Sacrifices and offerings you have not desired, but a body have you prepared for me." (Hebrews 10:3–5)[237]

…and to Jesus, the mediator of a new covenant, and to the sprinkled blood that speaks a better word than the blood of Abel. (Hebrews 12:24) [238]

Hidden for ages, each of these passages also reveals the image of Golgotha within the ancient Hebrew letter shapes.

OUR GREAT HIGH PRIEST

High Priest Connection to Passover

Now let's back up and briefly revisit that last Passover meal. In those passages of John 13, we find Yeshua revealing Himself in one of the most direct manners recorded in Scripture, as the fulfillment of the *Great High Priest*. As we observed in the opening narrative chapters of part one, this revelation takes place when Yeshua is preparing His disciples for their future priestly responsibilities through a foot-washing ceremony. This also happens in conjunction with the soon-coming betrayal through Judas. Both of these elements also point directly to Golgotha.

The following verses have the three-*tav* image of Golgotha within them:

> Now before the Feast of the Passover, when Jesus knew that His hour had come to depart out of this world to the Father, having loved His own who were in the world, He loved them to the end. (John 13:1)[239]

> Then He poured water into a basin and began to wash the disciples' feet and to wipe them with the towel that was wrapped around Him. (John 13:5)[240]

> He came to Simon Peter, who said to him, "Lord, do you wash my feet?" (John 13:6)[241]

> Simon Peter said to him, "Lord, not my feet only but also my hands and my head!" (John 13:9)[242]

> Jesus said to him, "The one who has bathed does not need to wash, except for his feet, but is completely clean. And you are clean, but not every one of you." (John 13:10)[243]

> After saying these things, Jesus was troubled in his spirit, and testified, "Truly, truly, I say to you, one of you will betray me." (John 13:21)[244]

GOLGOTHA'S GROANING

As soon as Judas took the bread, Satan entered into him. So Jesus told him, "What you are about to do, do quickly." (John 13:27, NIV)[245]

The final gears of Golgotha's groaning were set in motion by Judas' betrayal. And Yeshua Himself announced that betrayal during the priestly footwashing ceremony at their last Passover meal. Thus, we also find the three-*tav* imagery in those verses.

The holiness of what we are seeing is absolutely unearthly.

OUR GREAT HIGH PRIEST

High Priest Connection to Passover

Now let's back up and briefly revisit that last Passover meal. In those passages of John 13, we find Yeshua revealing Himself in one of the most direct manners recorded in Scripture, as the fulfillment of the *Great High Priest*. As we observed in the opening narrative chapters of part one, this revelation takes place when Yeshua is preparing His disciples for their future priestly responsibilities through a foot-washing ceremony. This also happens in conjunction with the soon-coming betrayal through Judas. Both of these elements also point directly to Golgotha.

The following verses have the three-*tav* image of Golgotha within them:

> Now before the Feast of the Passover, when Jesus knew that His hour had come to depart out of this world to the Father, having loved His own who were in the world, He loved them to the end. (John 13:1)[239]

> Then He poured water into a basin and began to wash the disciples' feet and to wipe them with the towel that was wrapped around Him. (John 13:5)[240]

> He came to Simon Peter, who said to him, "Lord, do you wash my feet?" (John 13:6)[241]

> Simon Peter said to him, "Lord, not my feet only but also my hands and my head!" (John 13:9)[242]

> Jesus said to him, "The one who has bathed does not need to wash, except for his feet, but is completely clean. And you are clean, but not every one of you." (John 13:10)[243]

> After saying these things, Jesus was troubled in his spirit, and testified, "Truly, truly, I say to you, one of you will betray me." (John 13:21)[244]

GOLGOTHA'S GROANING

As soon as Judas took the bread, Satan entered into him. So Jesus told him, "What you are about to do, do quickly." (John 13:27, NIV)[245]

The final gears of Golgotha's groaning were set in motion by Judas' betrayal. And Yeshua Himself announced that betrayal during the priestly footwashing ceremony at their last Passover meal. Thus, we also find the three-*tav* imagery in those verses.

The holiness of what we are seeing is absolutely unearthly.

Part Seven

FROM FIRST TO LAST

So then, men ought to regard us as servants of Christ and as those entrusted with the secret things of God. Now it is required that those who have been given a trust must prove faithful. (1 Corinthians 4:1–2, GOOD NEWS UK)

≡ 53 ≡

SHOW US THE FATHER

Yeshua's answer is still pointing to Golgotha's cross, a horror just hours away.

On the eve of the final Passover celebration, Yeshua solemnly assured His disciples everything He was doing had an eternal purpose. And it was there, in the upper room in downtown Jerusalem, where He most directly revealed the genuine nature of His divinity.

On that night, Yeshua comforted His disciples, telling them, "And if I go and prepare a place for you, I will come again and will take you to myself, that where I am you may be also" (John 14:3).

Yeshua assured them of these truths because He would soon be on Golgotha's cross—opening the "door" for them to come into His Father's House (the covenant house of *bereshith*). *That's* where he was "going."

The following is what we find in those precise words of John 14:3 as translated into Hebrew. In that verse, we again find the *tav* picture of Golgotha…with the *aleph-tav* in the middle of the three crosses.

JOHN 14:3

וְאַחֲרֵי אֲשֶׁר אֵלֵךְ וְאָכִין מָקוֹם לָכֶם שׁוּב אָשׁוּב וְלָקַחְתִּי אֶתְכֶם אֵלַי לְמַעַן תִּהְיוּ עִמִּי שָׁם בַּאֲשֶׁר אֶהְיֶה

† † †

GOLGOTHA'S GROANING

Thomas

It was immediately after Yeshua had made that promise when Thomas whimpered out the following words: "Lord, we do not know where you are going. How can we know the way?" (John 14:5).

Within the Hebrew translation of Thomas' words, there's the same image yet again, right where it might be expected, with the *aleph-tav* in the middle.

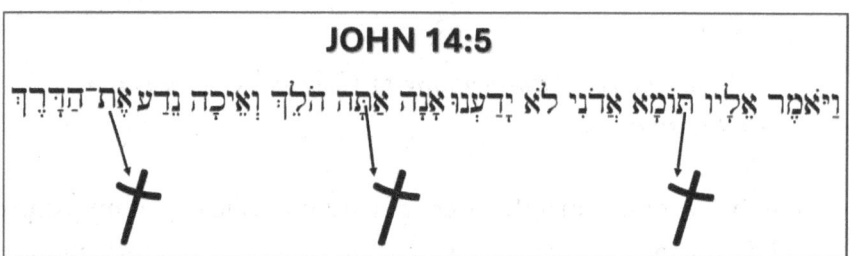

Philip

Next, Philip piped up with yet another objection to what Yeshua was trying to tell them. Philip framed it as a request, but it was one that shouldn't have been presented. But Philip asked it anyway, claiming to speak for the rest of the disciples as well: "Lord, show us the Father, and it is enough for us" (John 14:8).

Yeshua answered the request with a two-part response found within one verse. In each part of Yeshua's reply to Philip, we again find the three *tav* crosses. Yeshua's answer still pointed to Golgotha's cross, a horror that was then only hours away.

The first part of Yeshua's answer to Philip was, "Have I been with you so long, and you still do not know me, Philip?" In those words, here's the embedded code-speak:

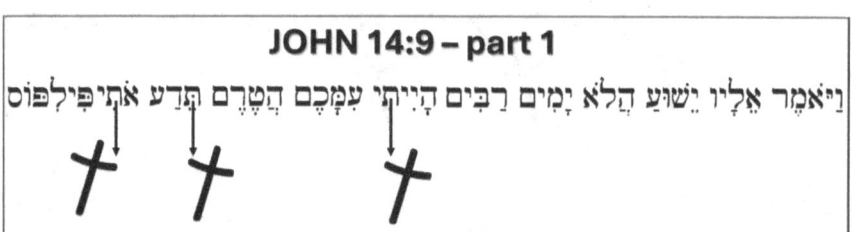

SHOW US THE FATHER

The second part of Yeshua's reply was, "Whoever has seen me has seen the Father." This is one of the most direct identifications of His Divinity.[246]

Following is the *tav* display found in those words. As you might guess, the arrangement of that display is absolutely what we anticipate—right down to the *aleph-tav* representing the middle cross.

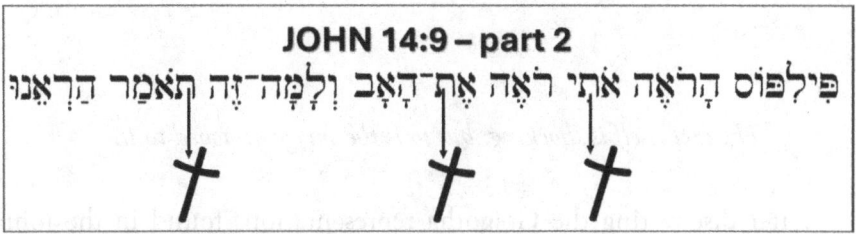

The Continuing Conversation

The discussion on that night includes two more links to Golgotha. Each has three *tavs/crosses* within the exact Hebrew-translated words:

> Believe me that I am in the Father and the Father is in me, or else believe on account of the works themselves. "Truly, truly, I say to you, whoever believes in me will also do the works that I do; and greater works than these will he do, because I am going to the Father. (John 14:11–12)[247]

> And now I have told you before it takes place, so that when it does take place you may believe. (John 14:29)[248]

These are astounding depictions of Golgotha's ultimate purpose. In this way, these pictures, like the others you have seen, are interconnected to one major theme: Golgotha's groaning, through Yeshua's sacrificial death, accomplished all of this for us!

≡ 54 ≡

THE WORD BECAME FLESH

The text itself is shocking, but so is the image attached to it.

After discovering the Golgotha representations found in the John 14 narrative, I immediately thought of the very first chapter of John. Not only is that chapter rich with the exaltation of Yeshua and His ultimate mission on earth, but it also begins with the word *bereshith*—as in Genesis 1:1.

As we discovered, the word *bereshith* has a lengthy embedded message, formed through the twelve Hebrew words found there. Also, the first word of the Scripture connects directly to the seven words in Genesis 1:1. Because of these facts, examining John 1 seemed another obvious place to search for the three *tavs* of Golgotha's groaning. Following is what I uncovered.

Just as *bereshith* possesses a code all of its own in the twelve embedded words, the code is also in John 1! You'll remember that a large part of the *bereshith* coded message spoke of Almighty God and Yeshua as being One from the beginning.[249]

John 1:1–2 presents the same complete thought, with which he opens his beloved Gospel. His opening salvo is expressed in the following words:

In the beginning was the Word, and the Word was with God, and the Word was God. He was in the beginning with God. (John 1:1–2)

When that statement of the Deity of *Yeshua HaMashiach* is translated to Hebrew, here is the coded display that is revealed:

THE WORD BECAME FLESH

As you can see, those opening words of John's Gospel are eerily similar to what we find in Genesis 1:1. Other than the number of words being different, the imagery is precisely the same...with Yeshua on the middle cross of the *aleph-tav* and the opening word being *bereshith*, the Hebrew word that forever contains a twelve-word, hidden message.

But there are still other instances. For example, in John 1:10–12, we again find the supernaturally implanted three *tavs* of Golgotha. You can see them by following the link in the endnote below.

> He was in the world, and though the world was made through Him, the world did not recognize Him. He came to his own, and his own people did not receive him. But to all who did receive him, who believed in his name, he gave the right to become children of God. (John 1:10–12, NIV)[250]

The next example is my favorite from the first chapter of John. It clearly defines Yeshua HaMashiach as God, the Word, manifest in the flesh.

The supernatural *Golgotha imprint* is found in John 1:14. There are exactly three crosses in that verse, and the *aleph-tav* is in the middle. The surface text itself reveals shocking information, but so does the attached iconic Golgotha image.

> And the Word became flesh and dwelt among us, and we have seen his glory, glory as of the only Son from the Father, full of grace and truth. (John 1:14)

JOHN 1:14

וְהַדָּבָר לָבַשׁ בָּשָׂר וַיִּשְׁכֹּן בְּתוֹכֵנוּ וְאֶת־כְּבוֹדוֹ רָאִינוּ כִּכְבוֹד בֵּן יָחִיד לְאָבִיו מָלֵא חֶסֶד וֶאֱמֶת

John 1 contains even a couple more hidden Golgotha messages, found in verses 17 and 18. Each verse features three *tav* crosses, respectively.

> For the law was given through Moses; grace and truth came through Jesus Christ. (John 1:17)[251]

> No one has ever seen God, but the one and only Son, **who is Himself God** and is at the Father's side, has made Him known. (John 1:18, BSB; emphasis added)[252]

So how are John 1:17 and 18 connected to Golgotha's cross? Have a look at the biblical answers. The first passage below addresses John 1:17, concerning the Law and Moses. The second one speaks to John 1:18, concerning the deity of Yeshua HaMashiach.

> And you, who were dead in your trespasses and the uncircumcision of your flesh, God made alive together with him, having forgiven us all our trespasses, **by canceling the record of debt** [the law[253]] that stood against us with its legal demands. This he set aside, **nailing it to the cross**. He disarmed the rulers and authorities and put them to open shame, by triumphing over them in him. (Colossians 2:13–15, emphasis added)

> And I [the LORD God Almighty] will pour out on the house of David and the inhabitants of Jerusalem a spirit of grace and pleas for mercy, so that, **when they look on me, on him whom they have pierced,** they shall mourn for him, as one mourns for an only child, and weep bitterly over him, as one weeps over a firstborn. (Zechariah 12:10, emphasis added)[254]

Incredible! And again…utterly holy.

55

GOD SO LOVED THE WORLD

This verse is directly tied to Golgotha's sacrifice.

The theme of John's first two chapters bursts right into the third, where we find some of the most recognizable words of the New Testament: John 3:16—specifically, the words that wrap up the promise of Golgotha: "For God so loved the world that He gave His only begotten Son."

Of course, we know God "gave" His Only Son on Golgotha's hill—on the cross of groaning agony. So then, how could there *not* be a picture of Golgotha in this verse? No need to worry, because it's there!

To repeat myself yet again…*these images are not there by coincidence*! They simply can't be.

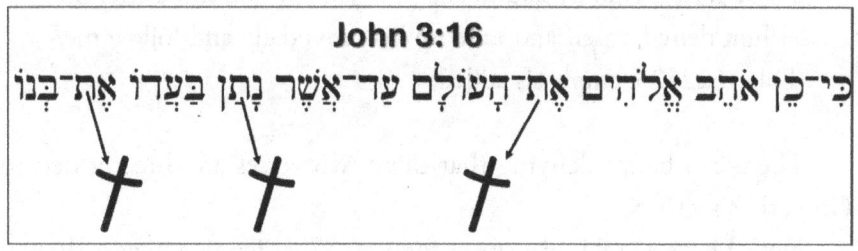

However, John's third chapter contains two more distinctive Golgotha *tav* displays. Each passage communicates a singular truth, and each contains only three *tav* crosses. Within the surface text, both tie directly to Golgotha's sacrifice.

For God did not send his Son into the world to condemn the world, but in order that the world might be saved through him. Whoever

GOLGOTHA'S GROANING

believes in him is not condemned, but whoever does not believe is condemned already, because he has not believed in the name of the only Son of God. And this is the judgment: the light has come into the world, and people loved the darkness rather than the light because their works were evil. (John 3:17–19)[255]

The Father loves the Son and has given all things into his hand. (John 3:35)[256]

It's unimaginable that the disciples missed so much in their understanding of exactly what Yeshua had come to do, especially on that Passover night in the upper room. Yet, the entire unfolding saga of Golgotha's cross and the resurrection was still beyond their wildest thoughts. At the time, not one of them understood it completely.

All of this was despite the fact that Yeshua had point-blank told them the truth many times throughout their ministry with Him. Luke's Gospel gives us a peek into one such conversation.

The **Son of Man must suffer** many things and **be rejected** by the elders and chief priests and scribes, **and be killed**, and on the third day **be raised**. And he said to all, "If anyone would come after me, let him deny himself and **take up his cross** daily and follow me." (Luke 9:22–23, emphasis added)

There can be no denying that these two verses are directly tied to Golgotha's sacrifice.

Now, I have a real brain-teaser for you: What iconic imagery do you think might be found within all the words of those verses?

Of course! The Golgotha icon is there again—exactly where we might expect to find it.[257]

≡ 56 ≡

THE ALPHA AND OMEGA

> *Worthy is the Lamb who was slain, to receive power and wealth and wisdom and might and honor and glory and blessing!* (Revelation 5:12)

In the opening chapters of this book, I assured you that the supernatural marvel of the Golgotha imagery could be found from the very first words of Genesis 1:1 all the way to some of the last words of Revelation. Now we'll look at those Golgotha-linked passages in Revelation.

Revelation includes almost two dozen passages related to Golgotha that have only three embedded *tavs*. As I've done in previous chapters, I'm listing the passages, with each including an endnote directing you to the *Delitzsch Hebrew New Testament* translation where you can see the *tav* placements for yourself.

I encourage you to read these passages in a meditative manner. I'm certain you'll feel their majesty, especially now that you know you're also seeing within your mind's eye the indisputable symbol of Golgotha in each passage.

> Behold, he is coming with the clouds, and every eye will see him, even those who pierced him, and all tribes of the earth will wail on account of him. Even so. Amen. (Revelation 1:7; this passage ties to Zechariah 12:10)[258]

> And in the midst of the lampstands one like a son of man, clothed with a long robe and with a golden sash around his chest. (Revelation 1:13)[259]

GOLGOTHA'S GROANING

Worthy are you, our Lord and God, to receive glory and honor and power, for you created all things, and by your will they existed and were created. (Revelation 4:11)[260]

And between the throne and the four living creatures and among the elders I saw a Lamb standing, as though it had been slain, with seven horns and with seven eyes, which are the seven spirits of God sent out into all the earth. And he went and took the scroll from the right hand of him who was seated on the throne. (Revelation 5:6–7)[261]

Then I looked, and I heard around the throne and the living creatures and the elders the voice of many angels, numbering myriads of myriads and thousands of thousands, saying with a loud voice, "Worthy is the Lamb who was slain, to receive power and wealth and wisdom and might and honor and glory and blessing!" (Revelation 5:11–12)[262]

And the four living creatures said, "Amen!" and the elders fell down and worshiped. (Revelation 5:14)[263]

Then the kings of the earth and the great ones and the generals and the rich and the powerful, and everyone, slave and free, hid themselves in the caves and among the rocks of the mountains. (Revelation 6:15)[264]

And they have conquered [Satan] by the blood of the Lamb and by the word of their testimony, for they loved not their lives even unto death. (Revelation 12:11)[265]

Therefore, rejoice, O heavens and you who dwell in them! But woe to you, O earth and sea, for the devil has come down to you in great wrath, because he knows that his time is short! (Revelation 12:12)[266]

And another angel came out from the altar, the angel who has authority over the fire, and he called with a loud voice to the one

THE ALPHA AND OMEGA

who had the sharp sickle, "Put in your sickle and gather the clusters from the vine of the earth, for its grapes are ripe." (Revelation 14:18)[267]

Who will not fear, O Lord, and glorify your name? For you alone are holy. All nations will come and worship you, for your righteous acts have been revealed. (Revelation 15:4) [268]

Then I saw heaven opened, and behold, a white horse! The one sitting on it is called Faithful and True, and in righteousness he judges and makes war. (Revelation 19:11)[269]

His eyes are like a flame of fire, and on his head are many diadems, and he has a name written that no one knows but himself. He is clothed in a robe dipped in blood, and the name by which he is called is The Word of God. (Revelation 19:12–13)[270]

Blessed and holy is the one who shares in the first resurrection! Over such the second death has no power, but they will be priests of God and of Christ, and they will reign with him for a thousand years. (Revelation 20:6)[271]

And he said to me, "It is done! I am the Alpha and the Omega, the beginning and the end. To the thirsty I will give from the spring of the water of life without payment. The one who conquers will have this heritage, and I will be his God and he will be my son." (Revelation 21:6–7)[272]

No longer will there be anything accursed, but the throne of God and of the Lamb will be in it, and his servants will worship him. They will see his face, and his name will be on their foreheads. (Revelation 22:3–4)[273]

"I am the Alpha and the Omega, the first and the last, the beginning and the end." Blessed are those who wash their robes, so that

GOLGOTHA'S GROANING

they may have the right to the tree of life and that they may enter the city by the gates. (Revelation 22:13–14)[274]

And if anyone takes away from the words of the book of this prophecy, God will take away his share in the tree of life and in the holy city, which are described in this book. (Revelation 22:19)[275]

That collection of Revelation's Golgotha imagery is quite overwhelming, isn't it?

Next, we'll have a look at where the Bible actually answers the question: *Where exactly did the Golgotha sacrifice take place?*

It's probably not where you might be thinking.

Part Eight

WHERE, OH WHERE?

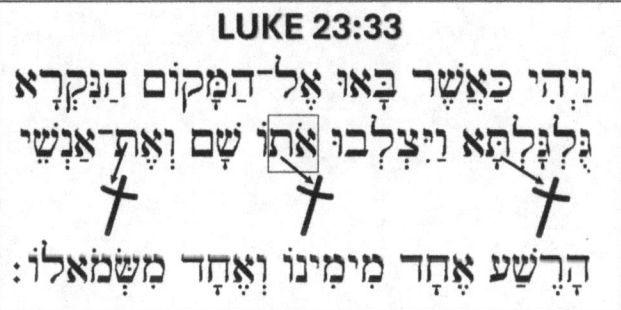

And when they came to the place that is called The Skull, there they crucified him, and the criminals, one on his right and one on his left. (Luke 23:33)

≡ 57 ≡

THE CAVERNOUS MYSTERY

The Scriptures actually reveal the very close proximity of where Yeshua's crucifixion occurred. Think of this: If the theme of Golgotha is so pervasive in the Scriptures, to the extent that its image has been supernaturally encoded in them, then why doesn't the Bible tell us *where* Golgotha was located? Why would that detail be left out of the Scriptures? Thus, the mystery. Considering all we've uncovered so far, it would be unthinkable not to settle this matter.

At first glance, it appears that the Scripture only tells us Yeshua was taken to "Golgotha, the place of the skull." However, these words only reveal what the name of the location *means, not where* it was situated.

Or so it would seem.

The truth is, the Bible does disclose much more than the meaning of the word "Golgotha." In fact, it reveals the close proximity of where Yeshua's crucifixion occurred. And, most likely, that location isn't where you've been led to understand—especially if you've believed the setting as often portrayed by most traditional and rather modern teachings.

However, the biblical answer does in fact highlight why the location of Golgotha is spiritually significant.

Before we begin to unpack this part of the Golgotha mystery, I urge you to read Messianic Rabbi Zev Porat's important work titled *Unmasking the Chaldean Spirit*. In that book, Rabbi Porat addresses in great detail the matter we're about to survey. Several weighty portions of the following material find their footings in Zev's extensive research.[276]

GOLGOTHA'S GROANING

Location, Location, Location

The foundational reason for the spotlight on Golgotha is the fact that the crucifixion of Yeshua HaMashiach, arguably the most earth-shaking occurrence in history, also has *everything* to do with a certain piece of prime real estate.

The property in question is what I call the "biblical ground zero."[277] Once we understand the truths we are about to unfold, everything we've explored thus far begins exploding to an even deeper level of insight.

When the Word of God is linked together in its proper context, it actually *does* solve the mystery of Golgotha's location. The answers have always been right there in the surface text—in the heart of God's Word—hidden in plain sight.

Sound familiar?

≡ 58 ≡

GOLGOTHA'S TRAIL

These factors alone very well could have been responsible for designating the Mount of Olives to be "the Place of the Skull."

Four New Testament references state that Yeshua was taken to a place called Golgotha (Matthew 27:33, Mark 15:22, Luke 23:33, John 19:17).[278] The most common understanding is that "Golgotha," in Greek, means the "place of *the/a* skull," which also most likely indicates the locale had to have been a well-known spot to the people of first-century Judea.[279]

Does the Bible give us any explicit information about the location of an area of land in or around Jerusalem that would have been widely known as "the place of *the skull*?"

Furthermore, does the Word of God tell us *whose skull* was so recognizable that a patch of land would signify its importance, even many years before Yeshua's crucifixion?

Both the Old and New Testaments give us pointers for uncovering the answers to those questions. Furthermore, the clues are the *only ones* in the entire Word of God that just happen to apply to the exact context of the questions at hand.

The Famous Skull

One of the first pieces of biblical evidence we'll examine is the account of young David's victory over the Philistine giant, Goliath:

> **So David prevailed** over the Philistine [Goliath] with a sling and with a stone, and struck the Philistine and killed him.... **Then David**

ran and stood over the Philistine and **took his sword** and drew it out of its sheath...and **cut off his head** with it.... And **David took the head** of the Philistine and **brought it to Jerusalem**, but he put his armor in his [own] tent. (1 Samuel 17:50–54, emphasis added)

This is the only reference in the Bible to the most famous head/skull ever brought to Jerusalem. And, of all things, it was transported there by the one who was to become a central figure in ancient Israel and in global history.[280]

The Famous Sword

Soon after slaying Goliath, the young David, who was being pursued by the insanely jealous King Saul, made his way to a specific place in Jerusalem proper (1 Samuel 21). It was in that place where David retrieved Goliath's sword.

Logically, the location of Goliath's sword would be the final resting place of his skull as well—since they were inseparable spoils of war and the most famous trophies the young nation of Israel had ever acquired. Now, look at the biblical verification of those facts:

> **Then David came to Nob**, to Ahimelech **the priest**. And Ahimelech came to meet David, trembling, and said to him, "Why are you alone, and no one with you?"...Then David said to Ahimelech, "Then have you not here a spear or **a sword** at hand? For I have brought neither my sword nor my weapons with me."
>
> And the priest said, "**The sword of Goliath** the Philistine, **whom you struck down** in the Valley of Elah, behold, **it is here** wrapped in a cloth **behind the ephod**. If you will take that, take it, for there is none but that here." And David said, "There is none like that; give it to me." (1 Samuel 21:1, 8–9, emphasis added)

In 1 Samuel 21, we discover that David is now at the Mount of Olives, not far from the East Gate of Jerusalem. He is at a holy place of worship called Nob.

Jamieson-Fausset-Brown Bible Commentary (1 Samuel 21):

Then came David to Nob to Ahimelech—**Nob, a city of the priests** (1Sa 22:19), was in the neighborhood of Jerusalem, **on the Mount of Olives**—a little north of the top, and on the northeast of the city.[281] (emphasis added)

Encyclopedia of the Bible:

It is easy to connect a religious sanctuary **on the Mt. of Olives** with the **references to Nob**, the city of priests, and Ahimelech the priest (1 Sam 21:1; 22:9, 11, 19).[282] (emphasis added)

International Standard Bible Encyclopedia ("Mount of Olives"):

There is **Old Testament evidence that there was a "high place"** here. In the account of **David's flight** mention is made of the **spot on the summit** "where he often went to worship God" (2 Samuel 15:32 margin). This is **certainly a reference to a sanctuary**, and there are **strong reasons** for believing that **this place may have been Nob** (which see) (see 1 Samuel 21:1; 1 Samuel 22:9, 1 Samuel 22:11, 1 Samuel 22:19; Nehemiah 11:32; but especially Isaiah 10:32).[283]

Anata (Anathoth) is 2 1/2 miles Northeast of Jerusalem. **Nob therefore lay between that and [Jerusalem]**, at a point where the city could be seen, apparently on the great road from Nob;... It quite **suits the requirements of...David's flight**.[284] (emphasis added, parenthesis in original)[285]

Goliath's Head at Nob

Nob was the most likely place for David to have first brought the head of Goliath, along with the giant's sword, to dedicate them to the Lord as offerings of that supernatural victory. These factors alone would be reasons for designating the Mount of Olives "the place of the Skull."

Please understand, I'm not attempting to read anything into the Scriptures regarding this matter. Nor am I stretching the principles of interpretation to arrive at this conclusion. Thus far, the fact is that we've only looked at what the Bible plainly states in the matter of a famous *head/skull*.

Several renowned scholars agree with what we've deduced thus far. Following is one example:

Cambridge Bible for Schools and Colleges:

David deposited [Goliath's] head as a votive offering in **the Tabernacle at** *Nob* which was **close to Jerusalem. We know** that he afterwards placed **Goliath's sword there**, and possibly the rest of his armor along with it.[286] (emphasis added)

The evidence we've examined to this point concerning Yeshua's crucifixion taking place somewhere on the Mount of Olives is only the beginning of this point in our investigation.

≡ 59 ≡

GOLIATH'S HEAD?

All of these words are oddly similar in appearance and sound.

In light of what we've learned about the word "Golgotha," let's consider the next possibility: What if that term is simply a corruption of a legitimate Hebrew word, a change that developed over a long period? And what if that word applies to the head/skull of Goliath himself?

A Common Occurrence

In all languages, over time, the process of word and phrase corruption occurs quite naturally. As examples, think about the following illustration from the acclaimed English language educators at *Pearson Language*:

> Decades ago, it would have been normal to ask, "Have you a moment?" Now, you might say "D'you have a sec?" Similarly, "How do you do?" has become "How's it going?" Not only have the sentences been abbreviated, but new words have been introduced to everyday questions.[287]

There is strong academic evidence, supplied by biblical and linguistic scholars, that this corruption scenario is likely the case with the word "Golgotha." Note the stark similarities in the Hebrew words for "Goliath," "Gath," and "skull" in the following Old Testament passages:

> A champion named **Goliath** (Heb. *Golyath*), who was from **Gath**, came out of the Philistine camp.[288] (1 Samuel 17:4, NIV; emphasis added)

GOLGOTHA'S GROANING

A woman dropped an upper millstone on his head and cracked his **skull** (Heb. *gulgōleṯh*).²⁸⁹ (Judges 9:53, NIV; emphasis added; see also 2 Kings 9:35)

Because of Judges 9:53 and 2 Kings 9:35, we know the word for "skull" in Hebrew is *gulgōleṯh*. However, the word used for the place of the crucifixion is the Greek *Golgotha*. "Golgotha" also reflects the *Syriac* word for skull: *gāgūlṯā*.²⁹⁰

Then, after we add to those linguistic similarities the fact that the Hebrew word for Goliath is *Golyath*, it's easy to see that all of these words are oddly similar in appearance and sound. It's also easy to hear how the Greek word *Golgotha* sounds a lot like the Hebrew word for "Goliath's skull."

Several scholars say this is precisely what the resultant corruption (Golgotha) means. For example:

Dr. Rick Shenk, who received his PhD in Systematic Theology from the University of Wales, Lampeter, has been (as of this writing) a professor at Bethlehem College & Seminary's Master of Divinity program since 2017.²⁹¹ Dr. Shenk believes the name *Golgotha* is most likely connected to Goliath:

> David took [Goliath's] severed skull to Jerusalem.... Hundreds of years later, Jesus was crucified at the "place of the skull" outside of Jerusalem. But why was that place called *Golgotha* in Jesus' day? The text does not tell us, but it is intriguing that **this place name sounds very much like, Goliath.**²⁹² (emphasis added)

Dr. Taylor Marshall, with a PhD from the University of Dallas, is a prominent theologian and author who's written a good deal about Golgotha's mystery. Here's what he has to say about the word *Golgotha:*

> **The "place of the skull" is where King David buried the head of the decapitated giant Goliath of Gath.** The Bible teaches that after David slew Goliath, he cut off his head and brought the skull

GOLIATH'S HEAD?

to Jerusalem. This would explain why the "place of the skull" is named "Golgotha."

The term [Golgotha] is a corruption of Hebrew for "Goliath Gath": Goliath Gath > GoliGath > GolGath > GolGatha.

The **slaying of Goliath** by David was one of the **most important events** in "Israelite history." …The **location of the giant's head would have been known by all.** Hence, **"Golgotha" is likely the place** of not just any old skull, but the place **of the skull of Goliath of Gath.**[293] (emphasis added)

Dr. James B. Jordan served for almost two decades, starting in 2000, as head of the Department of Biblical Studies at the Biblical Theological Seminary, St. Petersburg, Russia, where he taught Old Testament and eschatology. Here is what he has to add to our examination of the word *Golgotha*.

Golgotha is just a contraction of Goliath of Gath (Hebrew: Goliath-Gath). 1 Samuel 17:54 says that David took the head of Goliath to Jerusalem, but since Jerusalem was to be a holy city, this dead corpse would not have been set up inside the city, but someplace outside. **The Mount of Olives** was right in front of the city (1 Kings 11:7; 2 Kings 23:13), and a place of ready access. **Jesus was crucified at the place where Goliath's head had been exhibited.**[294] (emphasis added)

Based on the evidence we've uncovered, the name Golgotha most likely translated to the first-century Jewish mind as, "The place where Goliath's skull was offered as a trophy of war." That distinct possibility would also explain why there seems to be no other black-and-white definition of where the area might be. The reason is clear: the people who lived in and around Jerusalem in Yeshua's day already knew where it was. They simply had their first-century, modern way of expressing the earlier phrase, "the place of Goliath's skull." It merely transformed, over the centuries from 1000 BC to around AD 33, into the New Testament Greek word *Golgotha*.

Next we'll look at a New Testament clue that comes close to pinpointing the exact place of Golgotha.

≡ 60 ≡

NEW TESTAMENT CONFIRMATION

Jesus was crucified near the summit of the Mount of Olives about half a mile east of the Temple Mount.

A passage in the New Testament concerning Golgotha's proximity closes the circle even tighter. It's found in Hebrews chapter 13. Again, with permission, I am gleaning a portion of the following information from Messianic Rabbi Zev Porat's *Unmasking the Chaldean Spirit*.

The following is the New Testament description of Golgotha's location:

> **We have an altar** from which those who minister at the tabernacle **have no right to eat.** The **high priest** carries the **blood** of animals into the Most Holy Place as a sin offering, but **the bodies are burned outside the camp.** And so **Jesus also suffered outside the city gate** to make the people holy through his own blood. Let us, then, **go to Him outside the camp**, bearing the disgrace He bore. (Hebrews 13:10–13, NIV; emphasis added)

To properly understand the otherwise cryptic words of Hebrews 13, we would need in-depth knowledge about Old Testament worship ceremonies. That's because those rituals involved various burnt offerings unto the Lord, and this is inarguably one of those altars to which Hebrews 13 is referring.

Outside the Camp

Consider the words I've highlighted in the passage from Hebrews 13. They speak of the blood from the animal sacrifices being brought into

NEW TESTAMENT CONFIRMATION

the Holy Place of the Temple. Those words also assert that the *bodies* of the blood sacrifices were taken "outside the camp, and outside the gate." It was there where the bodies were to be burned up and the ashes used as sanctifying applications.

East of Jerusalem

The terms "gate" and "camp" refer to Jerusalem proper, specifically the *eastern* side, near the Temple Mount. However, the surrounding area, especially the Mount of Olives just east of the Old City of Jerusalem, was considered an important part of greater Jerusalem and even the city itself.[295]

The writer of Hebrews encourages the readers to go "outside the camp" and outside the "city gate." In so doing, he was narrowing the focus of the location of Golgotha. It was near the East Gate, and near the altar of the red heifer sacrifice—the altar to which Hebrews 13 refers (Numbers 19).[296]

Back to the Mount of Olives

This is an enormously important clue! And, of all places, the directions given in Hebrews 13 lead us right back to the Mount of Olives and the general locale of the "Place of the [Goliath's] Skull" and sword—otherwise known to first-century people as *Golgotha*.[297]

Remember that in Genesis 22:1–2, Abraham was instructed by the Lord to go to the *region* of Moriah. Moriah is where the Temple would eventually be built by King Solomon—but God didn't tell Abraham to go to that specific mountaintop for the purpose of offering the sacrifice of his son. He only said to Abraham, "Go to the region of Moriah," then said, "Sacrifice Isaac on *one of* the mountains I will tell you about."

The wording is pretty clear. If God wanted Abraham to sacrifice Isaac *on* Moriah itself, He probably would have simply said so. Instead, Abraham was told to go to the "region" of Moriah—and from *there* (near, or *on*, Moriah), God would reveal the exact place of sacrifice, which would be one of the *other* nearby mountains.

The fact is that there are three other mountains in that region, and all are in close proximity to Moriah. They are Ophel, Zion, and the

GOLGOTHA'S GROANING

Mount of Olives. The Mount of Olives is the tallest, at almost two hundred feet higher than Mount Moriah, and lays adjacent to it, on the east side of the city, just outside the gates of Old Jerusalem.[298]

It appears most likely that the mountain and place where God showed Abraham to sacrifice Isaac was indeed the Mount of Olives—especially since Moriah, Zion, and Ophel were "inside the gates" of Old Jerusalem.[299]

Since Hebrews 13 asserts that Yeshua was *sacrificed outside the gates*, then the only remaining mountain is the Mount of Olives! This is the mountain God pointed out to Abraham, and it's where Yeshua was crucified. The exact place would also be within direct eyesight of the future Temple of Yahweh, which would be situated on Mt. Moriah. The Temple was about two hundred feet below the crucifixion site.

Scholarship Matters

Once again, to assure you that this information is backed up by renowned biblical, archeological, and ancient Hebrew scholarship, I've listed three prominent sources below.

The work of Ernest L. Martin, PhD, author of *Secrets of Golgotha*, has long stood among scholars as one of the most definitive on this topic. His four-hundred-page book investigates the Hebrews 13 passage from about every angle, using not only reliable ancient sources but also the acclaimed works of several other respected modern scholars.

Dr. Martin concludes:

> Indeed, the important **sacrifice of the Red Heifer** was performed at this **eastern altar** which was located as Ezekiel says, "without the sanctuary." In the time of Jesus, Jewish records show that this outer altar was located **near the southern summit of the Mount of Olives** directly **east of the Temple**. It was also positioned just "outside the Camp" of Israel.
>
> There is no longer any doubt. Jesus was crucified near the summit of the Mount of Olives about half a mile east of the Temple Mount.[300] (emphasis added)

NEW TESTAMENT CONFIRMATION

James Tabor, PhD:

The basic case for **the Mt. of Olives being the site of Jesus' crucifixion** rests on several interrelated arguments. The first, and in my view, the **most weighty**, is a passage in the New Testament book of **Hebrews (13:10–13).**[301] (emphasis added)

Dr. Douglas Jacoby:

There is **substantial evidence** in the Old Testament **for a location** "outside the camp" devoted to the incineration of the bodies of sacrificial animals…(Leviticus 4:12, 6:11). In **Hebrews 13**…Jesus' death is symbolically **connected with this altar outside the Temple**…. Our "red heifer sacrifice" was "slaughtered" **on the Mount of Olives**, in roughly **the same location** as the original Red Heifer sacrifice.[302] (emphasis added)

Of all the pertinent biblical evidence, every piece points to the Mount of Olives as the general locale of Golgotha.[303]

By the way, the iconic Golgotha representation of the three *tav* crosses is also found in Hebrews 13:12–13. It is situated precisely in the following words:

> Jesus also suffered outside the gate in order to sanctify the people through his own blood. Therefore, let us go to Him outside the camp, bearing the disgrace He bore. (BSB)

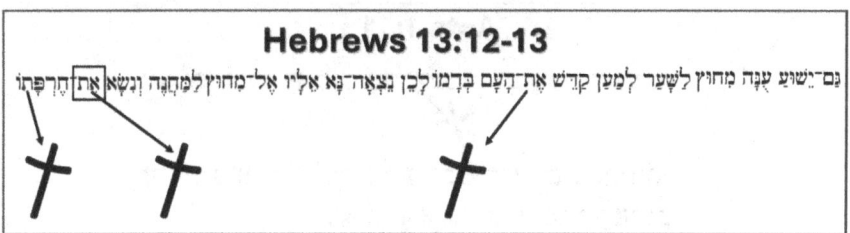

Even here, we find the supernaturally coded Golgotha icon, with the *aleph-tav* as the middle cross. Once more, we see the astounding image with our own eyes—right where it ought to be.

GOLGOTHA'S GROANING

The importance of the Mount of Olives in Israel's ancient history is huge. This fact is especially true as it relates to several of the most significant points of Yeshua's life and ministry. Yeshua even raised Lazarus from the dead there! Because of that miracle, the Sanhedrin council finally launched their demonically driven plot to murder Yeshua (John 11).

Furthermore, Yeshua and His disciples were on that mountain almost every time they were in Jerusalem, especially in the last week of His life. He went to the Garden of Gethsemane at the foot of the Mount of Olives, and was ultimately arrested there. Now we know He was crucified and resurrected there as well. Therefore, Satan's ultimate defeat was wrought on the Mount of Olives.

Yeshua also ascended into Heaven from there, and has promised He will return at His Second Coming…to the Mount of Olives![304] Two angels showed up on the Mount of Olives at Yeshua's ascension and assured the onlookers (perhaps several hundred) Yeshua would return to that spot (Acts 1:15).[305]

> "Men of Galilee," they said, "why do you stand here looking into the sky? This same Jesus, who has been taken from you into heaven, will come back in the same way you have seen him go into heaven." (Acts 1:11, NIV)

Following is Acts 1:11 in its Hebrew translation. We shouldn't be surprised at the imagery we find there.

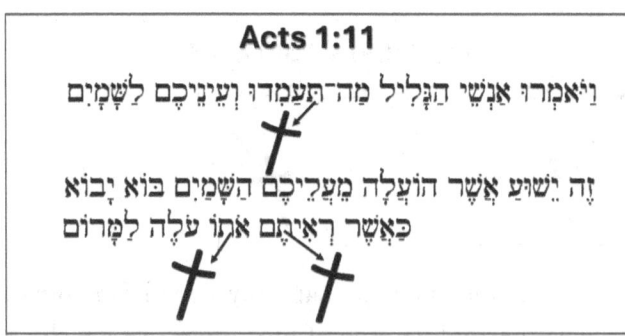

Part Nine

THE RELEVANCY

Who is like me? Let him proclaim it. Let him declare and set it before me, since I appointed an ancient people. Let them declare what is to come, and what will happen. (Isaiah 44:7)

61

WHAT WE DON'T KNOW

Our generation is now living in the most prophetically significant times since the first coming of Yeshua.

When the Golgotha prophecies were given, they were impossible for humans to accurately understand in their fullest sense—until they happened.

Further, every prophecy was written at least four hundred to five hundred years before it was fulfilled. Some were declared more than a thousand years before they came to pass, and others go all the way back to the beginning of earthly time. However, they *were fulfilled,* and they had always been about Yeshua and His preordained trek toward Golgotha's groanings.

It is also an absolute fact that only *one book* in all of history accurately catalogued each of those elements, encased within pages of pervasive detail and grandeur. Perhaps this is the reason the Bible is still the number-one, most-purchased book throughout the world, year after year, and has been since 1522.[306]

> Heaven and earth will pass away, but My words will not pass away. (Matthew 24:35)

> The grass withers and the flowers fall, but the Word of our God stands forever. (Isaiah 40:8, BSB)

However, the stark truth is that *no one*, not even the prophets who proclaimed the prophecies we've been examining or the angels in

GOLGOTHA'S GROANING

Heaven, knew exactly what the various elements of those prophecies were. They would never have dreamed that Golgotha would turn out to be the fulfillment, especially in the way we now know it as revealed in the New Testament. Those details would only become apparent *after* they had been satisfied.

In other words, often in the realm of biblical prophecy, *we don't know what we don't know* until it has been revealed to us in God's own season of precise timing.

The Apostle Peter wrote about this biblical truth in both of his letters to the churches of his day (1 and 2 Peter). Please pause over every sentence of these two Holy Spirit-anointed declarations and really "hear" what Peter is saying! His message goes directly to the journey we've just traveled through the pages of this book.

> **Concerning this salvation, the prophets who prophesied** about the grace that was to be yours **searched and inquired** carefully, inquiring what person or time the Spirit of Christ in them was indicating when he predicted the sufferings of Christ and the subsequent glories. It was **revealed to them that they were serving not themselves but you,** in the things that have now been announced to you through those who preached the good news to you by the Holy Spirit sent from heaven, things **into which angels long to look.** (1 Peter 1:10–12, emphasis added)

> We also have **the word of the prophets as confirmed beyond doubt.** And you will do well to pay attention to it, as to a lamp shining in a dark place, until the day dawns and the morning star rises in your hearts. (2 Peter 1:19, BSB; emphasis added)

Our Prophetic Times

Our own generation is immersed in the same kind of revelatory processes Peter was speaking of concerning his day. It is a historical and biblical fact that we are now living in the most prophetically unfolding times since the *First* Coming of Yeshua.[307]

WHAT WE DON'T KNOW

Now, numerous revelations of monumental proportions are emanating from the multidimensional depths of God's Word, and they're being revealed right before our eyes. Many of those revelations have been unveiled only in our lifetime. Some have been disclosed as recently as the past few decades. The truth of those biblical disclosures is now resounding throughout the world. *We are the ones* for whom they were originally intended—and they were prophesied thousands of years ago!

Peter admonished the first-century Church that they were accountable for what they had been shown. The same biblical warning holds true for our own generation. We are now accountable for what we've seen and for how we share those revelations with others.

The Purpose of the Presence

The types of supernatural phenomena we've been exploring in this book weren't revealed to our generation for us to merely ogle and *move on*. Rather, they're being unveiled for us to preach, teach, and fervently proclaim to the world. They are there so God's people might be in a perpetual state of awe. They're meant to be signs of *our* unprecedented prophetic times, as well as to display the glory of God's Word! We've now been gloriously assured from Heaven's throne, by ever-unfolding, divine revelations, that we truly can build every aspect of our lives upon His Word—without hesitation. And we can confidently encourage others to do so as well.

Right down to every single letter and word, the "biblical DNA" codes of Golgotha are there. As such, the symbols of God's divine fingerprints are also there, and they're found throughout the Scriptures.

Yahweh is verifying that there is no other Savior like *Yeshua HaMashiach*. He alone is the Lamb of God and the Lion of Judah. And it is through Golgotha's cross that we are saved. Those truths are the inarguable themes of the entire Word of God. We've now seen that fact emphasized repeatedly, and in dramatic detail, in the format of the iconic imagery of Golgotha's three crosses.

☰ 62 ☰

STICK A FORK IN IT

When the dishes of the main course were being cleared, someone would inevitably lean over and say, "Keep your fork."

As we conclude our journey together, take a look at two final Scripture verses. One is from the Old Testament, the other is from the New. Let's begin with the earlier passage:

> Who is like me? Let him proclaim it. Let him declare and set it before me, since I appointed an ancient people. Let them declare what is to come, and what will happen. (Isaiah 44:7)

What do you think might be the iconic image found in the midst of those words?

You guessed it again! Three Paleo-Hebrew *tavs* form the image of Golgotha to represent the ultimate *divine thing* that "was to happen," as revealed from the very first verse of Genesis all the way to Malachi. And, for two thousand years, the details of that prophesied event have been further verified from Matthew to Revelation.[308]

STICK A FORK IN IT

Now let's look at the New Testament passage that concerns two disciples of Yeshua—Cleopas and an unnamed disciple. They were on the road to Emmaus just after the resurrection of Yeshua.

> They said to each other, "Did not our hearts burn within us while He talked to us on the road, while He opened to us the Scriptures?" (Luke 24:32)

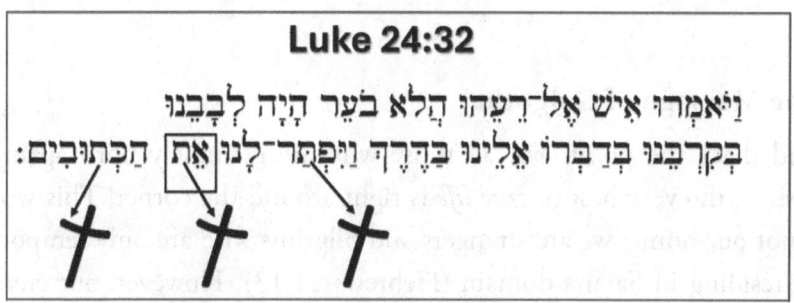

There it is again—a complete thought, containing three crosses. And the one in the middle is *aleph-tav/Yeshua*. Once again, we've come full circle, all the way back to the first Golgotha image we saw in Genesis 1:1.

A Closing Illustration

The following anecdote is attributed to Roger William Thomas. It appeared in a 2021 Ann Landers advice column as printed in the *Chicago Tribune*:

> A woman was diagnosed with a terminal illness and given three months to live. She asked her pastor to come to her home to discuss her final wishes. She told him which songs she wanted sung at her funeral, and what scriptures to read, and which outfit she wanted to be buried in. Then she said, "One more thing. I want to be buried with a fork in my hand."
>
> The pastor was surprised. The woman explained, "In all my years of attending church socials and potluck dinners, I always remember

that when the dishes of the main course were being cleared, someone would inevitably lean over and say, 'Keep your fork.'

"It was my favorite time, because I knew something better was coming, like velvety chocolate cake or deep-dish apple pie—something wonderful. So, I want people to see me there in that casket with a fork in my hand and wonder, 'What's with the fork?' Then, I want you to tell them, 'Keep your fork, because the best is yet to come!'"[309]

The Message of Golgotha

And that's the point. For all those who are genuinely born again in Yeshua, the very best of *true life* is right around the corner! This world is not our home; we are strangers and pilgrims who are only temporarily residing in Satan's domain (Hebrews 11:13). However, our eternal mission as we journey through this enemy territory is to be diligent and faithful ambassadors for the coming Kingdom of Yeshua HaMashiach and to accurately handle the Word of God (2 Corinthians 5:20). We are called to forever proclaim the good news of Golgotha's deliverance whenever the doors to do so are opened (2 Timothy 2:15). In that way, we too have become the Yeshua-ordained *priests* of His Kingdom that is soon to come!

After reading this book, you now possess one more colossal tool for helping others behold the wonders of God's Word. The encoded images of Golgotha will emphatically punctuate the invitation for all who have the eyes to "see" to humbly bow before the *One in the middle.*

From now on, every time you come across any passage in the Scripture directly related to Golgotha, I'm certain you will see the image of the three *tav* crosses in your mind's eye; it's likely to be forever imprinted upon your soul. The image in the passages will serve as divine confirmation that the Word of God is unique above all other *words, books, religions, and creeds,* and Yeshua has every detail of what is coming next under His control.

STICK A FORK IN IT

What a Journey!

Thank you so much for taking this excursion with me. I am humbled that you have done so. And now, because of Yeshua's sacrificial offering upon Golgotha's cross, we'll get to see each other in Glory, one day soon, perhaps somewhere around the throne of God, while singing songs of His magnificent wonders. I look forward to that day!

> Worthy is the Lamb to take the scroll and to open its seals, for you were slain, and by your blood you ransomed people for God from every tribe and language and people and nation, and you have made them a kingdom and priests to our God, and they shall reign on the earth!"… "Worthy is the Lamb who was slain, to receive power and wealth and wisdom and might and honor and glory and blessing!"
>
> To him who sits upon the throne and to the Lamb, be blessing and honor and glory and might forever and ever! (Revelation 5:9–10, 12–13)

The Lion of Judah has roared—Golgotha proves It!
Even so, *Yeshua Hamashiach Adonai, come*!

310

ABOUT THE AUTHOR

Carl Gallups has been the senior pastor of Hickory Hammock Church in Milton, Florida, since 1987.

He is a graduate of the Florida Law Enforcement Officer Academy, Florida State University (BSC in criminology), and New Orleans Baptist Theological Seminary (MDiv in theology, with studies in Hebrew and Greek), and has served on the Board of Regents at the University of Mobile in Mobile, Alabama.

He is a former decorated Florida law enforcement officer, having served under three sheriffs through two county offices, and has also worked in an administrative capacity in the Central Office of the Florida Department of Corrections in Tallahassee.

Pastor Gallups is also a critically acclaimed, Amazon Top 60 best-selling author. His book *Final Warning* was in the Top 60 of all Amazon books for several weeks. A number of his other popular books have made it into the Top 300s on Amazon's bestseller charts. Carl was also an internationally known talk radio host of *Freedom Friday with Carl Gallups*, 2002–2022 and has been heard by audiences around the globe on three live-streamed Gulf Coast radio stations (AM and FM), as well as on several popular podcast platforms.

He continues to be a regular guest on numerous television, radio, and podcast programs around the world, in addition to being a frequent guest speaker at national prophecy and Bible conferences. Carl has preached the gospel of Jesus Christ on three continents and in four nations, including Peru and Israel, and from the West Coast to the East Coast of the United States—including Hawaii and Alaska. He has also preached, on several occasions, in the Canadian provinces of British Columbia, Alberta, and Ontario.

Pastor Gallups lives in Milton, Florida, with Pam, his high school sweetheart who's now his wife. You can find more information about Pastor Carl at www.carlgallups.com.

Carl's life-promise Scripture is Romans 8:28, 31:

And we know that in all things God works for the good of those who love him, who have been called according to His purpose.... What, then, shall we say in response to these things? If God is for us, who can be against us?

ACKNOWLEDGMENTS

My deepest thanks to the following people:

To Donna Howell (CEO, Defender Publishing), Pennie Dutton (acquisitions, Defender Publishing), Angie Peters (editor), Jeffery Mardis (cover designer), and Katherine Lloyd (interior designer)—as well as to the entire Defender Publishing team. Thank you for your tireless efforts to consistently produce excellence in publishing—and most of all, for your patience with me!

To Joe Horn (CEO, SkyWatch TV) and his wife, Katherine. Also to their children: Katie, Nita, Becca, and Tommy. You have loved me, encouraged me, and believed in me since I first met all of you many years ago. What a sweet delight each of you has become to my life!

To Nita Horn, cofounder of SkyWatch TV and Whispering Ponies Ranch (an immersive ministry for children of abuse), as well as the loving wife of Dr. Tom Horn (February 28, 1957–October 20, 2023), founder of Skywatch TV and Defender Publishing. You and Tom have been such a wonderful influence, as well as great and loyal friends. Thank you for every good thing you have sown into my life!

Also to Messianic Rabbi Zev Porat of Tel Aviv, Israel, for your amazing contributions not only to this book and several others, but also to my own life and ministry endeavors…and to your precious and consistently thoughtful wife, Lian. The friendship and love the two of you have given me and my entire family has been a divinely appointed treasure. Praise Yeshua! You guys are the greatest!

To you, the reader! A number of you have purchased, read, and shared several of my other books as well. For that humbling honor, I am eternally grateful. I pray that you have been blessed by them, and especially by *this one*—to the glory of Yeshua!

GOLGOTHA'S GROANING

Finally, but certainly not the least, I want to thank my precious wife, Pam. You have been the love of my life since we were young teens. Without your decades of love, faith, patience, and grace, I would not be where I am today in my walk with Yeshua HaMashiach or in any other aspect of life itself. You are an immeasurable gift from the Lord! I love you.

NOTES

1. The Hebrew New Testament of the British and Foreign Bible Society (1883) is written by Franz Julius Delitzsch. This work is one of the most popular translations from English to Hebrew. Since its first publication by the British and Foreign Bible Society it has since become a vital resource for numerous scholars of the ancient biblical languages.
   Online Resources Here:
   1) Hebrew New Testament by Delitzsch, Franz,
   https://archive.org/details/hebrewnewtestam00deli/page/30/mode/2up.
   2) Delitzsch Hebrew New Testament,
   https://nocr.net/hbm/hebrew/hebdlz/index.php.
   3) Congregation Sar Shalom—Online Hebrew New Testament,
   http://sarshalom.us/resources/scripture/asv/bible.html.

2. To embark upon a search for **specific** Scriptures that contain three *tavs* (crosses) in the Hebrew language requires an exhaustive amount of research, especially when the investigation spans from Genesis through Revelation. However, to make that search credible at all, the three *tavs* of the Golgotha image must also be found in a Golgotha-related passage.

   In other words, to merely discover the presence of three *tavs* in any given passage is relatively meaningless and fairly easy to accomplish. After all, the *tav* is simply the last letter in the Hebrew alphabet. So, it makes sense that we would find untold numbers of *tavs* throughout Scripture. And that is exactly the case. So, unless the three *tavs* fall within a passage (or in a complete thought expressed in a larger passage) directly related to the Golgotha event, then their presence holds no credible weight for this study.

   Finally, when I speak of a *passage* of Scripture, I'm not necessarily talking about a *single verse* as it appears in our English translations. This is especially true if the Scripture is making a statement about Golgotha that spans more than one *verse*, and/or it is located within a longer passage. In that case, my search focused upon the entire message of that sentence (s). That element of the protocol I used was vital, because the placement of **numbers to denote chapters and verses in the Bible were not a part of the original writings.** The luxury of being able to locate a specific chapter and verse in either the Old or New Testaments didn't come along until **more than a thousand years after** the Christ event.

   (See Alyssa Roat, "Why Was the Bible Divided into Chapters and Verses?" 1/26/21, Christianity.com, https://www.christianity.com/wiki/bible/why-was-the-bible-divided-into-chapters-and-verses.html.)

   So, as you can see, we're not on a mere Easter egg hunt through all the passages

NOTES

in the Bible. I thoroughly searched the complete messages of the Golgotha prophecies (OT) and the fulfillment of those prophecies (NT) found within certain portions of the Scriptures where it made sense that the three *tavs* **might** appear.

I must confess that when I first began my research, I hadn't the slightest idea whether other Golgotha passages containing the three-cross image of Genesis 1:1 even existed. I suspected they might be there, but I was skeptical. It seemed humanly impossible from the outset that my speculation would prove to be correct.

As I began my tedious search for that answer, I was overwhelmed by what I was consistently finding. The several people around me whom I trusted with my research were also astonished by what they were seeing. What we were looking at seemed to be humanly impossible. We soon felt humbled, and began to realize that we were actually seeing what appeared to be a supernatural code that had been divinely placed in the Word of God.

Thank you for taking the time to read this important information. I want you to know that you can categorically trust the things the information I've uncovered. However, **what you do with what you see** is solely your decision. I am merely laying the images out for you with additional information to help you understand the passages in which the images are found. They are the images that undoubtedly tell the unified story of Golgotha's groanings—*our Salvation.*

3   Ibid.

4   Messianic Rabbi Zev Porat can be reached at www.messiahofisraelministries.com.

5   The narrative portion of this book (part one) draws its most vital elements from John 13–18 and Luke 22. Along the way, I've taken a few literary liberties in an attempt to present the dramatized account of God's Word in an impactful, yet biblically accurate, manner.

   For example, I've added dialogue that might not be explicitly stated in the biblical text; yet even that, along with other details, is either implied by the text or certainly *could* have been used in a similar manner in the real situation This is done with no violation of the overall message of God's Word, nor does it violate biblical doctrine.

   I pray the Lord uses this presentation for your spiritual edification and to help you experience the grandeur of all that you will soon see within the pages of this book, and most importantly, in the Word of God.

6   1) "In antiquity, crucifixion was considered one of the most brutal and shameful modes of death. Probably originating with the Assyrians and Babylonians, it was used systematically by the Persians in the 6th century BC. Alexander the Great brought it from there to the eastern Mediterranean countries in the 4th century BC, and the Phoenicians introduced it to Rome in the 3rd century BC. It was virtually never used in pre-Hellenic Greece. The Romans perfected crucifixion for 500 years until it was abolished by Constantine I in the 4th century AD."

   Retief, L Cilliers. "The History and Pathology of Crucifixion," PubMed, NIH, 12/9/03, https://pubmed.ncbi.nlm.nih.gov/14750495.

   2) From a *Christian Post* article:

   "In *The Case for Christ*, Lee Strobel provides in graphic detail this description of flogging from Dr. Alexander Metherell: 'The soldier would use a whip of braided

NOTES

leather thongs with metal balls woven into them. When the whip would strike the flesh, these balls would cause deep bruises or contusions, which would break open with further blows. And the whip had pieces of broken bone as well which would cut the flesh severely.

'The back would be so shredded that part of the spine was sometimes exposed by the deep, deep cuts. The whipping would have gone all the way from the shoulders down to the back, the buttocks, and the back of the legs.

'A third century historian by the name of Eusebius described a flogging by saying, "The sufferer's veins were laid bare and the very muscles, sinews and bowels of the victim were open to exposure."

'Jesus foretold His suffering with these words: "We are going up to Jerusalem, and everything that is written by the prophets about the Son of Man will be fulfilled. He will be handed over to the Gentiles. They will mock Him, insult Him, spit on Him, flog Him and kill Him. On the third day He will rise again" (Luke 18:31–33).

'When it was time for Christ to be crucified, nails were driven into His wrists and feet. The weight of His body was on the nails through the wrists. This caused compression on the lungs, which prevented Jesus from inhaling. In order to take a breath, Jesus had to push upward putting all the weight on His feet, causing unbearable pain. Try to imagine doing that for six seconds, let alone six hours.'" https://www.christianpost.com/voices/bible-truths-hell-jesus.html.

7 University of Chicago, "The Death of Jesus," accessed 10/25/24, https://penelope.uchicago.edu/encyclopaedia_romana/calendar/jesus.html.

"Jesus therefore died on Friday, April 3, AD 33 at about 3 p.m., a few hours before the beginning of Passover day and the Sabbath. This is the date in the Julian calendar, which had been introduced in 45 BC, and follows the convention that historical dates adhere to the calendar in use at the time. If, instead, the current Gregorian calendar were retroactively extended to a date prior to its introduction in 1582 (or 1752, when it was adopted by the United States and United Kingdom), such a proleptic date (a date retroactively calculated using a later calendar) would be different.

"The equivalent Jewish date for the death of Jesus is Nisan 14, 3793 *anno mundi* ('in the year of the world'), which is computed by adding 3761 to AD 33 and subtracting a year. In the Jewish calendar, AM 1 (or 3761 BC, its proleptic Julian date) is the traditional year of creation (a year before Adam and Eve themselves were created)—as determined by the sage Halafta, who used only the chronology of the Bible as his authority, and codified by the twelfth-century scholar Maimonides a millennium later."

8 Dr. Don Stewart, Blue Letter Bible, "What Precautions Were Taken to Keep the Tomb of Jesus Secure?"

"Pilate said to them, 'You **have a guard**; go, make it as secure as you know how.' And they went and made the grave secure, **and along with the guard** they set a seal on the stone" (Matthew 27:65, 66).

"There is a question as to which one of the two groups was watching over it. The context seems to favor **the Roman guard**. The Roman guard was a **sixteen-man unit** that was governed by very strict rules. Each member was responsible for six square feet of space. The guard members could not sit down or lean against anything while

NOTES

they were on duty. If a guard member fell asleep, he was beaten and burned with his own clothes. But he was not the only one executed, **the entire sixteen-man guard unit was executed** if only one of the members fell asleep while on duty."

9   See: 1 Peter 1:10–12.
10 Matthew 26:14–16, NIV: "Then one of the Twelve—the one called Judas Iscariot—went to the chief priests and asked, 'What are you willing to give me if I deliver him over to you?' So they counted out for him thirty pieces of silver. From then on Judas watched for an opportunity to hand him over."
11 See: Got Questions. "What is the significance of the thirty pieces of silver" gotquestions.org, accessed 10/26/24, https://www.gotquestions.org/thirty-pieces-of-silver.html.
12 See: John 6:64–65;70–71.
13 See Psalm 139.
14 Fatal flogging: "The Romans meted out whippings with particular zeal, inventing new tools to increase the misery: on the mild end, a flat leather strap; on the mortal end, long whips with, at their ends, balls of metal with protruding metal fragments or pieces of bone. It was not uncommon for the scourging that preceded a crucifixion to prove fatal."

   Ian Tuttle, "Flogging Through the Centuries," NationalReview.com, 1/14/2015, https://www.nationalreview.com/2015/01/flogging-through-centuries-ian-tuttle/.
15 You will discover this truth to be inarguable as we move along. This fact is one of the revealed elements of the theme of this book.
16 See Hebrews 12.
17 See Leviticus 23.
18 Jimmy Cox, "The Psalm Sang at the Last Supper," AOK Music and Arts, accessed 12/1/24, https://aokmusicandarts.com/news/2020/4/9/the-psalm-sang-at-the-last-supper.

   "At the end of the Passover meal, Matthew and Mark state that the disciples sang a hymn with Jesus before departing. While Scripture doesn't explicitly state which hymn was sung, Jewish tradition reveals that the Passover meal was concluded by singing the last portion of the *Hallel*. The *Hallel* is comprised of Psalms 113 through 118. It is a joyous celebration of praise and thanksgiving to God. Why is this significant to the events of Holy Week? By looking at these Psalms, we see that there were many references to the eventual salvation of the Lord's people brought by the death and resurrection of Christ. This is especially true of Psalm 118, which served as the conclusion of the Passover meal."
19 See Luke 22:14–16.
20 In this ancient culture, to have freshly cleaned feet was a stimulating part of sitting down to a meal. One's whole body felt cleansed and invigorated when the dirt, crust, and muck from spending all day in sandals, or bare feet, had been cleansed away. This was a fairly routine procedure for most households, a mere part of daily life and tradition in the first century Middle East. From "Footwashing for Domestic Comfort purposes":

   "Footwashing occurs frequently in the Old Testament. Footwashing is observed in domestic settings for hygiene and comfort, and domestic settings devoted to

NOTES

hospitality. Footwashing also prepared you for a variety of activities, like a meal for example. Footwashing was also used for personal hygiene and comfort. Footwashing was so common that the lack of adequate preparation could be expressed by the phrase 'with unwashed feet.' Also, footwashing is generally the responsibility of servants. A host or hostess can offer the hospitable act, but it is ordinarily carried out by slaves. Those who receive footwashing are almost always the social superiors of those who render the service. See: Carmine Permini, "Footwashing in the Old and New Testament, the Graeco Roman World, the Early Church, and the Liturgy," 4/15/2014, http://www.zionlutherannj.net/footwashing-in-the-old-and-new-testament-the-graeco-roman-world-the-early-church-and-the-liturgy-2/#_ftn10.

Also see: John Christopher Thomas, *Footwashing in John 13 and the Johannine Community*, (Sheffield: JSNT Publishers, 1991), pages 26–131.

21 Footwashing for initiation of Priests: "In the Old Testament it is common to associate footwashing with the priestly admission into the tabernacle and temple.... In the Torah, **priests are required to wash their hands and feet before entering the holy place** of the tabernacle to offer sacrifice on the altar. Moses receives these commands in Exodus 30:17–21. Exodus 40:30–32 describes these instructions. 1 Kings 7:38 and 2 Chronicles 4:6 mention ten basins (40 baths) in which the priests were to wash. Also, the high priest is expected to wash his hands and feet on the Day of Atonement (Lev. 16:24).... Philo says, 'One should not enter with unwashed feet on the pavement of the temple of God.' ...Footwashing has a lengthy history associated with cultic rituals and purity in the Old Testament."

See Carmine Permini, "Footwashing in the Old and New Testament, the Graeco Roman World, the Early Church, and the Liturgy," 4/15/2014, http://www.zionlutherannj.net/footwashing-in-the-old-and-new-testament-the-graeco-roman-world-the-early-church-and-the-liturgy-2/#_ftn10.

Also see John Christopher Thomas, *Footwashing in John 13 and the Johannine Community*, (Sheffield: JSNT Publishers, 1991), pages 26–131.

22 Did Yeshua wash Judas' feet? (*Yes,* He did.)

Some commentators think Judas had already left before the footwashing occurred. But that's not the opinion of the majority of scholars, and for good reason. John 13:2 says, in almost every modern translation, that *during supper* Judas left to betray Yeshua. The KJV and NKJV say "after supper." However, the Greek text does not say "after," it says, "as supper was taking place" (see: https://biblehub.com/interlinear/john/13-2.htm). It appears the more scholarly translation of the Greek wording in John's rendition of the matter is specifically accurate, clearly indicating Judas left "during the meal" and after the foot-washing ceremony (which had taken place sometime in the middle of the meal.) The meal would have essentially been the central focus of the entire evening before they went out to the Garden of Gethsemane.

23 Moses receives these ritualistic commands in Exodus 30:17-21. Exodus 40:30–32 describes these instructions. 1 Kings 7:38 and 2 Chronicles 4:6 mention ten basins (40 baths) in which the priests were to wash. Also, the high priest is expected to wash his hands and feet on the Day of Atonement (Lev. 16:24).... Philo says, "One should not enter with unwashed feet on the pavement of the temple of God."... See Carmine Permini, "Footwashing in the Old and New Testament, the Graeco Roman

NOTES

World, the Early Church, and the Liturgy," 4/1/14, http://www.zionlutherannj.net/footwashing-in-the-old-and-new-testament-the-graeco-roman-world-the-early-church-and-the-liturgy-2/#_ftn10.

24 Footwashing as an act of humility and love for another person: "A host or hostess can offer the hospitable act, but it is ordinarily carried out by slaves. Those who receive footwashing are almost always the social superiors of those who render the service. Lastly, and very rarely, in cases of deep love or devotion a host might wash the feet of another."

See Carmine Permini, "Footwashing in the Old and New Testament, the Graeco Roman World, the Early Church, and the Liturgy," 4/15/2014, http://www.zionlutherannj.net/footwashing-in-the-old-and-new-testament-the-graeco-roman-world-the-early-church-and-the-liturgy-2/#_ftn10.

Also see: John Christopher Thomas, *Footwashing in John 13 and the Johannine Community*, (Sheffield: JSNT Publishers, 1991), pages 26–131.

25 Psalm 41:9.

26 See Jeremiah 31:31.

27 See Matthew 26:22.

28 Both Matthew and Mark record that when Judas led the arresting entourage in the Garden of Gethsemane that night, he kissed Yeshua on the cheek and said "Rabbi!" This was the signal to the mob that the Man he kissed was in fact Yeshua. However, neither Luke nor John mention that Judas even spoke to Yeshua. Matthew has Judas saying, "Greetings rabbi!" Mark has him saying only, "Rabbi!" There's no other mention of Judas ever speaking to Yeshua in any kind of conversation on that night, or ever again.

29 *Benson Commentary* on John 13:27: "**The devil having now put it into the heart of Judas to betray him**—By this version the English reader would be led to apprehend, that it was at this paschal-supper that the devil first tempted Judas to betray Christ: but the original expression may be properly rendered, the devil having already put it into the heart of Judas, &c., for the participle βεβληκοτος is of the perfect tense, and denotes an action done at some time past, and the particle ηδη, rendered now, often signifies already, or before: so that what Christ says here concerning Judas, may refer to what had passed between him and the chief priests, after the reproof given him in the supper at Bethany. And therefore when John says afterward, (John 13:27), that after the sop was given him, Satan entered into Judas, the meaning must be, that he was then again incited by the devil to execute the treachery which he had before resolved upon, by a like instigation of the same evil spirit. https://biblehub.com/commentaries/john/13-2.htm.

30 See John 13:29.

31 Matthew 16: 1: "Show us the Father, Give us a sign from Heaven…Mark 8:11–12: "And the Pharisees and Sadducees came, and to test him they asked him to show them a sign from heaven."

Luke 11:16: "The Pharisees came and began to argue with him, seeking from him a sign from heaven to test him. And he sighed deeply in his spirit and said, 'Why does this generation seek a sign? Truly, I say to you, no sign will be given to this generation."

32 The following teaching session is not in the Scriptures. But the absolute truth of my invented words are reflected throughout the Word of God. And since Yeshua's own words, in John 14, instruct Philip and the others to at least believe in his

NOTES

"works"—another word for "miracles"—this teaching session could have been exactly what Yeshua did, but John simply didn't record it all, because the possibility of it would have spoken for itself.

In other words, Jesus would have them think back on all the things He did that only God Himself could do—according to the clear Word of God. In this manner, He was answering their request by encouraging them to acknowledge to their own hearts and minds that they actually had been *seeing Father God, Yahweh, Elohim, El Shaddai*…all along. Therefore, He could punch it home that, "If you've seen me (and the miracles I did before your eyes) then you have been looking squarely at the Father ever since you first laid eyes on Me."

33   See Psalm 77:16; Psalm 107:24; Proverbs 30:4ff; Job 9:6–8.
34   See Luke 8:25.
35   The three people raised from death were Jarius' daughter, the son of the widow of Nain, and Lazarus of Bethany (Mary and Martha's brother).
36   Those healed include the man with the shriveled hand (Matthew 12), the ten lepers, the woman with the issue of blood, the lame, the deaf, and many more.
37   *Expositor's Greek Testament:* "John 14:9. Jesus corrects the error, and guides the craving to its true satisfaction.… The manifestation which Philip craves had been made, and made continuously for some considerable time; for so long that it was matter of surprise and regret to Jesus that Philip needed still to be taught that he who saw Jesus saw the Father. It is implied that not to see the Father in Jesus was not to know Him. See https://biblehub.com/commentaries/john/14-9.htm.
38   Matthew 26:20. *Ellicott's Commentary for English Readers*, Biblehub.com. https://biblehub.com/commentaries/matthew/26-30.htm.

   Ellicott's Commentary: "This was probably the received Paschal series of Psalms (Psalms 115–118, inclusive), and the word implies a chant or musical recitative. Psalms 113, 114, were sung commonly during the meal. The Greek word may mean "when they had sung their hymn," as of something known and definite.
39   Nighttime temperatures in late March to early April at the Jerusalem elevation is typically in the low- to mid-forties Fahrenheit. Add a breeze to that temperature, and it can be extremely uncomfortable, enough so that a good warm fire would usually be needed. The Scriptures actually speak of men in Jerusalem warming themselves by fires on that night.
40   See https://www.bibleref.com/2-Peter/1/2-Peter-1-15.html.
41   Matthew 27:24–26.
42   There is scriptural evidence, however, that Peter and the other disciples actually were at the scene of the crucifixion, but were watching from the back of the crowd, probably with cloaks covering their faces. See Luke 23:49.
43   See John 19:25–26.
44   "Joseph of Arimathea," BBC.co.uk, accessed in archives on 2/12/25, https://www.bbc.co.uk/thepassion/articles/joseph_of_arimathea.shtml.
45   1 Corinthians 15:6.
46   "And having disarmed the powers and authorities, He made a public spectacle of them, triumphing over them by the cross" (Colossians 2:15).
47   See Revelation 12 (entire chapter).

NOTES

48 L. Cilliers Retief, "The History and Pathology of Crucifixion," PubMed, NIH, 12/9/03, https://pubmed.ncbi.nlm.nih.gov/14750495.

49 This description of our unprecedented prophetic times (other than the days of the First Coming of Jesus) is one that I use prolifically in my media interviews, preaching/teaching, and writing. I have contextually proven the truth of this declaration numerous times, most recently in my books *Yeshua Protocol* and *Eyes to See*.

50 1) *Enduring Word Commentary:* "On the surface, it seems clear that the rulers of this age must refer to human rulers, because only they didn't know what they were doing when they incited the crucifixion of Jesus. However, one could say that demonic powers were ignorant of what would result from the crucifixion of Jesus—the disarming and defeat of demonic powers (Colossians 2:15)—and had they known they were sealing their own doom by inciting the crucifixion, they would not have done it." David Guzik, "1 Corinthians 2," *Enduring Word Commentary*, https://enduringword.com/bible-commentary/1-corinthians-2.

   2) *Revised English Version Commentary:* "Which none of the rulers of this age knew." The "rulers of this age" are the Devil and his demons. https://www.revisedenglishversion.com/1-Corinthians/chapter2/8.

   3) *Clarke's Commentary:* "Then entered Satan into Judas—The **devil filled the heart of Judas** with avarice; and that infamous passion **led him to commit the crime** here specified [Jesus' crucifixion!] ...**What Satan could not do** by the envy and malice of the high priests and Pharisees, **he effects by Judas**" (emphasis added); https://biblehub.com/commentaries/clarke/luke/22.htm.

51 I call it a "coded" message because it couldn't have been until after the events of Golgotha occurred that the images we now find would have made sense to anyone. Yet, *after* Jesus suffered on the cross and arose from the dead, the images made by the ancient Hebrew letters and words all of a sudden made perfect sense; they came to life, right before our eyes. This book, along with *Yeshua Protocol* and *Eyes to See*, is taking these images and the message they represent to the entire world—preparing God's people and all who will come for the return of Yeshua HaMashiach.

52 "The Bible mentions the *scarlet cord or thread* in several significant instances, revealing the Bible is one unified story."
    Bible Journal Class. "The Scarlet Thread: The Depth of God's Redemptive Love," Accessed 9/17/24, https://www.biblejournalclasses.com/blog/the-scarlet-thread.

53 "351 Old Testament Prophecies Fulfilled in Jesus Christ." Accessed 12/8/24. https://www.newtestamentchristians.com/bible-study-resources/351-old-testament-prophecies-fulfilled-in-jesus-christ.

54 E. Schuyler English, *A Companion to the New Scofield Reference Bible* (New York: Oxford University Press, 1972), 26. Quoted in Boice, *Standing on the Rock*, 61. See https://www.2pc.org/media/is-the-bible-relevant-for-modern-day-people.

55 Dr. David Jeremiah, "What the Bible Says about Christ's Second Coming," davidjeremiah.blog, accessed 12/22/24, https://davidjeremiah.blog/the-second-coming-of-christ.

56 There are arguably more than fifty like these between Deuteronomy and Zechariah. Some include entire chapters—i.e., Isaiah 49, Ezekiel 37, 38, 39, and more. The entire list would be too long to reproduce here; however, following are some from

NOTES

Deuteronomy and Zechariah, the *first* and *last* ones of the Old Testament.

"And it will be, when all these things come upon you the blessing and the curse which I have set before you that you will consider in your heart, among all the nations where the Lord your God has banished you, and you will return to the Lord, your God, with all your heart and with all your soul, and you will listen to His voice according to all that I am commanding you this day you and your children, then, the Lord, your God, will bring back your exiles, and He will have mercy upon you. He will once again gather you from all the nations, where the Lord, your God, had dispersed you. Even if your exiles are at the end of the heavens, the Lord, your God, will gather you from there, and He will take you from there. And the Lord, your God, will bring you to the land which your forefathers possessed, and you will take possession of it, and He will do good to you, and He will make you more numerous than your forefathers" (Deuteronomy 30:1–5).

"This is what the Lord Almighty says: 'I will save my people from the countries of the east and the west. I will bring them back to live in Jerusalem; they will be my people, and I will be faithful and righteous to them as their God.... Just as you, Judah and Israel, have been a curse among the nations, so I will save you, and you will be a blessing. Do not be afraid, but let your hands be strong'" (Zechariah 7:7–8, 13, NIV).

57 As this book is being written in 2024–2025, Israel and Iran are still in the throes of a dangerously growing war. I, along with numerous other students of God's prophetic Word, believe this at least points to the very beginning of the ultimate fulfillment of the Ezekiel 38 prophecies. As a matter of historical fact, every map and globe prior to 1935 showed the area of what is now Iran, as Persia. The two words are synonymous.

58 The Old and New Testament predictions of an exponential growth of technology in the very last days is thoroughly proven and documented from biblical, historical, statistical, and tech sites filled with the scientific verifications of that fact. They are each referenced for your review and further study in my books *Yeshua Protocol* and *Eyes to See* (Defender Publishing). I have spoken about these facts on national and international television and radio broadcasts, prophecy conferences, biblical teaching seminars, and in my pulpit on numerous occasions (globally live-streamed).

59 All of these prophetic revelations, and many more, are outlined in detail, and referenced by scholarly attestations of every imaginable ilk within the theological and professional realms, in my bestselling books *Yeshua Protocol* (Defender Publishing, 2023) and *Eyes To See* (Defender Publishing, 2024).

60 I do not set dates for Yeshua's return, and never have. I am only stating the obvious. With so many already-fulfilled end-time prophecies, and being the first generation to see them colliding at once, how could His return not be relatively soon?

61 Michael Handelzalts, "In the Beginning: The Origins of the Hebrew Alphabet," *Haaretz*, 8/4/13, https://www.haaretz.com/jewish/.premium-why-hebrew-should-be-called-jewish-1.5316745.

62 *Hebrew Today. Who We Are:* "Hebrew Today is a reputable publication house, specializing in the highly professional and unique fusion of linguistics and journalism. Our products are developed and written by professionals in the fields of education, linguistics, and the Hebrew language.... Many teachers use our newspapers to teach

NOTES

Hebrew both in classes and in private lessons, because they find that we offer an easy and effective way to learn the Hebrew alphabet and grammar."

See: "Who We Are," HebrewToday.com, accessed 4/21/22, https://hebrewtoday.com/company-overview. Also see: https://hebrewtoday.com/content-our-approach-learning-hebrew.

63   Yigal Tzadka. "The Book of Hebrew Letters, HebrewToday.com. Accessed 5/3/22, https://hebrewtoday.com/product/the-book-of-hebrew-letters.

64   Alexander Poltorak, "History and Customs," Chabad.org. Accessed 4/12/22, https://www.chabad.org/library/article_cdo/aid/310887/jewish/History-and-Customs.htm.

65   **Mezuzah also spelled Mezuza** (Hebrew: 'doorpost'), plural Mezuzoth, Mezuzot, Mezuzahs, or Mezuzas, small folded or rolled parchment inscribed by a qualified calligraphist with scriptural verses (Deuteronomy 6:4–9, 11:13–21) to remind Jews of their obligations toward God. The parchment is placed in a metal, wooden, or glass case so that the word Shaddai ('Almighty') can usually be seen on the back of the parchment. After a special blessing is recited, the mezuzah is firmly fixed to the main doorpost of the home (to the right as one enters). It is a custom with some Jews to kiss the mezuzah as they pass it." *Encyclopedia Britannica*. "Mezuzah: Judaism." Accessed 4/8/22, https://www.britannica.com/topic/mezuzah.

66   *Hebrew Today.* "The Hebrew Alphabet—The Letter Shin (ש)." Accessed 4/8/22, https://hebrewtoday.com/alphabet/the-letter-shin-%D7%A9. Also see: https://en.wikipedia.org/wiki/Mezuzah.

67   "Who has performed this and carried it out, calling forth the generations from the beginning? I, the Lord—the first and the last—I am He. ...For I myself will help you, declares the Lord, your Redeemer, the Holy One of Israel" (Isaiah 41:4, 14, BSB).

"This is what the Lord says—Israel's King and Redeemer, the Lord Almighty: I am the first and I am the last; apart from me there is no God" (Isaiah 44:6).

"I am he; I am the first and I am the last. My own hand laid the foundations of the earth, and my right hand spread out the heavens; when I summon them, they all stand up together.... This is what the Lord says—your Redeemer, the Holy One of Israel: 'I am the Lord your God'" (Isaiah 48:12–13, 17).

68   See Romans 3:22–25; Titus 2:13–14. "Redeemer" is a synonym for "Savior" and "Jesus." See https://thesaurus.yourdictionary.com/redeemer.

69   Frank Moore Cross, Jr., "Yahweh and the God of the Patriarchs," *Harvard Theological Review*, Vol. 55, No. 4 (October 1962), pp. 225–259. Published by Cambridge University Press on behalf of Harvard Divinity School. https://www.cambridge.org/core/journals/harvard-theological-review/article/abs/yahweh-and-the-god-of-the-patriarchs/53A54441CCD6A43C5514077D8857CA07.

70   Studylight.org. "Ancient Hebrew Alphabet," (*Al-Aleph*). Accessed 6/23/18, https://www.studylight.org/lexicons/hebrew/ahl_alphabet.html.

71   "The Hebrew Alphabet," Britannica.com, accessed 5/2/22, https://www.britannica.com/topic/Hebrew-alphabet.

72   "Meaning 1. **Truth** 2. **sign** 3. life or death…also found pertaining to the '**Covenant between the Parts**,' when G-d caused Abraham to fall into a deep slumber and told him that his children would reside in a foreign land (the land of Egypt) for four hundred years and afterwards go out with great wealth and an outstretched arm"

NOTES

(emphasis added). Rabbi Aaron L. "Tav—The twenty-second letter of the Hebrew alphabet." Accessed 11/25/23, Raskinhttps://www.chabad.org/library/article_cdo/aid/137287/jewish/Tav.htm.

73   See Psalm 22:16–18; Zechariah 12:10; and Isaiah 53:5–6.
74   Michael Handelzalts, "In the Beginning: The Origins of the Hebrew Alphabet," *Haaretz*, 8/04/13, https://www.haaretz.com/jewish/.premium-why-hebrew-should-be-called-jewish-1.5316745.
75   Carl Gallups, with Zev Porat, *The Rabbi, the Secret Message, and the Identity of Messiah (The Aleph and the Tav)*, (Crane, MO: Defender Publishing, 2019), 45–49.
76   Ibid.
77   Reading the *aleph-tav* in English (left to right) requires the Hebrew letters to be represented as את. However, they are correctly rendered as תא when written in correct Hebrew styled script, reading right to left.
78   OT 853. "Eth," Biblehub.com, https://biblehub.com/hebrew/853.htm.
79   Depending upon the font used, there are about twelve thousand pages of the Old Testament in modern English translations. But the word *eth* is found almost eleven thousand times in the Old Testament, averaging being used about ten times for every single page of the Old Testament.
80   Zechariah 12:10.

   1) "Dr. Constable's Expository Notes," Studylight.org, https://www.studylight.org/commentary/zechariah/12-10.html.

   2) *Keil and Delitzsch Biblical Commentary on the Old Testament:* "The historical fulfilment of this prophecy commenced with the crucifixion of the Son of God, who had come in the flesh…. The fulfilment has continued with less striking results through the whole period of the Christian church, in conversions from among the Jews; and it will not terminate till the remnant of Israel shall turn as a people to Jesus the Messiah, whom its fathers crucified. On the other hand, those who continue obstinately in unbelief will see Him at last when He returns in the clouds of heaven, and shriek with despair (Rev. 1:7, Matt. 24:30)." https://biblehub.com/commentaries/zechariah/12-10.htm.

81   A Hebraic Explanation of the word *Eth*.

   Oxford Jewish Thought—Essays by Rabbi Eli Brackman: "An extra word in the Bible: finding the mystical in the simple," OxfordChabad.org, 8/27/09, https://www.oxfordchabad.org/templates/blog/post.asp?aid=708481&PostID=14343&p=1.

   Also see Harry Goldtmann, *Biblical Word Studies,* ""Eth (אֵת) and the three Crosses." Accessed 3/23/22, https://goldtmann.wordpress.com/2016/02/11/eth-%D7%90%D6%B5%D7%AA-and-the-three-crosses.

Harry Goldtmann is a chemical engineer with a master's degree in Lean Six Sigma, a born-again believer, and a student of Hebrew; https://goldtmann.wordpress.com/author/zachariah28/.

"I have learned the use of this word in Hebrew may have had more meaning in the primitive Hebrew language, and that over time as languages improved, the meaning lost its significance. Today, *eth*, is generally used to point out more definitely the object of a verb or preposition. Reading through the scholars on the linguistics of this word, they struggled to define a use. One states, "This word by degrees lost much of its primitive force, so that

NOTES

as set before nouns and pronouns already definite, it scarcely increases the demonstrative power. What I gathered from reading the scholars, basically, this is a Hebrew word that doesn't belong in the Bible today, for its use was in the primitive times.... I've been told every word of the Bible is precious and has a purpose. I have also been told how God can take the littlest of things and turn them into something big. Is there a message in this little word, which linguistically no longer applies? Was this a primitive method of placing emphasis on the noun, in today's world, putting a word in BOLD font?"

82 Ibid.

From the article: "We will therefore approach this question from an exegetical point of view first **followed by a mystical perspective**, which **ultimately proves most satisfactory** in our case.

"**This interpretation is found in a Jewish mystical text** of 1905 by Rabbi Sholom Dov Ber of Lubavitch (Sefer Hamamorim 5665 p. 15). Rabbi Sholom Dov Ber analyses **the word 'Eth'** in the context of love of G-d, **whereby he resolves the question posed at the beginning of this essay.**

"In **the simple interpretation of this word** it **emphasizes a deep mystical meditation** that all of existence is nullified before G-d's existence" (emphasis added).

83 This photograph of the Siloam Inscription is found on the website of Dr. David Graves, PhD, archeologist. Accessed 10/2024, https://biblicalarchaeologygraves.blogspot.com/2014/12/figure-19.html.

84 The picture of Jesus on the cross in this image is the property of Defender Publishing and was created by cover designer Jeffrey Mardis. Used with permission.

85 The magnified letters usually don't exist in most modern renditions of the Hebrew Scriptures, but they are found in ancient scrolls (i.e., the Dead Sea Scrolls) and even in modern Scripture collections used in some synagogues.

86 The First Five Books (Torah?)—Referred to by the Orthodox Jews as the *Torah*—however, the word *torah* literally means "teaching or instruction," and is often used in the Bible to mean the whole Word of God. Even Yeshua used the word *torah* in that sense. See Matthew 5:17.

From *Strong's Concordance:* "Word Origin: often used in the context of teaching or instruction. Often used in the New Testament to refer to the Law of Moses or the broader concept of law and commandments. In a broader sense, 'Torah' can refer to the entire body of Jewish religious teachings, including both written and oral traditions. It is often translated as 'law' but carries a deeper connotation of divine instruction and guidance for living a life pleasing to God" (emphasis added). See https://biblehub.com/hebrew/8451.htm.

87 *Hebrew Resources Admin:* "The Extra Large 'Bet' in the First Letter of the Hebrew Bible," 4/3/09, https://hebrewresources.com/the-extra-large-bet-in-the-first-letter-of-the-hebrew-bible.

88 Ibid.

89 Ibid.

90 "The letter RESH," Gabriel Levy. Accessed 11/24/23, https://gabrielelevy.com/pages/the-letter-resh.

91 "The letter ALEPH," Gabriel Levy. Accessed 11/24/23, https://gabrielelevy.com/pages/the-letter-aleph.

NOTES

92   *Your Jewish Journey*. "SHIN (HEBREW LETTER)." Accessed 11/24/23, https://bje.org.au/knowledge-centre/jewish-languages/hebrew-alphabet/shin.

93   Rabbi Aaron L. Raskin. "Yod—The Tenth Letter of the Hebrew Alphabet." Accessed 11/25/23, https://www.chabad.org/library/article_cdo/aid/137082/jewish/Yod.htm.

94   "Meaning 1. Truth 2. **sign** 3. life or death.... also found pertaining to the 'Covenant between the Parts,'12 when G-d caused Abraham to fall into a deep slumber and told him that his children would reside in a foreign land (the land of Egypt) for four hundred years and afterwards go out with great wealth and an outstretched arm."

     Rabbi Aaron L. "Tav—The Twenty-second Letter of the Hebrew Alphabet." Accessed 11/25/23, Raskinhttps://www.chabad.org/library/article_cdo/aid/137287/jewish/Tav.htm.

95   Most of these words are used multiple times in the Hebrew Old Testament. I have included only one example for each of the twelve words. I provide this information to prove that these are real (and in use) Hebrew words.

96   No. 8, *Ashuyah*. Pillar/Buttress: (Messianic Rabbi Zev Porat, who speaks Hebrew as his first language, has verified the following, in writing):

     1) *Brown-Driver-Briggs*: [אֲשֻׁיָה] (aleph-shin-yud-tav) noun feminine (support) **Buttress** (Arabic—*column, support*). https://biblehub.com/hebrew/803.htm. Used in Jeremiah 50 with **the plural suffix**.

     2) *Klein Dictionary*: אֲשֻׁיָה f.n. **pillar**; **foundation**, base (a hapax legomenon in the Bible, occurring Jer. 50:15 in the pl. אֲשֻׁיוֹתֶיהָ). [Prob. **a loan word** from Akka. *asītu* (= pillar), whence also Aram.–Syr. אֲשִׁיתָא (= pillar). Arab. *'āsiya* (= pillar) is an Aramaic loan word.] https://www.sefaria.org/Klein_Dictionary%2C_%D7%90%D6%B8%D7%A9%D6%B0%D7%81%D7%99%D6%B8%D7%94.1?lang=bi&lookup=hapax%20legomenon&with=Lexicon&lang2=en.

     For other Hebrew *hapax legomena*, and a deeper understanding of this phenomenon, see this excellent article: https://www.jewishencyclopedia.com/articles/7236-hapax-legomena#:~:text=Saadia's%20Treatise.-,%E2%80%94Biblical%20Data%3A,meaning%20from%20other%20occurring%20stems.

97   No. 12, *Ahsheet*. Messianic Rabbi Zev Porat, who speaks Hebrew as his first language, has verified the following in writing:

     "The word for 'I will cause, or I will put' in Genesis 3:15 is אָשִׁית (*aleph-shin-yud-tav*). The original verb form, (*to put*) according to Strong's Concordance is שִׁית (*shin-yud-tav*). There are **nine instances** of the use of אָשִׁיָה (to: put, bring about, make, etc.)." See https://biblehub.com/hebrew/ashit_7896.htm. Also see https://biblehub.com/hebrew/7896.htm, and https://biblehub.com/interlinear/genesis/3-15.htm.

98   In this book, I often use several English translations of the Bible when quoting Scripture. This is my attempt to present what I deem to be the best and most readable English word arrangement of a particular verse or passage. However, it must be noted that no matter which English translation is used, the Hebrew version was translated from the Greek arrangement of words—the original text of the New Testament. So the Hebrew images of the three *tav* crosses are always accurate, regardless of the English translation used.

99   Ibid.

100   The imagery of the three-cross *tav* is found in Yeshua's statement of John 10:18. You will see the image of it in the first chapter of part five.

NOTES

101 *Ashuyah*. **Pillar/Buttress:** (Messianic Rabbi Zev Porat, who speaks Hebrew as his first language, has verified the following in writing.)

Brown-Driver-Briggs Hebrew Lexicon (aleph-shin-yud-tav) noun, Feminine (support) Buttress (Arabic—*column, support*). https://biblehub.com/hebrew/803.htm. It is used in Jeremiah 50 with **the plural suffix.**

The NASB 1995, NASB 1997, Legacy Standard, Amplified Bible, and the International Standard Version (ISV) translations use the word "pillar" as the translation. See https://biblehub.com/jeremiah/50-15.htm.

102 "A **pillar** is any isolated, **vertical structure used in architecture** or construction to serve an aesthetic or structural purpose in a building. They are **often referred to as** a pier, **column**, or post and can be built from a wide array of materials, including wood, stone, or bricks. In architecture, it is **frequently used for aesthetic purposes** but always **has a stabilizing or structural purpose** in load-bearing and weight distribution. Pillars can stand alone or be grouped" (emphasis added).

See Logan Etheredge, "Pillars in Architecture | Definition, Purpose & Characteristics." Accessed 2/3/25, https://study.com/academy/lesson/pillars-architecture-overview-function.html.

103 Jeremiah 50:15, "Raise your battle cry against her on every side! She has given herself up, her pillars (Heb.—*ashuyah*) have fallen." (NASB 1995) See https://biblehub.com/jeremiah/50-15.htm.

104 This passage is repeated in 2 Chronicles 3:17.

105 *Ammud. Strong's Hebrew Lexicon* #5982.

"**Usage:** The Hebrew word ('ammud) primarily refers to a pillar or column. It is used in the Bible to describe physical structures that provide support or serve as a monument. Additionally, it is used metaphorically to describe divine presence, guidance, and protection, as seen in the pillar of cloud and fire that led the Israelites during the Exodus." https://biblehub.com/hebrew/5982.htm.

106 *Yakin. Hebrew Strong's* #3199.

"**Usage:** The name 'Jachin' means 'He will establish' or 'He establishes.' In the Bible, Jachin is primarily known as the name of one of the two bronze pillars erected at the entrance of Solomon's Temple in Jerusalem. The name signifies stability and the establishment of God's presence and covenant with His people." See https://biblehub.com/hebrew/3199.htm.

107 *Boaz. Hebrew Strong's* #1152.

"**Usage:** The name Boaz is traditionally understood to mean 'strength' or 'swift.' In the Bible, Boaz is a significant figure in the Book of Ruth, where he is depicted as…a kinsman-redeemer." See https://biblehub.com/hebrew/1162.htm.

108 1 Kings 7:21, *Benson Commentary*, Biblehub.com, https://biblehub.com/commentaries/1_kings/7-21.htm.

109 Wyatt Graham, executive director, Davenant Institute. "How Is Jesus the Temple?" November 11, 2019, https://www.wyattgraham.com/p/how-is-jesus-the-temple.

110 Jachin, the priest. https://biblehub.com/topical/naves/j/jachin--a_priest,_head_of_one_of_the_shifts_of_priests.htm.

111 Noel Vincent, "Concept of Goel: Kinsman-Redeemer," Apolgiaveritas.org, 10/12/2007, https://apologiaveritas.org/2007/12/10/concept-of-goel-kinsman-redeemer.

112 Yahweh as Redeemer. See Job 19:25; Psalm 19:14; Psalm 78:35; Isaiah 41:14; 43:14; 44:6, 24; 47:4; 48:17; 49:7,26; 54:5,8; 59:20; 60:16; 63:16; and Jeremiah 50:34.

NOTES

113 Edward L. Greenstein (2019), *Job: A New Translation*. (Yale University Press). p. xxvii. ISBN 9780300163766: "Determining the time and place of the book's composition is bound up with the nature of the book's language. The Hebrew prose of the frame tale, notwithstanding many classic features, shows that it was composed in the post-Babylonian era (after 540 BCE). The poetic core of the book is written in a highly literate and literary Hebrew, the eccentricities and occasional clumsiness of which suggest that Hebrew was a learned and not native language of the poet. The numerous words and grammatical shadings of Aramaic spread throughout the mainly Hebrew text of Job make a setting in the Persian era (approximately 540-330) fairly certain, for it was only in that period that Aramaic became a major language throughout the Levant. The poet depends on an audience that will pick up on subtle signs of Aramaic." See https://books.google.com/books?id=W8KmDwAAQBAJ&pg=PR27#v=onepage&q&f=false.

Also see GOOGLE AI. When the search parameter is "Is the book of Job one of the oldest books in the world?" ANSWER: "Yes, the Book of Job is considered one of the oldest books in the world, belonging to the Hebrew Bible and often dated to the Persian period (between 540–330 BCE)."

114 See these four references for verification of the reliability of the Hebrew New Testament version used in this work.

1) https://www.tbsbibles.org/page/TheBiblicalTranslationPrinciplesoftheNewHebrewTranslation.

2) https://www.scribd.com/document/216172183/Hebrew-New-Testament-Franz-Delitzsch.

3) https://ffoz.org/messiah/articles/a-1888-review-of-delitzschs-hebrew-new-testament.

4) https://www.goodreads.com/book/show/7465318-the-hebrew-new-testament-of-the-british-and-foreign-bible-society.

115 Franz Julius Delitzsch: "As a young adult Franz Delitzsch commenced his studies of language, literature and philosophy and eventually completed a doctorate in philosophy. Influenced by missionaries of the London Society for the Propagation of the Gospel to the Jews, and especially by the Jewish Christian Johann Peter Goldberg, he came to a living faith in Jesus Christ. From then on he turned to theology. He also began to intercede for Jews and supported them, and through Franz's ministry, his godfather Levy Hirsch came eventually to the conclusion that Jesus is the Messiah.

"Apart from theology Franz did research in the entire body of Jewish-religious literature, accompanied by studies of Hebrew, Aramaic and Arabic, plus Oriental studies. **Franz's outstanding literary achievement is the Berit HaHadashah, the translation of the New Testament into the Hebrew language**, edited in 1877. During more than fifty-one years of labor he poured his efforts into this work." https://dep-israel.nl/wp-content/uploads/2020/10/3.-Biografie-Franz-Delitzsch.pdf. (See also https://dep-israel.nl/introduction).

116 *Keil & Delitzsch Old Testament Commentary:* "**Karl Keil (1807–1888) and Franz Delitzsch (1813–1890)** stand as towering figures in the world of biblical scholarship, particularly renowned for their collaborative work on the **Old Testament Commentary**, a seminal series that has left a lasting impact on Christian theology

NOTES

and biblical exegesis. Their partnership bridged the gap between the rigorous academic analysis of Scripture and the spiritual nourishment sought by believers, blending scholarly depth with a profound respect for the biblical text's divine inspiration." https://www.studylight.org/commentaries/eng/kdo.html.

117 *Ellicott's Commentary for English Readers:* "[Groans and Travail] In view of the physical evil and misery prevalent in the world, the Apostle attributes a human consciousness of pain to the rest of creation. It groans and travails *together*.... The idea of travailing, as in childbirth, has reference to the future prospect of joyful delivery. (Comp. John 16:21.)

"Until now.—This consciousness of pain and imperfection has been continuous and unbroken (nor will it cease until an end is put to it by the Coming of Christ.)." (Brackets added; parentheses in original). https://biblehub.com/commentaries/romans/8-22.htm.

118 Romans 8. "Barclay's Daily Study Bible Commentary," https://www.studylight.org/commentary/romans/8-22.html.

119 Romans 8. "Kelly Commentary on Books of the Bible," https://www.studylight.org/commentary/romans/8-22.html.

120 In the *Delitzsch Hebrew Translation of the New Testament*, this verse is listed as Romans 8:21. But in our modern translations, it is marked as 8:22. Therefore, I reference it in this image as 8:22.

121 *Keil and Delitzsch Biblical Commentary on the Old Testament:* "If then the promise culminates in Christ, the fact that the victory over the serpent is promised to the posterity of the woman, not of the man, acquires this deeper significance, that as it was through the woman that the craft of the devil brought sin and death into the world, so it is also through the woman that the grace of God will give to the fallen human race the conqueror of sin, of death, and of the devil. And even if the words had reference first of all to the fact that the woman had been led astray by the serpent, yet in the fact that the destroyer of the serpent was born of a woman (without a human father) they were fulfilled in a way which showed that the promise must have proceeded from that Being, who secured its fulfilment not only in its essential force, but even in its apparently casual form." https://biblehub.com/commentaries/genesis/3-15.htm.

122 The Genesis 3:15 prophecy:

1) *Coffman's Commentaries on the Bible:* "And I will put enmity between thee and the woman, and between thy seed and her seed: he shall bruise thy head, and thou shalt bruise his heel."

"Many scholars cannot recognize this as the great Protoevangelium of the O.T., which of course, it surely is. Their blindness is due to their failure to recognize that the key to understanding the O.T. is Jesus Christ (2 Corinthians 3:15–16). The terminology of this verse is such that it cannot apply to anything in heaven or upon earth except the long spiritual conflict between Christ and Satan." https://www.studylight.org/commentary/genesis/3-15.html.

2) Elliott E. Johnson: "When Christ died on the cross and rose from the dead, the details of the climax were filled in and specified, but the [Genesis 3:15] text does not demand to be reinterpreted. Nor does it demand interpretation in a way not

NOTES

suggested in context." [Elliott E. Johnson, "Premillennialism Introduced: Hermeneutics," in *A Case for Premillennialism: A New Consensus*, p. 22. See also Darrell L. Bock, "Interpreting the Bible—How Texts Speak to Us," in *Progressive Dispensationalism*, p. 81; and Wenham, pp. 80–81.]

3) *Spurgeon's Verse Expositions of the Bible:* "This is the first gospel sermon that was ever delivered upon the surface of this earth. It was memorable discourse indeed, with Jehovah himself for the preacher, and the whole human race and the prince of darkness for the audience. It must be worthy of our heartiest attention. Is it not remarkable that this great gospel promise should have been delivered so soon after the transgression? As yet no sentence had been pronounced upon either of the two human offenders, but the promise was given under the form of a sentence pronounced upon the serpent [Satan—see Revelation 12]. https://www.studylight.org/commentary/genesis/3-15.html.

123 It is true that not *every passage* in the Bible that has any relationship to Golgotha has precisely three *tavs* (the picture of Golgotha). However, a significant number do—and those are our primary focus in this book. It appears that the coded message of these Golgotha images follow the central storyline of the entire Word of God. For those of us who observe this picture-format storyline, it becomes all too obvious that this unfolding message was placed there by the Holy Spirit of Yahweh. A reasonable person would have to believe that the statistical chances of this phenomenon occurring by mere happenstance is utterly impossible.

124 To have the middle *tav* appear directly under the *aleph-tav* is certainly dramatic, but the point is that practically every single time the *tav* is not found under an *aleph-tav* arrangement, it is indeed found in concert with other letters around that middle *tav*. There we discover that *tav* encased within a Hebrew ideographic meaning formed by the letters the *tav* is attached to; that will also make it clear that the "one in the middle" is Yeshua! I will actually give an example of this phenomenon in a subsequent chapter. The endnote at that example will demonstrate other similar letter arrangements that punctuate the truth I've just laid out in this endnote.

125 I have documented almost seventy places wherein the *aleph-tav* is the middle *tav* cross in the Golgotha image made by three Paleo-Hebrew crosses. All are connected to surface-text Golgotha verses and passages. All of the passages listed below are illustrated in this book.

Old Testament

The first verse: "In the beginning God created the Heavens and the earth" (Genesis 1:1; this is the first image of Golgotha in the Bible).

God's prophecy of the coming male child that will destroy Satan's kingdom: Genesis 3:15.

Abraham's sacrifice of Isaac: Genesis 22:2; Genesis 22:4–5; Genesis 22:6; Genesis 22:9

The Exodus Passover: Exodus 12:6; Exodus 12:13

Job's vision: Job 19:25–27

The Temple pillars: 1 Kings 7:21

The Day of Atonement ritual with the high priest and the scapegoat: Leviticus 16:6; Leviticus 16:7; Leviticus 16:9–10; Leviticus 16:30; Leviticus 16:33

NOTES

Leviticus 16:34: The first words of this entire verse establishes Yom Kippur as an everlasting covenant. In those words are three crosses; the *aleph-tav* presents in the middle.

Jesus' words on the cross: Rather than the *aleph-tav* symbol, Yeshua's *actual name* is in it, right next to the *tav* in the middle—Psalm 22:1

The Shepherd's Psalm—The Valley of Death: Psalm 23:4

More prophecies of Messiah's coming: Isaiah 52:10 (rather than the *aleph-tav* symbol, Yeshua's *actual name* is in it, right next to the Tav in the middle); Isaiah 53:9; Zechariah 9:9

New Testament

Yeshua is our Great High Priest of Leviticus 16: Hebrews 4:15–16; Hebrews 9:6; Hebrews 9:28; Hebrews 11:19

Golgotha/resurrection: Matthew 21:5; Matthew 26:35; Matthew 26:50; Matthew 26:57; Matthew 27:11; Matthew 27:15–16; Matthew 27:27; Matthew 27:35–36; Matthew 27:43–44; Mark 14:30; Mark 14:47; Luke 22:42; Luke 23:33; Luke 23:33; Romans 8:32; Galatians 4:4

Yeshua's last Passover meal: John 13:27; John 13:30; John 14:3; John 14:5; John 14:11–12

More Golgotha details: John 3:35; John 8:56–57; John 18:4; John 19:1–3; John 19:15; John 19:16; John 19:26; John 20:5; Hebrews 13:12–13 (The image is found within these precise words: "Jesus also suffered outside the gate in order to sanctify the people through his own blood. Therefore let us go to Him outside the camp, bearing the disgrace He bore.")

Direct ties to Genesis 1:1 and *bereshith*: John 1:1–2; John 1:14; Luke 24:32; Colossians 1:20

The glory of Golgotha and the coming Kingdom: Revelation 1:7; Revelation 4:11; Revelation 12:11; Revelation 14:18; Revelation 15:4; Revelation 22:3–4; Revelation 22:13–14; Revelation 22:19 (the last *tav* image of Golgotha in the Bible)

126 5254. *Nasah.* "Biblehub.com—Concordance, dictionaries, and lexicons," Biblehub.com, https://biblehub.com/hebrew/5254.htm.

127 "The *walkabout* is a *spiritual journey* that is meant to challenge young people to develop the skills and knowledge needed to become a responsible adult within their unique culture." Walkabout.org. Accessed 10/4/23, https://walkabout.org/history.

128 "It was revealed to [the prophets] that they were serving not themselves but you, in the things that have now been announced to you through those who preached the good news to you by the Holy Spirit sent from heaven, **things into which angels long to look.**" (1 Peter 1:12, emphasis added)

Question: Did the angels (Heaven's host) actually weep at the crucifixion of Jesus?

From an article at Stack Exchange: "There is no biblical basis to answer this question in any direction pro or con. But there may be a few small glimmers of light on this subject that come from the Scriptures....

"We see the Angels administering to the needs of Jesus on at least two separate occasions during his earthly ministry—His temptation in the wilderness and His passion in the Garden of Gethsemane (Matthew 4, Luke 22)....

"Now if the Angels appeared to Jesus on the eve of his Passion in order to

NOTES

strengthen him, it would likewise make sense that during his Crucifixion on the Cross, the Heavenly Hosts were supporting the second person of the Sacred Trinity in his human nature through their prayer and admiration of the Divine Sacrifice that being unfolded. This is not the time for rejoicing, but of awe and reverence. Although Angels are pure spirit, traditional art have them 'weeping' at the Crucifixion of Jesus. In the Crucifixion, angels are seen lamenting, wringing their hands, averting or hiding their faces.

"It makes the most logical sense that during the Most Holy Passion of Our Lord Jesus Christ there was in heaven nothing but silence and reverence at that moment.

"There is a time for everything and the time for heaven and earth to rejoice would have been first felt is at the Resurrection of Christ. It is not wholly known if the Angels fully knew how the redemption of mankind was going to be transpired here below! God has secrets." https://christianity.stackexchange.com/questions/74759/was-there-silence-in-heaven-when-our-lord-and-saviour-was-crucified.

129 This detail will be described fully in the closing chapters of this book.

130 John 8:56. *Ellicott's Commentary for English Readers*, Biblehub.com, https://biblehub.com/commentaries/john/8-56.htm.

131 YRM.org. "The Sixth Letter, Waw or Vav?," 7/5/22, https://yrm.org/the-sixth-letter-waw-or-vav.

132 Ideographic meanings of the *waw* or *vav*. Hebrew Today. "The Letter Vav (ו) In the Hebrew Alphabet." Accessed 3/12/22, Hebrewtoday.com, https://hebrewtoday.com/alphabet/the-letter-vav-%D7%95/.

133 These kinds of imageries, evoked by the precise arrangement of certain Hebrew letters around the middle *tav*, are almost always present. Like the illustration we are examining now, there are also others that are *exactly* like it.

Still other Golgotha images have the *shin* ("God Almighty") next to the *tav*. That meaning would be: "This is God Almighty (in the person of Yeshua) on the covenant/cross." Others have the *waw* (nails/spear) attached to the *tav*. The meaning in that case is obvious.

Still others have the *tav* enclosed within the Hebrew letters *yud* and *heh*. That idiographic meaning would therefore be: "Behold the outstretched arms/hands upon the cross."

Still others have the *tav* next to the *ayin*. The ideographic meaning of that combination would be: "In this *covenant/cross* the world will see the salvation of the Lord."

On and on the combinations present themselves. To have the middle *tav* appear directly under the *aleph-tav* is certainly dramatic, but practically every single time the *tav* is not under an *aleph-tav* arrangement, it is indeed found in concert with other letters whose ideographic meanings still make it clear that the "one in the middle" is Yeshua! However, because of space limitations, I don't examine each of the occurrences as presented in the Golgotha *tav* images.

134 See Exodus 12 for the first month of the new year falling on Passover—the month of Nisan.

135 Compound prophecy:

The biblical principle of *compound prophecy* interpretation is well-known among

NOTES

biblical scholars and serious students of God's Word. A compound prophecy starts off talking about the prophet's own days, but then, almost on a dime, morphs into a prophecy of Jesus Christ, or Satan, or even the end time.

Just a few examples of some compound prophecies are Psalm 22, Isaiah 14, and Ezekiel 28. One of the most certain instances of a compound prophecy is found in Habakkuk 1. Then, the next few verses in Habakkuk 2 declare that the words of Habakkuk 1 have a double meaning, one concerning the end times. There are many other examples as well. In most cases however, they're not as easy to discern as the one in Habakkuk. Therefore, one has to be intimately familiar with this style of prophetic writing, or else the intended meaning of it can quickly be lost on the researcher.

See Dr. Lehman Strauss, "Bible Prophecy (A Principle of Prophetic Interpretation; Isaiah's Prophecies; Micah's Prophecies)," Bible.org. Accessed 11/4/17. https://bible.org/article/bible-prophecy.

Example statement of Dr. Strauss on the compound nature of Genesis 3:15: "What we now desire to emphasize in the Edenic prophecy in Genesis 3:15.... We have already stated that this verse contains a compound prophecy combining both the first and second appearances of Christ on earth."

136 "Son of God, "righteous man, innocent man, etc.": See Poole on 'Matthew 27:51' and following verses to Matthew 27:56. This passage noted by Matthew and Mark; only they say he said, *Truly this was the Son of God.* Luke saith that he said, *Certainly this was a righteous man.* Possibly the sense is the same, and the centurion by *the Son of God* did not mean the Son of God by eternal generation, but one highly favored of God, a righteous than, and very dear to God, and highly beloved of him; for it must be by a very extraordinary revelation and impression if he, had so early a faith in Christ as God blessed for ever. I think Mr. Calvin, on **Matthew 26:54**, expounds it well. The centurion determined that Christ was no ordinary person, but one stirred up by and sent of God. It is observable, that Christ had a testimony from all orders of men almost, except the scribes, and priests, and Pharisees. Pontius Pilate and Herod declared him innocent. Pilate's wife acknowledged him a righteous person. The thief on the cross testified he had *done nothing amiss.* Judas the traitor confessed he had *betrayed innocent blood.* The centurion [claimed] him to be no ordinary man, but *a righteous man, the Son of God.* The multitude always [claimed] him [to be righteous, or the Son of God]. https://biblehub.com/commentaries/luke/23-47.htm.

137 Following are the words of mocking recorded in Matthew 27:43–44. "He trusts in God; let God deliver him now, if he desires him. For he said, 'I am the Son of God. And the robbers who were crucified with him also reviled him in the same way.'" These two verses display the three *tav* crosses, and the *aleph-tav* is in the middle! See http://www.sarshalom.us/resources/scripture/asv/html/matthew.html#27.

138 John 19:19. *MacLaren's Expositions,* Biblehub.com, https://biblehub.com/commentaries/john/19-19.htm: "This title is recorded by all four Evangelists, in words varying in form but alike in substance. It strikes them all as significant that, meaning **only to fling a jeer at his unruly subjects,** Pilate should have written it, and proclaimed this Nazarene visionary to be He for whom Israel had longed through weary ages."

NOTES

139 Mark 15:23. Accessed 11/12/24, http://www.sarshalom.us/resources/scripture/asv/html/mark.html#15.

140 Mark 15:24–25. Accessed 11/12/24, http://www.sarshalom.us/resources/scripture/asv/html/mark.html#15.

141 Mark 15:26. Accessed 11/12/24, http://www.sarshalom.us/resources/scripture/asv/html/mark.html#15.

142 Matthew 27:38–39. Accessed 11/12/24, http://www.sarshalom.us/resources/scripture/asv/html/matthew.html#27.

143 For confirmation, see Psalm 22 and the following verses: 7–8, 12–13, 16, and 18.

144 These four verses complete one thought. They include the casting of lots and the crowd that mocked Him with specific words from Psalm 22. The first verse contains no *tav* at all. The next three contain one *tav* each. This complete thought reflects Psalm 22—containing precisely three *tavs*—the picture of Golgotha!

Luke 23:34–37. Accessed 11/12/24, http://www.sarshalom.us/resources/scripture/asv/html/luke.html#23.

145 The Forbidden Chapter (a well-documented and historical fact) :1) Jewish Voice, "Forbidden Chapter in the Tanakh," (Isaiah 53), 6/2/16, https://www.jewishvoice.org/read/blog/forbidden-chapter-of-the-tanakh.

2) Rabbi Frydland has also written about Isaiah 53 in an article titled, "The Rabbis' Dilemma: A Look at Isaiah 53." Following are a couple of pertinent excerpts: "The subject was never discussed in my pre-war-Poland Hebrew school. In the rabbinical training I had received, the fifty-third chapter of the book of Isaiah had been continually avoided in favor of other, 'weightier' matters to be learned. Yet, when I first read this passage, my mind was filled with questions.... Who is this chapter speaking about? The words are clear—the passage tells of an outstanding Servant of the Lord whose visage is marred and is afflicted and stricken.... Rashi (Rabbi Shlomo Itzchaki, 1040–1105) and some of the later rabbis, though, interpreted the passage as referring to Israel. They knew that the older interpretations referred it to Messiah.... This verse presented an insurmountable difficulty to those who interpreted this passage as referring to Israel." (emphasis added)

Rabbi Rachmiel Frydland, "The Rabbis' Dilemma: A Look at Isaiah 53," Jews for Jesus. Accessed 6/12/18, https://jewsforjesus.org/publications/issues/issues-v02-n05/the-rabbis-dilemma-a-look-at-isaiah-53/.

3) Also see the book *The Rabbi, the Secret Message, and the Identity of Messiah* by Carl Gallups and Zev Porat (Defender Publishing). That book catalogues a plethora of scholarly evidence, as well as personal testimony from renowned and former Orthodox Jewish people who also affirm that that Isaiah 53 is the "forbidden chapter" and not read in synagogue services.

146 As an important side note, almost every time we see the word "salvation" in English translations of the Old Testament, we're looking at the Hebrew word *yeshua*. I've addressed this in depth in several previous books.

147 *Yod* is the Aramaic pronunciation. *Yud* is the Hebrew pronunciation. Most Israelis pronounce the letter as *yud*. https://hebrewtoday.com/alphabet/the-letter-yud-%D7%99/.

148 Hebrew for Christians. "Yod" represents the arm, or hand. See https://www.hebrew4christians.com/Grammar/Unit_One/Aleph-Bet/Yod/yod.html.

NOTES

Chabad.org, "The Yud," (The Meaning), the hand, a Jew, arm. Accessed 4/3/22, https://www.chabad.org/library/article_cdo/aid/137082/jewish/Yod.htm.

149 This Hebrew letter ו (*waw/vav*) is the sixth letter in the Hebrew *aleph-bet*, and is pronounced differently in various dialects of Hebrew. Modern Hebrew uses a *vav* ("v") for the sixth letter of its alphabet, but in ancient days this wasn't the case. Originally it had a "w" (double "u") sound. See https://yrm.org/the-sixth-letter-waw-or-va.

150 The *waw/vav* represents a hook, tent peg (spike), nail, or spear. See https://hebrewtoday.com/alphabet/the-letter-vav-%D7%95.

151 Rabbi Aaron L. Raskin. "Ayin: The sixteenth letter of the Hebrew alphabet," Chabad.org. Accessed 4/12/22, https://www.chabad.org/library/article_cdo/aid/137088/jewish/Ayen.htm.

152 There are no *tavs* in verse 13, but that verse is connected to the thought of the three verses put together. There are two *tavs* in verse 14 and one in verse 15. Three verses= one thought/message=three crosses.

For verification, see https://biblehub.com/interlinear/isaiah/52-13.htm, https://biblehub.com/interlinear/isaiah/52-14.htm, https://biblehub.com/interlinear/isaiah/52-15.htm.

153 There is one *tav* in verse 2, associated with the word "form/appearance." There are two *tavs* in verse 3, associated with the words "hid and sorrow." There are no *tavs* in verse 4, but that verse completes the running thought. For verification, see https://biblehub.com/interlinear/isaiah/53-2.htm, https://biblehub.com/interlinear/isaiah/53-3.htm, and https://biblehub.com/interlinear/isaiah/53-4.htm.

154 There are two *tavs* in verse 5, associated with the words "for our iniquities" and "by his stripes." There is one *tav* in verse 6, associated with the word the second "gone astray." For verification, see https://biblehub.com/interlinear/isaiah/53-5.htm and https://biblehub.com/interlinear/isaiah/53-6.htm.

155 To see a user-friendly, letter-by-letter display of the ideographic meanings of the ancient Hebrew letters, see https://www.ancient-hebrew.org/learn/learn-the-ancient-pictographic-hebrew-script.htm.

The Hebrew letter *heh* means "behold," or "look at this." See https://www.chabad.org/library/article_cdo/aid/137077/jewish/Heh.htm.

The Hebrew letter *waw* (as referenced in an earlier chapter) means "the nails" or "spear."

The Hebrew letter *yud* (as referenced in an earlier chapter) means "hand" or "arm(s)."

This amazing truth is detailed through scholarly references as well as vivid imagery within the pages of my books *Yeshua Protocol* and *The Rabbi, The Secret Message, and the Identity of Messiah* (Defender Publishing). The *Rabbi* book was co-authored by Messianic Rabbi Zev Porat of Tel Aviv, Israel. His website is www.messiahofisraelministries.com.

156 Andrew Case, "Does God Want Us to Use His Divine Name?" Text and Canon Institute, Phoenix Seminary, accessed 12/1/24, https://textandcanon.org/does-god-want-us-to-use-his-divine-name-part-1.

157 There are *two tavs* in verse 7 and one in verse 8. For verification, see https://biblehub.com/interlinear/isaiah/53-7.htm, and https://biblehub.com/interlinear/isaiah/53-8.htm.

NOTES

158 *Jamieson-Fausset-Brown Bible Commentary* "Rather, 'His grave was appointed,' or 'they appointed Him His grave' [Hengstenberg]; that is, they intended (by crucifying Him with two thieves, Mt 27:38) that He should have His grave 'with the wicked.' Compare Joh 19:31, the denial of honorable burial being accounted a great ignominy (see on [854]Isa 14:19; Jer 26:23). (Mt 27:57; Mrk 15:43-46; Joh 19:39, 40); two rich men honored Him at His death, Joseph of Arimathea, and Nicodemus." https://biblehub.com/commentaries/isaiah/53-9.htm.

159 Isaiah 53:10–11. "Pulpit Commentary," biblehub.com, https://biblehub.com/commentaries/isaiah/53-11.htm.

160 One *tav* in verse 10, and two *tavs* in verse 11. For verification, see https://biblehub.com/interlinear/isaiah/53-10.htm and https://biblehub.com/interlinear/isaiah/53-11.htm.

161 "Your Heart Will Live Forever":

Strong's Lexicon: "the heart"—Hebrew—Lebab: "Cultural and Historical Background: In ancient Hebrew culture, the heart was considered the **seat of life and the core of one's being**." https://biblehub.com/hebrew/3824.htm.

162 1) *Cambridge Bible for Schools and Colleges:* "If the primary and **immediate reference is to a sacrificial feast**, it is clear that **the words reach** far beyond the outward rite **to the spiritual communion of which it was the symbol**; while the Christian reader cannot but see the counterpart and **fulfilment** of the words in **the Holy Eucharist** [the Lord's Supper]." (Emphasis added) https://biblehub.com/commentaries/psalms/22-26.htm.

2) *Pulpit Commentary:* "Psalm 22:26—The meek shall eat and be satisfied. In the Eucharistic feasts [The Lord's Supper] of Christ's kingdom it is "the meek" especially who shall **eat, and be satisfied**, feeling that they have all their souls long for—a full banquet, of the very crumbs of which they are not worthy. They shall praise the Lord that seek him. **The service shall be emphatically one of praise.** Your heart shall live forever. **The result shall be life for evermore**; for the **body and blood** of the Lord Jesus Christ, worthily received, preserve men's bodies and souls to everlasting life." (Emphasis added) https://biblehub.com/commentaries/psalms/22-26.htm.

163 *MacLaren's Expositions on the Scripture* (Psalm 22:26), https://biblehub.com/commentaries/psalms/22-26.htm.

164 Here again is another example of a beautiful ideographic message (other than the *aleph-tav*) that characterizes the *tav* in the middle. The word in which the middle *tav* is located is the Hebrew word that translates to "and drink." That Hebrew word is spelled *waw, heh, shin, tav, heh* (right to left in Hebrew). The ideographic meaning of it could be iterated as "Behold the nail/spear and behold God Almighty on the cross of the covenant!"

165 Got Questions, "What does it mean that Jesus is the son of David?" gotquestions.org. Accessed 10/21/24, https://www.gotquestions.org/Jesus-son-of-David.html.

166 Jesus enters Jerusalem on Nisan 10.

1) Karen Engle, "Palm Sunday, and Why the 'Date' Is So Significant," Logos.com, 3/3/23, https://www.logos.com/grow/palm-sunday-and-why-the-date-is-so-significant.

2) Indiana District, Lutheran Church-Missouri Synod. "A Lamb Riding a Donkey." Accessed 10/12/24, https://in.lcms.org/a-lamb-riding-a-donkey.

NOTES

167 Ibid.
168 I highly recommend Messianic Rabbi Zev Porat's book *Blood Alliance* (Defender Publishing). It goes into great and relevant detail about the biblical concept of threshold covenants/blood covenant. Zev's website is www.messiahofisraelministries.com.
169 This illustration was made from joining two images designed by Jeffrey Mardis, Defender Publishing's cover designer. The images are owned by Defender Publishing and are used here with permission.
170 "In antiquity, crucifixion was considered one of the most brutal and shameful modes of death. Probably originating with the Assyrians and Babylonians, it was used systematically by the Persians in the 6th century BC. Alexander the Great brought it from there to the eastern Mediterranean countries in the 4th century BC, and the Phoenicians introduced it to Rome in the 3rd century BC. It was virtually never used in pre-Hellenic Greece. The Romans perfected crucifixion for 500 years until it was abolished by Constantine I in the 4th century AD."
L. Cilliers Retief, "The History and Pathology of Crucifixion," PubMed, NIH, 12/9/03, https://pubmed.ncbi.nlm.nih.gov/14750495.
171 Between Malachi and the first New Testament book of Matthew, there are a little more than four hundred years of biblical history.
Drew Haninger, "What Happened Between the Old and New Testament?" OliveTree.com. Accessed 2/1/25, https://staging-blog.olivetree.com/what-happened-between-old-and-new-testament.
172 Malachi 3:1. *Pulpit Commentary*, Biblehub.com, https://biblehub.com/commentaries/malachi/3-1.htm.
173 Malachi 3:1. *Barnes' Notes on the Bible*, Biblehub.com, https://biblehub.com/commentaries/malachi/3-1.htm.
174 The Tav: "Meaning 1. **Truth** 2. **sign** 3. **life or death**.... also found pertaining to the '**Covenant** between the Parts,' when G-d caused Abraham to fall into a deep slumber and told him that his children would reside in a foreign land (the land of Egypt) for four hundred years and afterwards go out with great wealth and an outstretched arm." (emphasis added)
Rabbi Aaron L. "Tav–The Twenty-second Letter of the Hebrew Alphabet." Accessed 11/25/23, Raskinhttps://www.chabad.org/library/article_cdo/aid/137287/jewish/Tav.htm.
175 Read Matthew 21–26 for a vivid account of this truth.
176 Following is only an abbreviated list of New Testament passages that speak of Exodus 12 Passover being connected to Yeshua, Golgotha, the early Church, the centrality of the gospel message, etc.: Luke 22:19–20; 1 Peter 1:19; John 19:33, 36; Matthew 26:26; Mark 14:22; Luke 22:19–20, 1 Corinthians 5:7–8.
177 See http://sarshalom.us/resources/scripture/asv/html/mark.html#14.
178 See http://sarshalom.us/resources/scripture/asv/html/matthew.html#21.
179 See http://sarshalom.us/resources/scripture/asv/html/matthew.html#26.
180 Ibid.
181 Ibid.
182 Ibid.
183 Ibid.

NOTES

184 See http://sarshalom.us/resources/scripture/asv/html/mark.html#14.
185 See http://sarshalom.us/resources/scripture/asv/html/john.html#13.
186 Ibid.
187 See http://sarshalom.us/resources/scripture/asv/html/luke.html#22.
188 See http://sarshalom.us/resources/scripture/asv/html/john.html#18.
189 Ibid.
190 Ibid.
191 See http://sarshalom.us/resources/scripture/asv/html/matthew.html#26.
192 See http://sarshalom.us/resources/scripture/asv/html/luke.html#22.
193 See http://sarshalom.us/resources/scripture/asv/html/matthew.html#26.
194 See http://sarshalom.us/resources/scripture/asv/html/mark.html#14.
195 Ibid.
196 Ibid.
197 See http://sarshalom.us/resources/scripture/asv/html/matthew.html#26.
198 Ibid.
199 Ibid.
200 See http://sarshalom.us/resources/scripture/asv/html/matthew.html#27.
201 Ibid.
202 Ibid.
203 See http://sarshalom.us/resources/scripture/asv/html/mark.html#14.
204 See http://sarshalom.us/resources/scripture/asv/html/matthew.html#27.
205 See http://sarshalom.us/resources/scripture/asv/html/john.html#19.
206 See http://sarshalom.us/resources/scripture/asv/html/luke.html#23.
207 See http://sarshalom.us/resources/scripture/asv/html/matthew.html#27.
208 Ibid.
209 See http://sarshalom.us/resources/scripture/asv/html/john.html#19.
210 See http://sarshalom.us/resources/scripture/asv/html/matthew.html#27.
211 Ibid.
212 See http://sarshalom.us/resources/scripture/asv/html/john.html#19.
213 Ibid.
214 See http://sarshalom.us/resources/scripture/asv/html/mark.html#16.
215 Ibid.
216 Ibid.
217 See http://sarshalom.us/resources/scripture/asv/html/john.html#20.
218 Ibid.
219 Ibid.
220 Rehearsal: The Hebrew word *miqra* is associated with all seven feasts of the Lord, and also with the celebration of the weekly Sabbath (Leviticus 23). That word *miqra* is often translated into English versions as "convocation, assembly, or public gathering." But it is also used to speak of a *rehearsal*.

Not only was there the idea of meeting together, but also that these feasts, and even the Sabbath itself, were mere *rehearsals* of something greater that was to come—namely, *Yeshua HaMashiach*. He is the fulfillment of all the *miqras!*

Strong's Exhaustive Concordance: "From qara'; **something called out**, i.e. A public meeting; **also a rehearsal**—assembly, calling, convocation, reading." See https://biblehub.com/hebrew/4744.htm.

NOTES

221 1) The following comes from *Matthew Henry's Commentary* entry on Leviticus 16:15–34: "Here are typified the two great gospel privileges, of the remission of sin, and access to God, both of which we owe to our Lord Jesus. Christ is both the Maker and the Matter of the atonement; for he is the Priest, the High Priest, that makes reconciliation for the sins of the people. And as Christ is the High Priest, so he is the Sacrifice with which atonement is made; for he is all in all in our reconciliation to God.

"Thus he was figured by the two goats [of Leviticus 16]. The slain goat was a type of Christ dying for our sins; the scape-goat a type of Christ rising again for our justification. The atonement is said to be completed by putting the sins of Israel upon the head of the goat, which was sent away into a wilderness, a land not inhabited; and the sending away of the goat represented the free and full remission of their sins. He shall bear upon him all their iniquities.

"Thus Christ, the Lamb of God, takes away the sin of the world, by taking it upon himself, John 1:29. The entrance into heaven, which Christ made for us, was typified by the high priest's entrance into the most holy place. (See Hebrews 9:7)

"The high priest was to come out again; but our Lord Jesus ever lives, making intercession, and always appears in the presence of God for us.

"Here are typified the two great gospel duties of faith and repentance. By faith we put our hands upon the head of the offering; relying on Christ as the Lord our Righteousness, pleading his satisfaction, as that which alone is able to atone for our sins, and procure us a pardon. By repentance we afflict our souls; not only fasting for a time from the delights of the body, but inwardly sorrowing for sin, and living a life of self-denial, assuring ourselves, that if we confess our sins, God is faithful and just to forgive us our sins, and to cleanse us from all unrighteousness.

"By the atonement we obtain rest for our souls, and all the glorious liberties of the children of God. Sinner, get the blood of Christ effectually applied to thy soul, or else thou canst never look God in the face with any comfort or acceptance. Take this blood of Christ, apply it by faith, and see how it atones with God. Leviticus 16:15–35." Biblehub.com, https://biblehub.com/commentaries/leviticus/16-32.htm.

2) *Keil and Delitzsch Biblical Commentary on the Old Testament:* "The yearly repetition of the general atonement showed that the sacrifices of the law were not sufficient to make the servant of God perfect according to this own conscience. And this imperfection of the expiation, made with the blood of bullocks and goats, could not fail to awaken a longing for the perfect sacrifice of the eternal High Priest, who has obtained eternal redemption by entering once, through His own blood, into the holiest of all (Hebrews 9:7–12).

"And just as this was effected negatively, so by the fact that the high priest entered on this day into the holiest of all, as the representative of the whole congregation, and there, before the throne of God, completed its reconciliation with Him, was the necessity exhibited in a positive manner for the true reconciliation of man, and his introduction into a perfect and abiding fellowship with Him, and the eventual realization of this by the blood of the Son of God, our eternal High Priest and Mediator, prophetically foreshadowed." https://biblehub.com/commentaries/leviticus/16-32.htm.

222 See http://sarshalom.us/resources/scripture/asv/html/leviticus.html#16.

NOTES

223 Ibid.
224 Ibid.
225 Ibid.
226 Ibid.
227 Ibid.
228 Ibid.
229 See http://sarshalom.us/resources/scripture/asv/html/hebrews.html#4.
230 See http://sarshalom.us/resources/scripture/asv/html/hebrews.html#6.
231 See http://sarshalom.us/resources/scripture/asv/html/hebrews.html#7.
232 Ibid.
233 See http://sarshalom.us/resources/scripture/asv/html/hebrews.html#9.
234 Ibid.
235 Ibid.
236 Ibid.
237 See http://sarshalom.us/resources/scripture/asv/html/hebrews.html#10.
238 See http://sarshalom.us/resources/scripture/asv/html/hebrews.html#12.
239 See http://sarshalom.us/resources/scripture/asv/html/john.html#13.
240 Ibid.
241 Ibid.
242 Ibid.
243 Ibid.
244 Ibid.
245 Ibid.
246 "Show us the Father":

    1) *Ellicott's Commentary for English Readers:* "That Father has been manifested in the person of the Son. In the Life and Truth revealed in Him is the full revelation of God. In Him is the Bread of Life to satisfy every want of every man. He that hath seen Him hath seen the Father. How then can men say, Show us the Father?" See https://biblehub.com/commentaries/john/14-9.htm.

    2) *Cambridge Bible for Schools and Colleges:* "The Gospels are full of evidence of how little the Apostles understood of the life which they were allowed to share: and the candor with which this is confessed, confirms our trust in the narratives. Not until Pentecost were their minds fully enlightened. Comp. John 10:6, John 12:16; Matthew 15:16; Matthew 16:8; Mark 9:32; Luke 9:45; Luke 18:34; Luke 24:25; Acts 1:6; Hebrews 5:12."

247 See http://sarshalom.us/resources/scripture/asv/html/john.html#14.
248 Ibid.
249 Remember...*bereshith* is Hebrew. John's Gospel was written in Greek. Yet he opens his Gospel with the phrase, "in the beginning." This is the exact way Genesis 1:1 opens. In the Hebrew translation of the Greek language, "in the beginning" is written as *bereshith*. Therefore, the same encoded message of *bereshith* of Genesis 1:1 is also in the first word of John's Gospel—with its decoding found in Paul's words recorded in Colossians 1:15–20.
250 See http://sarshalom.us/resources/scripture/asv/html/john.html#1.
251 Ibid.

NOTES

252 Ibid.
253 *Thayer's Greek Lexicon* (GK—1378. Dogma): "**Of the rules and requirements of the law of Moses**, carrying a suggestion of severity, and of threatened punishment, **the law containing precepts** in the form of decrees (A. V. **the law of commandments contained in ordinances**)." https://biblehub.com/greek/1378.htm.
254 Zechariah 12:10

   1) *Dr. Constable's Expository Notes*, Studylight.org, https://www.studylight.org/commentary/zechariah/12-10.html.

   2) *Keil and Delitzsch Biblical Commentary on the Old Testament:* "The historical fulfilment of this prophecy commenced with the crucifixion of the Son of God, who had come in the flesh…. The fulfilment has continued with less striking results through the whole period of the Christian church, in conversions from among the Jews; and it will not terminate till the remnant of Israel shall turn as a people to Jesus the Messiah, whom its fathers crucified. On the other hand, those who continue obstinately in unbelief will see Him at last when He returns in the clouds of heaven, and shriek with despair (Rev. 1:7, Matt. 24:30)." https://biblehub.com/commentaries/zechariah/12-10.htm.
255 See http://sarshalom.us/resources/scripture/asv/html/john.html#3.
256 Ibid.
257 See http://sarshalom.us/resources/scripture/asv/html/luke.html#9.
258 See http://sarshalom.us/resources/scripture/asv/html/revelation.html#1.
259 Ibid.
260 See http://sarshalom.us/resources/scripture/asv/html/revelation.html#4.
261 See http://sarshalom.us/resources/scripture/asv/html/revelation.html#5.
262 Ibid.
263 Ibid.
264 See http://sarshalom.us/resources/scripture/asv/html/revelation.html#6.
265 See http://sarshalom.us/resources/scripture/asv/html/revelation.html#12.
266 Ibid.
267 See http://sarshalom.us/resources/scripture/asv/html/revelation.html#14.
268 See http://sarshalom.us/resources/scripture/asv/html/revelation.html#15.
269 See http://sarshalom.us/resources/scripture/asv/html/revelation.html#19.
270 Ibid.
271 See http://sarshalom.us/resources/scripture/asv/html/revelation.html#20.
272 See http://sarshalom.us/resources/scripture/asv/html/revelation.html#21.
273 See http://sarshalom.us/resources/scripture/asv/html/revelation.html#22.
274 Ibid.
275 Ibid.
276 As a disclaimer, I was blessed to have been asked by Zev to write the foreword to *Unmasking the Chaldean Spirit*, and also to supply him with some of my own research on the important matters. I have Rabbi Porat's permission to use and refer to any of the material in his book.

   Rabbi Porat's *Unmasking the Chaldean Spirit* is academically and biblically sound, based on well-studied scholarship and including abundant references for further study and verification. The fact that Rabbi Porat speaks Hebrew as his first

NOTES

language is a huge advantage when exploring God's Word, especially the documents of the Old Testament.

Zev Porat, *Unmasking the Chaldean Spirit* (Crane, MO: Defender Publishing, 2022), pp. 241–297. http://www.messiahofisraelministries.com.

277 For further study on the topic of the biblical ground zero, see my book *Gods of Ground Zero* (Crane, MO: Defender Publishing). http://www.carlgallups.com.

278 Luke includes this description. The words "the Skull" is Greek is *kranion*. It was referred to in Yeshua's day as "Golgotha." See *Strong's Lexicon*, https://biblehub.com/greek/2898.htm.

"And when they came to the place that is called The Skull, there they crucified him, and the criminals, one on his right and one on his left" (Luke 23:33).

279 A number of English translations of the Greek manuscripts use the article "the," while others use the article "a." The point is, regardless of which article is used, the name denotes the place of a specific skull, not of a collection of skulls, or a boneyard filled with skulls. This was a special place that memorialized a single skull. See examples at https://biblehub.com/matthew/27-33.htm.

280 More than 55 percent of today's global population is made up of Christians, Jews, and Muslims. All three of these major world religions regard David as a very important figure. A huge additional number of the world's population at least knows of ancient Israel's King David. See https://www.britannica.com/biography/David.

Also see "The Global Religious Landscape," *The Pew Forum on Religion & Public Life*. Pew Research center. 12//12. Archived from the original on 12/25/18. Retrieved 3/18/13. https://web.archive.org/web/20181225045352/http://www.pewforum.org/2012/12/18/global-religious-landscape-exec.

281 See "Jamieson-Fausset-Brown Bible Commentary," https://biblehub.com/commentaries/1_samuel/21-1.htm.

282 See: "Encyclopedia of the Bible," Biblegateway.com, https://www.biblegateway.com/resources/encyclopedia-of-the-bible/Mount-Olives.

283 See *International Standard Bible Encyclopedia*, Studylight.org, https://www.studylight.org/encyclopedias/eng/isb/o/olives-mount-of.html.

284 See *International Standard Bible Encyclopedia* (Nob), biblestudytools.com, https://www.biblestudytools.com/dictionary/nob.

285 As an important side note about Nob, we discover that *King* David would later return to this very location when he was fleeing from his son Absalom years later.

Smith's Bible Dictionary: "There is Old Testament evidence that there was a 'high place' here. In the account of David's flight mention is made of **the spot on the summit** 'where he often went to **worship God**' (2 Sam 15:32 margin). This is certainly a reference to **a sanctuary**, and there are **strong reasons** for believing that **this place may have been Nob** (see 1 Samuel 21:1; 22:9, 11, 19; Nehemiah 11:32; but especially Isaiah 10:32)."

286 1 Samuel 17:54. *Cambridge Bible for Schools and Colleges*, Biblehub.com, https://biblehub.com/commentaries/1_samuel/17-54.htm.

287 Steffanie Zazulak, "How the English Language Has Changed over the Decades," *Pearson Language*, 6/15/20, https://www.pearson.com/languages/community/blogs/2020/06/how-the-english-language-has-changed-over-the-decades.html.

NOTES

288 OT:1555. Golyath, Accessed 1/21/21, (*Biblesoft's New Exhaustive Strong's Numbers and Concordance with Expanded Greek-Hebrew Dictionary*. Copyright © 1994, 2003, 2006 Biblesoft, Inc. and International Bible Translators, Inc.).

289 OT:1538. Gulgoleth. Accessed 1/ 21/21. (*Biblesoft's New Exhaustive Strong's Numbers and Concordance with Expanded Greek-Hebrew Dictionary*. Copyright © 1994, 2003, 2006 Biblesoft, Inc. and International Bible Translators, Inc.).

290 See https://en.wiktionary.org/wiki/Golgotha. Accessed 10/23/2024.

291 Richard A. Shenk, PhD (biographical profile), https://bcsmn.edu/profile/rick-shenk.

292 For Dr. Shenk's statements on this, see:

   1. Henry Holloway, "Bible Bombshell as 'David vs Goliath Skull Found Where Jesus Was Crucified'," *UK Star*, 10/19/19, https://www.dailystar.co.uk/news/weird-news/bible-bombshell-david-vs-goliath-20649333.

   2. Conny Waters, "Skull of Biblical Giant Goliath Is Buried on the Hill Golgotha in Jerusalem—New Claim," *Ancient Pages*, 11/7/2019, https://www.ancient-pages.com/2019/11/07/skull-of-biblical-giant-goliath-is-buried-on-the-hill-golgotha-in-jerusalem-new-claim.

293 Dr. Taylor Marshall, "Golgatha: The Word Symbolizes a Beautiful Reality." Accessed 2/2/21, https://taylormarshall.com/2013/03/golgatha-word-symbolizes-beautiful.html.

294 *Biblical Horizons Newsletter* No. 84: "Christ in the Holy of Holies, the Meaning of the Mount of Olives," by James B. Jordan (April 1996), and as quoted at: "Kill Goliath and Save His Skull," Kuyperian.com. Accessed 10/11/24, https://kuyperian.com/kill-goliath-and-save-his-skull.

295 The Meaning of the Mount of Olives to Jesus in the Bible: "The second most **famous mountain in Jerusalem** (the Temple Mount on Mount Moriah or Mount Zion being the first) **is the Mount of Olives. The Mount of Olives served the city in making olive oil to anoint** Israel's kings and temple priests" (emphasis added). See https://firmisrael.org/learn/meaning-mount-of-olives-jesus-in-the-bible.

296 Altar of the Red Heifer on the Mount of Olives:

   1) Mélbourne O'Banion, "The Law of the Red Heifer: A Type and Shadow of Jesus Christ," *Studia Antiqua*, Volume 4, Number 1, 4/2005, https://scholarsarchive.byu.edu/cgi/viewcontent.cgi?article=1041&context=studiaantiqua.

297 2) Eli Shiller, "The Site of the Burning of the Red Heifer," 2/29/16, https://mountofolives.co.il/en/%D7%9B%D7%9C%D7%9C%D7%99-en/the-site-of-the-burning-of-the-red-heifer-on-the-mount-of-olives.

   Rabbi Eliezer ben Hurcanus had actually seen the Second Temple before its destruction in AD 70. He was one of the most prominent Hebrew sages of the first and second centuries in the Roman region of Judea. He is the sixth most-mentioned sage in the Mishnah.

   See Drew Kaplan, "Rabbinic Popularity in the Mishnah VII: Top Ten Overall Final Tally" *Drew Kaplan's Blog* (July 5, 2011). http://drewkaplans.blogspot.com/2011/07/rabbinic-popularity-in-mishnah-vii-top.html.

   See also Wikipedia, "Eliezer ben Hurcanus." Accessed 2/3/21, https://en.wikipedia.org/wiki/Eliezer_ben_Hurcanus.

   Rabbi Eliezer ben Hurcanus' commentary on the issue of "Outside the Camp":

NOTES

"It is said here [in Leviticus 4: 12]: Without the Camp, and it is said there [in Numbers 19:3]: Without the Camp. Just as here [in Leviticus] it means outside the three Camps [of the priests, of the Levites, and of the Israelites], so does it mean there [in Numbers] outside the three Camps; and just as there [Numbers 19:3—the burning of the Red Heifer Sacrifice] it means TO THE EAST OF JERUSALEM, so does it here [Leviticus 4:12] TO THE EAST OF JERUSALEM" (caps and brackets in original).

See Dr. Ernest L. Martin, PhD, "Secrets of Golgotha: The Lost History of Jesus' Crucifixion" (Second Edition), Academy for Scriptural; 2nd edition (6/1/96), (Chapter 1). Read the entire book online here: https://www.askelm.com/golgotha/Golgotha%20Chap%2000.pdf.

298 Various sources of information on Jerusalem's mountain heights differ slightly, but this list reflects consensus estimates: Mount of Olives—2,684 feet; Mount Zion—2,510 feet; Mount Moriah—2,520 feet; Mount Ophel—2,300 feet.

299 It is indisputable that these three mountains (Zion, Moriah, and Ophel) were inside the Old Jerusalem City gates during the time of Yeshua: "Mount Zion was enclosed within Jerusalem's city wall at the end of the governorship of Nehemiah and during the Herodian period." See "The Conservation of Jerusalem's City Walls," antiquities.org. Accessed 12/1/24, https://www.antiquities.org.il/jerusalemwalls/preservation_e08zion_hstry.asp.

300 Dr. Ernest L. Martin, PhD, *Secrets of Golgotha: The Lost History of Jesus' Crucifixion* (Second Edition), Associates of Scriptural Knowledge; 2nd edition (6/1/96), pp. 14–15. Read relevant portions of the book online here: https://www.askelm.com/golgotha/Golgotha%20Chap%2000.pdf.

301 Dr. James D. Tabor served as chair (2004–2014) of the Department of Religious Studies at the University of North Carolina, where he has taught since 1989. He is currently professor of ancient Judaism and early Christianity. Previously he held positions at the University of Notre Dame and the College of William and Mary. He received his PhD from the University of Chicago in 1981 in ancient Mediterranean religions. See https://jamestabor.com/about-dr-tabor/.

302 Dr. Douglas Jacoby, *The Red Heifer Sacrifice and the Crucifixion*, (1997, Revised 2001), https://www.douglasjacoby.com/the-red-heifer-sacrifice-and-the-crucifixion.

303 I am not at all concerned about identifying the specific *piece of ground*, that can be measured in square feet, as it would relate to the location of the actual site of Golgotha. It seems that the Lord has hidden that information for a reason. Nevertheless, as we've discovered, the biblical site *has* to be located on the Mount of Olives. Hebrews 13 settles the matter.

304 Got Questions. "What happened on the Mount of Olives?" Accessed 2/2/25, https://www.gotquestions.org/Mount-of-Olives.html.

305 How many were at the ascension of Yeshua? See: Acts 1:1–9, 15, KJV—120 were meeting regularly, right after the ascension. Also, the Apostle Paul wrote in 1 Corinthians 15:6 that more than five hundred people at one time witnessed the Risen Christ. Scholars agree it was highly possible some of those were present at the Ascension as well.

306 Jeffrey Kloha, "The Day the Bible Became a Bestseller." Textandcanon.org, 9/21/22, https://textandcanon.org/the-day-the-bible-became-a-bestseller.

NOTES

307 Several of my books go to great lengths to detail the proof of that statement. The proof comes from the Word of God, the historical/prophetic happenings of our own days, scientific sites, technology sites, DNA research sites, and more. My two books before this one (*Yeshua Protocol* and *Eyes to See*) are prime examples of that research and its biblical conclusions. They are produced by Defender Publishing—a major Christian publisher and have been featured on many TV, radio, and podcast outlets—both Christian and secular. You can get them at www.carlgallups.com/store.

308 See https://biblehub.com/interlinear/isaiah/44-7.htm.

309 Ann Landers, "Keep Your Fork, Best Is Yet to Come," *Chicago Tribune*, 8/20/21, https://www.chicagotribune.com/2000/08/12/keep-your-fork-best-is-yet-to-come.

310 Image designed by Defender Publishing Company's cover designer, Jeffrey Mardis. Used with permission.

www.ingramcontent.com/pod-product-compliance
Lightning Source LLC
Chambersburg PA
CBHW011408070526
44586CB00021B/2578